J F K VS. C I A

THE CENTRAL INTELLIGENCE AGENCY'S

ASSASSINATION OF THE PRESIDENT

J F K V S. C I A — *The Central Intelligence Agency's Assassination of the President*

© 1998 by Michael Calder

ISBN: 0-9660749-0-4

LIBRARY OF CONGRESS CATALOG CARD NO. : 97-061809

West LA Publishers
P.O. Box 641339
Los Angeles CA 90064

So a wild tartar, when he spies
A man that's handsome, valiant, wise
If he can kill him, think to inherit
His wit, his beauty, and his spirit:
As if just so much he enjoyed
As in another is destroyed.

—Samuel Butler, "Hudibras," 1646

DEDICATION

This book is dedicated to Lee Bowers.
A man who witnessed treason, spoke out against it,
and paid the ultimate price for his courage.

"But I see in the near future a crisis approaching that un-nerves me and causes me to tremble for the safety of my country. As a result of war, corporations have been en-throned and an era of corruption in high places will follow, and the money power of the country will endeavor to pro-long its reign by working upon the prejudices of the people until all wealth is aggregated in a few hands, and the Republic is destroyed. I feel at this moment more anxiety for the safety of my country than ever before, even in the midst of war. God grant that my suspicions prove groundless."

—Abraham Lincoln
November 21, 1863

The little girl next to me blurted out in that saucy, imperious manner that only little girls have, "President Kennedy has been shot and I'm glad. I voted for Nixon." Whereupon she burst into tears.

—Michael Calder
November 22, 1963

ACKNOWLEDGEMENTS

In every family there is one responsible person. The one we run to when our nightmares catch up with us. Aunt Emma Jean Wallace demanded that I return to U.C. Berkeley to "get my degree," bribing me with free room and board. It was at Berkeley where I encountered government documents which led to my thesis which became this book.

I'd also like to thank that attractive daughter of the South and ex-Rainbow girl, Rebecca Calder, my mother, for being there when the home runs were hit, the impossible catches made, and who stamped my character, which now compels me to stand, point and "cry treason." Thanks, Mom.

My thanks to my brother Cory who shared my vision from the start and saw the possibilities at a glance. With your courage, intelligence and daring, between the two of us, the bad guys don't stand a chance. I almost feel sorry for them. Almost. Thanks as well to Ruth C. Moore for her financial advice and for otherwise helping me navigate real life.

Finally, my deep appreciation to Bill Becker of BB Communications in Los Angeles, who applied his editorial skills to the production of this book. He took a diamond in the rough and rendered a polished stone. He might say that's merely to be expected from a Yalie. As luck would have it, he's also the Yale Club's secretary and publisher of the *IvyNews.Org*.

* * *

CONTENTS

PREFACE

Once a shot was fired and heard around the world. It signaled the beginning of the American Revolution. Another shot heard around the world almost brought an end to our Republic. Only now, in retrospect, can we see how very close we came, at that time, to losing our democracy.

Shortly before completing my studies at the University of California, Berkeley, I came across the 26 volumes of evidence upon which the Warren Commission based its conclusions. While reading through those historical documents, I became especially fascinated by the testimony of participants who were directly touched by the assassination. The stories of Secret Service agents in the motorcade; the firsthand accounts of eyewitnesses in Dealy Plaza; the testimony of Dallas Police Department officers; that of the beautiful and shy wife of the accused assassin, as well as Lee Harvey Oswald's own testimony in custody, all these came alive. My interest became a passion. My passion became a compulsion. The truth became my quest, with government documents my Bible. I couldn't let go of it, though I tried.

This book is an extension of my University thesis as a social science field major. The title of my thesis was *The Assassination of President John F. Kennedy: An Analysis of the Social, Political and Economic Factors which led to his assassination by the CIA.*

My conclusion is that the CIA assassinated the President because he was perceived as a threat to national security. I believe that, as you journey through this book, you will come to the same inescapable conclusion. The replacement of the rule of law with the rule of force at the apex of our political system has removed a fundamental building block in our political culture. Until the mechanism for treason is terminated, the country will remain in jeopardy.

* * *

PART I—THE WARREN COMMISSION

1

A BRIEF SUMMARY OF THE WARREN COMMISSION'S FINDINGS & CONCLUSIONS

The President was traveling in a motorcade through downtown Dallas. His vehicle turned right onto Houston Street from Main Street and traveled one block. Next it turned left off of Houston onto Elm. The purpose of these turns was to place the President's vehicle on Elm because Elm Street flows into the Stemmons freeway access road which turns onto the Stemmons freeway. Once reaching the Stemmons Freeway, it is a short ride to the Trade Mart where the President was scheduled to give a speech.

After the vehicle passed the front of the Texas School Book Depository (hereinafter referred to as the book depository), located at the corner of Elm and Houston, three shots rang out. All of the shots were fired from a position that was behind the vehicle. One shot missed. One shot entered the back of the President's neck and exited his throat. This same bullet then entered Governor Connally's back, snapped off a rib, exited his chest, broke his right wrist and lodged in his left thigh. The third shot hit the President in the back of his head causing the fatal injury. No shots were fired from the front, notwithstanding the overpass which the President's vehicle was approaching when the shots erupted.

Only one man did the shooting and that man was Lee Harvey Oswald. He was determined to be the sole assassin because the rifle found on the sixth floor of the book depository was traced to his ownership. A Chicago gun firm had sent this particular weapon to an A. Hidell at the same post office address that was rented to Oswald. The request for the rifle was in the handwriting of Oswald. A palm print was on the rifle found in the book depository and the palm print belonged to Oswald. Fingerprints on the boxes in the sniper's nest from where the gunman fired belonged to Oswald.

Therefore the commission concluded that Lee Harvey Oswald was on the sixth floor of the book depository when the President's motorcade turned onto Elm Street and that he alone shot the President.

* * *

2

REBUTTAL TO THE WARREN COMMISSION'S FINDINGS & CONCLUSIONS

Direction of the Shots. The Warren Commission has concluded that the shots which killed President Kennedy and wounded Governor Connally were fired from the sixth-floor window at the southeast corner of the book depository building.[1]

The evidence, though, throughout the 26 volumes of testimony and exhibits produced by the Warren Commission, points to an ambush of the President involving multiple assassins firing from the front as well as behind.

Forrest Sorrels. Forrest Sorrels was the Secret Service agent in charge of the Dallas Office of the Secret Service. While driving over the route the President's motorcade was to follow in a few days, he made a remark that horribly foretold the future. His comment was, "Someone wanting to get the President of the United States could do it with a high powered rifle and a telescopic lens from some building or some hillside."[2] Sorrels rode in the lead car which was just

ahead of the President's in the motorcade. His testimony to
the Warren Commission when he heard the first report of the
rifle was, "I said, 'What's that?'" And turned around to look
upon the terrace part there, because the sound, sounded like
it came from back and up in that direction. At that time, I did
not look back up to the building, because it was way in the
back."[3] The terrace Sorrels was speaking of was in front of
and just to the right of the President as the shots erupted.

When challenged by the Commission lawyer later on in
his testimony as to the source of the shots, Sorrels once
again gave his distinct impression: "And, as I said, the noise
from the shots sounded like they may have come back up on
the terrace there...but the report seemed so loud that it
sounded like to me—in other words, that was my first
thought, *somebody up in the terrace*, and that is the reason I
looked there."[4]

Roy Kellerman. Roy Kellerman was the assistant special
agent in charge of the White House Detail. He was in charge
of security for President Kennedy's trip to Dallas. Kellerman
was riding in the same vehicle as the President. He was sitting in the front passenger seat. William Greer, a Secret
Service Agent was driving the President's vehicle. Kellerman
heard what he described as a firecracker noise and heard a
voice from the back seat say "My God, I'm hit." As he
turned around to look at the President, he saw the President's
hands go up toward his throat in a choking gesture.
Kellerman yelled to the driver Greer, "Let's get out of here!
We are hit!".[5] He then grabbed the mike and ordered the lead
car to guide them out of the ambush and to the hospital.
Kellerman testified that as he was speaking a "flurry of shells
came into the car." He described the second and third shots
as a double bang—like that of a plane breaking the sound
barrier.[6] When challenged about the rapidity of the last two
shots by the Warren Commission lawyer, Agent Kellerman
replied, "These shells all came in all together."[7] When asked
by Representative Ford about any noise coming from the

crowd, thus implying that the noise of the crowd might have caused a hearing impairment at the time of the shooting, Kellerman replied, "We are in an open field area, so to speak, and everything was just clear." [8]

The Commission was having a problem with a Secret Service agent in the vehicle with Kennedy telling them that the sound of the shots was like a sonic boom and came in a flurry. With a bolt-action rifle that Oswald supposedly had in the sixth floor window of the Book Depository, it is impossible to fire in so rapid a fashion. The Warren Commission was trying to derail Secret Service Agent Kellerman's testimony. The Commission also tried to raise doubt in the mind of Agent Forest Sorrels when he testified the shots were coming from in front and not from behind. To the credit of both agents, they stuck to the truth.

S.M. Holland. S. M. Holland was a railroad man standing on the overpass and facing the President's vehicle as it approached when the shots rang out. He testified that he saw smoke coming from the trees atop the grassy knoll that lay in front and to the right of the President's vehicle. "There was a shot, a report, a puff of smoke came out 6 to 8 feet above the ground."[9] "...I have no doubt about seeing that puff of smoke come out from under those trees either."[10] The trees that he was referring to were under him and to his left. These trees are exactly where Secret Service Agent Sorrels said he thought the shots were coming from." I definitely saw the puff of smoke and heard the report from under those trees."[11]

Frank Reilly. Frank Reilly was also on the overpass, awaiting the President's passing underneath him. He also was definite about the direction of the shots. "It seemed to me like they come out of the trees....Well, it's at that park where all the shrubbery is up there...up the slope." [12]

William Newman. Mr. Newman was standing alongside the President's vehicle at the moment the fatal head shot occurred. He was on the sidewalk immediately to the right of the President. The car had stopped in the middle of the street by this time. In his affidavit, taken the afternoon of the assassination, Mr. Newman stated as follows:

> By this time he was directly in front of us and I was looking directly at him when he was hit in the side of the head...I thought the shot had come from the garden directly behind me, on an elevation from where I was, as I was right on the curb. I do not recall looking toward the book depository. I looked back into the vicinity of the garden.[13]

Mr. Newman pinpointed the shot that killed the President as coming from the garden. The garden that he is referring to is the shrubbery and trees atop the grassy knoll which is in front of and slightly to the right of the President. It is the same clump of trees to which the men on the overpass referred. The fact that Mr. Newman also said that the President was shot on the side of the head will have strong implications as we proceed.

Abraham Zapruder. Abraham Zapruder was standing atop the grassy knoll to the right of the President as the motorcade traveled down Elm Street. Zapruder, a dress manufacturer, was filming the procession with his movie camera, which his secretary had urged him to go back and get. His film starts off with the motorcycles preceding the President's vehicle down Elm Street. The President's vehicle disappears behind a sign that is between Zapruder and the vehicle. As the President's vehicle emerges from the sign, the President is dramatically raising his hands to his throat. He has been hit by the first shot. As the horrible seconds ticked by, Zapruder held his camera steady and recorded the entire assassination on film, including the fatal head shot. Zapruder testified that at the time of the assassination, he cried out, "They killed him! They killed him!" He said, "And I just felt that somebody had ganged up on him and I was still shooting the pictures until he got under the underpass."[14]

Zapruder felt that the shots came from behind him.[15] This is significant because the book depository is in front of and to the left of Zapruder, almost 100 yards away. Yet Zapruder, who is filming the President's assassination, believed that the shots came from behind him. His statement concerning where the shots originated from coincides with the testimony of so many other eyewitnesses who explicitly said the shots were coming from the same general area.

Even more significant is what Zapruder captured on film. The film shows the President clutching at his throat as the vehicle emerges from behind the freeway sign. A few seconds later the President starts to lean forward. At this point, the driver of the vehicle, Secret Service agent Will Greer, had come to a complete stop in the middle of the street.[16] What we see next on the film is the president's head exploding as it is being violently jerked backward and his torso is rising up from the seat. Whether the film is viewed in slow motion or at normal speed, it is clear that at one moment the President's entire body is leaning forward and that in the next instant his whole upper body is violently thrown back and up against the car seat. After colliding with the back seat, he rebounds forward and falls limp and motionless on the floor of the automobile. The only way the President's body could have jerked backward so quickly and violently would have been if a bullet had struck him from the front. The driving force of a bullet is what propelled the President's body backward.

Joe Marshall Smith. Dallas police officer Joe Marshall Smith received instructions at 9:00 a.m. to station himself at the corner of Elm and Houston and to hold up traffic when the motorcade approached Dealey Plaza. This intersection is directly in front of the book depository. He was also stationed there for crowd control and to make sure nothing was thrown from the crowd.[17] He testified that at the moment of the assassination, a woman came up to him in hysterics yelling, "They're shooting the President from the bushes."[18]

He also believed the shots came from the bushes beside the overpass.[19]

Paul Landis. Paul Landis was one of the Secret Service agents in the vehicle behind the President's. In his testimonial, written a few days after the assassination, he stated that "The shot came from somewhere toward the front, right hand side of the road." [20]

* * *

3

OSWALD'S ACTIONS IN THE BUILDING AFTER THE ASSASSINATION

The commission has concluded that Oswald's movements are consistent with his having been at the window at 12:30 P.M.[21]

Altgens Photograph. Let's look retrospectively at the few seconds before the assassination. As President Kennedy is being gunned down on Elm Street, Oswald is supposed to be on the sixth floor of the book depository shooting at the President. At the very moment the President clutched up to his throat in reaction to the first bullet, award-winning photographer James Altgens was snapping his camera. Mr. Altgens, standing in front of the President's vehicle as it made its way toward the overpass, caught the President's first reaction to being hit. In the background of the photograph, clearly and graphically standing by himself in the entrance to the book depository is Lee Harvey Oswald.[22] Another photograph taken at the time of his arrest one hour later shows him to be wearing similar clothes to those of the

man in the Altgens photograph.[23] The central question therefore becomes, how it is possible for Lee Harvey Oswald to
be standing in the doorway of the book depository watching
the President's motorcade go by and at the same time be on
the sixth floor of the building shooting at the President?

The Warren Commission, concerned that a photograph
existed apparently showing Lee Harvey Oswald standing outside the book depository as President Kennedy was being
shot, ordered the FBI to find the identity of the man in the
photograph. Mind you, this was months after the FBI had already seen the photograph and closed the case. The FBI
came back with the identity of the man in the photograph. It
wasn't Lee Harvey Oswald after all. It was a fellow employee of the book depository, Billy Lovelady. Well, I'm glad
we got that straight. But do we?

William Shelley, the foreman for the book depository,
was outside the building watching the Presidential motorcade
pass down Elm Street. A part of his affidavit written just after the assassination follows:

> As the Presidential motorcade passed, I was standing just
> outside the glass doors of the entrance. At the time President
> John F. Kennedy was shot, I was standing at this same place.
> Billy Lovelady, who works under my supervision for the
> book depository, was seated on the entrance steps just in
> front of me. I recall Wesley Frazier, Mrs. Sarah Stanton, and
> Mrs. Carolyn Arnold were also standing in the entranceway
> near me at the time President Kennedy was shot.[24]

Well, that's funny. In the photograph that shows what
appears to be Lee Harvey Oswald, the man in the photograph
is standing all alone. If the man in the photograph is really
Billy Lovelady, where is William Shelley? Where is Sarah
Stanton? Where is Wesley Frazier? Where is Carolyn Arnold?

What does Sarah Stanton have to say? Let's take a look
at her affidavit written the afternoon of the assassination:
"When President John F. Kennedy was shot, I was standing

on the front steps of the book depository with William Shelley, Otis William, and Billy Lovelady."[25]

Once again, we don't see any of these people in the Altgen's photograph. Why not? The explanation comes from the testimony of Wesley Frazier, whose affidavit was taken shortly after the assassination: "At the time President Kennedy was shot I was standing on the front steps of the book depository building. I was with William Shelley and Billy Lovelady when the President was shot."[26]

Furthermore, Wesley Frazier said he was standing one step down from the top by the rail and stood there until the motorcade went by. He said he was next to a heavy set lady named Sarah. Wesley added he was just standing and talking to Mr. Shelley and the boy Billy Lovelady, commenting on what a nice day it turned out to be. "I was standing one step down from the top, and Mr. Shelley was standing, you know, back from the top steps and over toward the side of the wall there. Billy was a couple of steps down from me over more toward the wall also."[27]

The Warren Commission lawyer asked him if he could identify himself in the Altgens photograph. Frazier answered, "No sir, I don't, because I was way in the back up in more or less the black area here."[28]

In the James Altgens photograph, above the man who looks like a dead ringer for Lee Oswald, is an area that is blackened out. You cannot make out anything in this blackened out area as the steps reach the entrance of the book depository. It is in this area that Wesley Frazier was standing. This means that since Billy Lovelady was standing next to him, Billy Lovelady was also invisible in this darkened area. This is also why we cannot see Mr. Shelley or Sarah Stanton as well. What does Billy Lovelady have to say about his position at the time the President was struck down? Let's look at Bill Lovelady's affidavit, written the afternoon of the assassination:

At this time the Presidential motorcade passed the depository building heading west on Elm Street. I was standing on the top step to the far right against the wall of the entrance to the book depository. At this time I recall that William Shelley, and Mrs. Sarah Stanton, both of whom are likewise employed by the book depository, were standing next to me.[29]

So not only was Billy Lovelady standing among friends at the top steps of the entrance to the building which would place him in the darkened portion of the photograph, he was leaning against the far right wall. To further make life hell for the dauntless FBI and CIA, on the day of the assassination, Billy Lovelady was wearing a red and white striped sports shirt buttoned up near the neck.[30]

The man in the photograph is wearing a t-shirt and a workshirt over the t-shirt with the top three buttons unbuttoned. This photograph of Oswald standing on the steps of the book depository should have brought the conspiracy to its knees right from the start. The FBI's obfuscation in this matter shows the depths to which the cover-up ran in order for the CIA to pull off the crime of the century. Things get even more interesting a minute and a half after the Altgens' photograph is snapped.

Officer Marrion Baker. As soon as the last shot was fired, Officer Marrion Baker rushed into the Texas School Book Building. Running up the stairs, he noticed the movement of a swinging door and entered a room. He noticed a man at a Coke machine. With his gun drawn and pointed at the man's stomach, he was about to question him. Just then, Roy Truly, the building manager came into this second-floor lunchroom and identified the man as an employee of the building. The officer and the building manager continued up the stairs to the roof of the building.

The man Officer Baker confronted was Lee Harvey Oswald.[31] Officer Baker arrived at the second-floor lunchroom from one minute to one minute and thirty seconds from the time the shots ceased.[32] Officer Baker said Oswald did not seem out of breath and was calm.[33] Oswald was standing next to the Coke machine.

Whoever shot at the President from the sixth floor ran across the length of the floor, laid down the rifle, put a box filled with books on top of it in order to hide it from casual view, and then paused long enough to build a semicircle of cartons of books around the location of the rifle, half again as high as a man.[34]

Officer Eugene Boone. Officer Eugene Boone described to the Warren Commission how he found the rifle: "There were a row of windows there and a slight space between some boxes and the wall. I squeezed through them...I caught a glimpse of the rifle stuffed down between two rows of boxes with another box or so pulled over the top of it...There was a row of boxes that came across there...Then the rifle was behind that first row of boxes."[35]

The gunman didn't need an extraordinary amount of time to run across the sixth floor from the sniper's nest to the northwest corner, set the rifle down, pull a box of books over the rifle and then commence building a mini-fortress of boxes surrounding and protecting the rifle from casual view. Officer Boone described how he had to squeeze through this barrier of boxes before being able to glance down at the weapon. Someone had to have built that stack of boxes in a manner which takes time. The amount of time necessary to do this precludes Oswald being on the sixth floor because he was on the second floor by the Coke machine with a gun pointed at his stomach a minute or so after the shots had been fired. After Officer Baker and Superintendent Roy Truly left the lunchroom and continued up the stairs toward the roof of the building, Lee Harvey Oswald took his Coke and walked out the front door of the building.

Mrs. Reid. Mrs. Reid next saw Lee Harvey Oswald. Thirty seconds after the confrontation in the lunchroom, Mrs. Reid saw Lee Harvey Oswald walk past her.[36] He had a

Coke in his hand.[37] She spoke to him about the President getting shot and said hopefully his injuries were not fatal. In answer to her, Lee mumbled something indecipherable. Mrs. Reid testified that Lee walked past her in a slow, calm manner.[38]

William Whaley. The Commission determined that after leaving the book depository, Oswald boarded a bus and remained on the bus a short time. In any event, it is certain that Oswald entered a taxi driven by William Whaley. William Whaley had been driving a cab for 37 years.[39] He said Oswald approached his cab and slowly walked up to the window. Mr. Whaley said he wasn't in any hurry nor was he nervous.[40] He described Lee as being dressed in a t-shirt and a shirt over the t-shirt which had the first three buttons undone.[41] This is exactly how Lee Oswald looked in the Altgens photograph—he has the top buttons of his shirt unbuttoned.

Mr. Whaley described his encounter with Oswald to the Warren Commission: "He said, 'May I have this cab?' He opened the front door, which is allowed, and got in; and about this time an old lady sticking her head down past him in the door and said, 'Driver, will you call me a cab down here?' And he opened the door a little bit like he was going to get out and he said, 'I will let you have this one,' and she says 'No the driver can call me one.'"[42]

The driver then took Oswald to 500 N. Beckley.[43] Lee Oswald lived at 1026 N. Beckley.

* * *

4

DESCRIPTION OF THE RIFLE

The Warren Commission concluded the following about the rifle found on the sixth floor of the book depository shortly after the assassination: It was a 6.5 mm Mannlicher-Carcano Italian military rifle. It was a bolt-action, clip-fed rifle with various markings on it including the words "CAL 6.5," "Made Italy," "Terni," "Rocca," the numerals "1940," and "40" and the serial number "C2766." The rifle bore a very inexpensive Japanese four-power sight, stamped "Hollywood California" and "Made in Japan' and a sling consisting of two leather straps, one of which had a broad patch. The sling was not a standard rifle sling, but appeared to be a musical instrument strap or a sling from a carrying case or camera bag.[44] The Warren Commission has given us a full and detailed description of the rifle found on the sixth floor of the book depository, so rich in detail there can be no mistaking it. The sling itself seems to be of unique origin. But what do the police officers say about the rifle they found on the sixth floor?

Seymour Weitzman. Seymour Weitzman and Eugene Boone came across the gun on the sixth floor of the book depository simultaneously. Both deputy sheriffs were searching the sixth floor. Weitzman told the Warren Commission lawyer taking his deposition in Dallas the following:

"We saw the gun, I would say simultaneously, and I said, 'There it is!' and he started hollering "We got it!" It was covered with boxes. It was well protected as far as the naked eye because I would venture to say eight or nine of us stumbled over that gun a couple of times before we thoroughly searched the building."[45] Weitzman told the Warren Commission lawyer the gun was a 7.6 German Mauser. When challenged by the attorney on this point as to what his expertise was as far as rifles were concerned, Weitzman laconically replied that he was "fairly familiar because I was in the sporting goods business awhile."[46] Weitzman had also flown combat missions during WWII. He was shot down and ended up in a Japanese prison camp.[47] Before he became a deputy sheriff for Dallas County, he was a district supervisor for a chain of 26 Holly's dress shops in New York City for 15 years.[48] When it became apparent Weitzman was not going to waver in his testimony or be intimidated, the Warren Commission lawyer got down to business. Weitzman confirmed the gun he found had one round in the chamber. He described the gun as follows:

a. The gun had a 2.5 weaver scope.
b. It was blue-metal gun color.
c. The rear portion of the bolt was visibly worn.
d. The wooden portion of the rifle was brown, not mahogany brown but dark oak brown.[49]
e. The wood was rough wood.[50]
f. It had a thick, brownish-black sling.[51]

The gun that Seymour Weitzman described looks nothing like the rifle that the Warren Commission says was found on the sixth floor of the Book Depository. In effect,

Weitzman said the rifle he found was a German Mauser. The Commission said it was an Italian Mannlicher-Carcano. Weitzman said the scope was a 2.5 Weaver. The Commission said it was an inexpensive Japanese four-power scope. Weitzman said the sling was a thick, brownish-black sling. The Commission said the sling consisted of two leather straps, one of which had a broad patch. The sling appeared to be a strap from a musical instrument or camera bag carrying case. Finally, Weitzman described the gun as being a blue-metal gun color, the wood portion was brown, not mahogany brown but dark brown and it was of a rough wood texture. He also added that the rear portion of the bolt was visibly worn. Yet Weitzman, noticing the rifle in such detail, seemed to miss all the various writing on the rifle including its caliber and origin which was clearly stamped on the rifle. He also missed all the writing on the scope and he somehow confused two leather straps, one of which had a broad patch, that clearly came from a camera carrying case or some other makeshift material for a thick, brownish-black sling. Perhaps Eugene Boone, the co-discoverer of the rifle, provided a description more akin to the one the Warren Commission says was found on the sixth floor of the book depository.

Eugene Boone. When Deputy Sheriff Eugene Boone was brought to Washington to appear before the Warren Commission (unlike Seymour Weitzman, who was deposed in Dallas), he reiterated that the rifle he found was a 7.6 German Mauser. Officer Boone actually had a chance to view the Italian Mannlicher-Carcano. After viewing the rifle he was unable to positively identify it.[52]

The Italian Mannlicher-Carcano. Obviously, the two deputy sheriffs found a German Mauser. The appearance of the Italian Mannlicher-Carcano was to frame Oswald through circumstantial evidence. The German Mauser was not supposed to be found by law enforcement officers. May I suggest the following scenario: The professional assassin, firing from the sniper's nest, was using the weapon of choice among members of his profession—the German Mauser rifle. The weapon was a superior one for its time. The assassin fired at the President, paused to admire his handiwork, and departed the sniper's nest. He ran across the sixth floor from the southeast corner where the sniper's nest was located, to the northwest corner to a prearranged spot to leave the actual murder weapon. He covered the weapon with a 50-lb. box and built a small fortress of boxes five feet high, surrounding the weapon to keep it from casual view. The assassin then ran down the stairs and out the back of the building.

In the meantime, CIA agents holding falsified Secret Service identification ran into the building and up to the sixth floor. Many citizens as well as police officers told of plain-clothes men and Secret Service men rushing into the building. There were no Secret Service agents on foot in Dealey Plaza at anytime during the assassination and its immediate aftermath.

I suggest that the CIA team rushing up to the sixth floor had two jobs. The first job was to spirit the real murder weapon off the floor. The assassin couldn't very well take the rifle with him. Anyone seen running out of the building with a gun would have been shot on sight. By leaving the rifle at the opposite end of the sixth floor from where the sniper's nest was, this rifle could be picked up and carried clandestinely out of the building. The local law enforcement officers would be searching for a weapon at the other end of the floor.

The second job the CIA team had to do was leave the Italian Mannlicher-Carcano in the sniper's nest to frame Oswald. But the CIA made a mistake. Either the professional assassin left his weapon in the wrong spot or he forgot to leave a marker for the CIA men who were to follow. He also may have done too good of a job in hiding the rifle. Officers Boone and Weitzman stumbled across the rifle several times before accidentally discovering it. The way those floors are arranged with row after row of boxes, they all begin to look the same.

In any event, after the two deputy sheriffs found the rifle and the chief of homicide came over to take a look, things became more complicated for the conspirators. When the two Dallas Police officers found the 7.6 caliber German Mauser, this initially confounded the conspirators. But less than 24 hours later, some clever boy in the CIA managed to turn a potentially devastating deficit into a brilliant gain. The decision was made to pretend the found German Mauser was Oswald's Italian Mannlicher-Carcano. Only a handful of people would know the true identity of the weapon, including the two police officers who found the gun; the other 160 million citizens would believe whatever they were told.

The Warren Commission desperately tried to prove that Oswald went home to Mrs. Paine's residence the night before the assassination specifically to retrieve that murder weapon in order to shoot the President the next day. Oswald could not shoot the President unless he smuggled the weapon into the book depository. His coming home the night before the assassination was unusual because he would usually hitch a ride home with a fellow employee, Wesley Frazier, on Friday evenings after work. This time he asked Mr. Frazier for a ride home on Thursday evening. Wesley Frazier was surprised at the request. Over the previous six weeks, Oswald had stayed at a boarding house during the week and only needed a ride home Friday evenings to spend the weekends with his wife and children at Mrs. Paine's home.

The morning of the assassination, while Wesley Frazier and his sister, Linnie Mae Randall, were eating breakfast, Lee passed by the window. It was Oswald's way of showing them he was on time and ready to go to work. Both Wesley Frazier and Linnie Mae Randall saw that Lee was carrying a package. While driving to work, Mr. Frazier asked Lee what was in the package. Lee replied it was curtain rods which he was going to hang in his rented room. When they reached the parking lot of the book depository, Oswald hurriedly walked ahead of Mr. Frazier. Again, this was unusual in that the two of them would walk together from the parking lot into the building.

The Warren Commission, in attempting to prove that Oswald was carrying a disassembled Italian Mannlicher-Carcano in this package, had the FBI make another package that could contain an Italian Mannlicher-Carcano and this package was shown to Wesley Frazier. Frazier said the package was entirely too long. He told the Warren Commission that while Oswald was hurriedly walking ahead of him from the parking lot, he held the package cupped in his right hand. "He had this cupped in his hand because I remember glancing at him when he was walking up ahead of me."[53]

The Warren Commission lawyer had the six-foot tall witness stand up and place the FBI package in his right hand. The lawyer then made this comment: "When you have cupped the package, the package is not under the armpit, the top of the package extends almost up to the level of your ear."[54] The Warren Commission lawyer had just proven that the package Oswald carried into the book depository was not a disassembled Italian Mannlicher-Carcano, since Lee was several inches shorter than Mr. Frazier and had held the package cupped in his hand under his armpit.

The Warren Commission lawyer next interviewed Linnie Mae Randall who had also seen the package Oswald was carrying that day and asked her if the FBI-made package resembled the one Lee was carrying. Her reply was the following: "Well, it wasn't that long, it definitely wasn't that long."[55] She told the Warren Commission that the package Lee was carrying was a little more than two feet, perhaps 27 inches, long.

One thing is for certain. Whatever was in the paper sack, it was not a disassembled Italian Mannlicher-Carcano. Perhaps it was curtain rods that Oswald was carrying, although living in a small rented room wasn't the time for Lee to show off his interior decorating skills. The package was something Lee wanted to keep hidden from his co-worker as he hurriedly rushed into the building ahead of Mr. Frazier. If the package did not contain a rifle, and perhaps did contain curtain rods, what else may Lee have been hiding in the package? It must have been something important enough for him to make a trip home for and it may have had something to do with the impending assassination. I believe that whatever was contained in the package was discovered at the time of Oswald's arrest in the Texas theater, a little more than an hour after the President's assassination. As Oswald was being handcuffed, a pistol was taken from him which had been tucked inside his belt. I think it would have been unwise for Lee to leave his pistol in his room at the boarding house where an old lady housekeeper could come across it, thus causing his expulsion from the residence. Earlene Roberts, the housekeeper, told the Warren Commission she cleaned Oswald's room and never saw a gun. I think it is much more logical that Oswald would have kept his pistol in Mrs. Paine's garage along with the rifle that he actually owned. Oswald came back the night before the assassination to fetch his pistol perhaps because he wanted the gun for his own personal protection.

The assassination was to take place the following day and Oswald was a party to the assassination. However, if he felt his life was in danger, he must have had some suspicion about the unfolding scenario. Certainly he could take one look at the assassination and realize that, as an ex-defector and self-proclaimed Marxist, he could easily become a suspect in the President's assassination, especially since he worked at the book depository.

We know that the package did not hold an Italian Mannlicher-Carcano but, even more importantly, Oswald's return home the night before the assassination injects another twist in the plot to kill the President. If the gun found on the sixth floor of the book depository was the actual gun used to shoot the President from the building, but wasn't the Italian Mannlicher-Carcano, then where and when was Oswald's Italian Mannlicher-Carcano supposed to be found?

I suggest Oswald's return home the night before the assassination gives us the origin of the Italian Mannlicher-Carcano. This rifle, ordered through the mail, was a backup rifle the Agency was prepared to use if access to Oswald's own rifle was unattainable. Lee did own a rifle and it was this rifle that the Agency was going to use to frame Oswald. However, when Lee came home unexpectedly, the CIA agents who were about to enter the Paine garage and lift Oswald's rifle to frame him for the assassination had to withdraw. Mrs. Paine's garage was a small, one-car affair and the Oswalds slept in a bedroom that was just off the garage entrance from the inside of the house. The CIA agents could hardly risk breaking into the garage at night for fear of spooking Oswald. If Oswald suspected anything, he might not show up for work the next day and complicate the assassination.

So the agents withdrew and Plan B was initiated. The Italian Mannlicher-Carcano would be employed to frame Lee. Since the rifle had been ordered the previous spring in Lee Oswald's handwriting and delivered to a post office box that was rented by him, circumstantially, he could be convicted of murdering the President, especially if he wouldn't be around to defend himself. If the CIA agents had entered the garage on the morning of the assassination, following Oswald's departure for work, they would have been met with a startling surprise. There wasn't any weapon wrapped in the blanket. The Warren Commission wants us to believe that the weapon was not in the blanket because Lee Harvey

Oswald took the weapon with him to the book depository. In any event, Lee's rifle was not in that blanket the morning of the assassination. So where was it?

Glen Emmet Smell was interrogated by the Warren Commission. He worked at Jack's Super Shell located at Rock Island and Story Road in Irving, Texas. Mr. Smell told the Warren Commission lawyer that his mechanic, Robert Taylor, had mentioned that he had bought a rifle from Lee Harvey Oswald. The Warren Commission lawyer said that Robert Taylor was scheduled to testify but had canceled because he had been sick for about a week and a half. Robert Taylor's testimony never made it into the 26 volumes of Hearings and Exhibits prepared for the Warren Commission. Perhaps Robert Taylor's "sickness" proved fatal. If Lee Harvey Oswald had actually sold his rifle in the weeks prior to the assassination, then he did not have a rifle with which to shoot anyone the day of the assassination. The absence of Robert Taylor's testimony is a red flag and lends credence to the statements of Glen Emmet Smell.

There is also evidence from the FBI crime lab that the Italian Mannlicher-Carcano was never wrapped in the blanket that supposedly held the rifle. Logic dictates that if a disassembled rifle is wrapped inside a blanket for several weeks, microscopic fibers from the blanket would attach to the rifle. Threads from the blanket would be found on the rifle or in the rifle, perhaps in the trigger mechanism or in the gun barrel. Paul Morgan Stombaugh, the FBI's hair and fiber expert, told the Warren Commission: "I did find limb hair and head hair in the blanket which were dissimilar to Oswald's and definitely did not come from him."[56] Allen Dulles, the ex-CIA director and Warren Commission member, then asked Special Agent Stombaugh: "And you found no other pieces of fabric or other foreign material from the gun?" To which Stombaugh replied, "Nothing I could associate with the blanket or the shirt or the paper bag."[57]

Therefore, no hair or fibers can be associated between the blanket and the gun, and no hair or fibers can be associated with the blanket and Lee Harvey Oswald! A prosecutor would be hard pressed to prove that the blanket even belonged to Oswald. Still, this does not tell us when the Italian Mannlicher-Carcano was supposed to make its original appearance. We can deduce the answer when we look at the radio log and testimony of the detective who first broadcast the description of the suspect in the President's assassination.

It was Inspector Sawyer of the Dallas Police Department who made the original broadcast of the man suspected as the President's assassin. Inspector Sawyer told the Warren Commission he went to the book depository in response to a radio dispatch made by Sheriff Decker who was in the motorcade: "I heard Sheriff Decker come on the radio and tell the dispatcher to get all his men over to, and I thought he said the book depository. The book depository was mentioned in the broadcasts that were made at the time."[58]

The Warren Commission lawyer pointed out to Inspector Sawyer that there was no mention in the police radio log of the book depository by Sheriff Decker. Here is what Sheriff Decker actually said in his dispatch immediately after the shots were fired at the President: "Get a man on top of that triple underpass and see what happened up there..."[59] He continued, "Have my office and all available men out of my office into the railroad yard to try to determine what happened in there and hold everything secure until homicide and other investigators should get there."[60]

As we see, Sheriff Decker made no mention whatsoever of the book depository. In fact, Sheriff Decker thought the shots fired at the President were coming from in front of the motorcade, perhaps from the overpass or the railroad yards. Sheriff Decker was two cars in front of the President when the shooting erupted. The dispatcher responded to Sheriff

Decker's orders with the following: "All units and officers vicinity of the station report to the railroad tracks area, just north of Elm."[61]

The actual broadcasts contradict Sawyer's testimony because they make no mention of the book depository. Inspector Sawyer gave the first description of the suspect at 12:40 p.m. Dispatch broadcasted it at 12:43 p.m. "The wanted person in this is a slender white male, about thirty, 5'10", 165 lbs., carrying what looks to be a .30 .30 or some type of Winchester."[62]

The first thing one notices is that the description of the suspect is practically identical to the eyewitness description of the man who shot Officer Tippit 45 minutes later. The second thing one notices is that the suspect is carrying his rifle with him as he makes his getaway. However, this gets even more interesting as Inspector Sawyer is grilled by the Warren Commission lawyer. Inspector Sawyer was asked where he got the description of the suspect. Inspector Sawyer replied that an unidentified man came up to him and gave Sawyer the description. The Warren Commission lawyer pressed Inspector Sawyer on this point. Inspector Sawyer's answers were entirely evasive. "I can't remember that much about him. I was real hazy about that."[63]

Let us bring some reality to Inspector Sawyer's testimony. Here is an inspector in the Dallas Police Department who is given a description of the assassin of the President of the United States, but he doesn't remember anything about this eyewitness. At the time he is given the description of the suspect by the citizen, but Inspector Sawyer does not bother to get the person's name, address, or telephone number. He does not bother to hold the person as a material witness to a homicide. Sawyer does not know anything about anyone. He, in my opinion, is the real suspect in the President's assassination. His actions and testimony are entirely suspect. If Inspector Sawyer is one of the conspirators, then what he said at the time of the assassination is vital. Let us look at the description of the gun the "suspect" was carrying.

It was previously mentioned that the suspect was "...carrying what looks to be a .30 caliber or some type of Winchester." If Inspector Sawyer is part of the conspiracy, then the first broadcast of the suspect is part of the plot. Inspector Sawyer was merely mouthing the words of a script written perhaps months before the assassination took place. With the "suspect" carrying his rifle with him, this means that there was never any plan to put a rifle in the sniper's nest. It also means that Lee's rifle, if all had gone according to plan, would have been found at a different location sometime after the assassination. Perhaps it would have turned up in a locker at the Greyhound bus station or some other public storage area.

Hence the mystery of the suddenly appearing Italian Mannlicher-Carcano is solved. The CIA was originally going to use the rifle Oswald actually owned, but in case it was not accessible at the time of the assassination, the CIA had ordered a backup gun through the mail which could be used to frame Oswald for the President's murder. Between the two weapons, one would be found shortly after the crime and be used to implicate Oswald as the assassin. But with the discovery of the real assassin's 7.6 caliber German Mauser on the sixth floor of the book depository, the CIA had to improvise. The Agency combined the German Mauser with Oswald's Italian Mannlicher-Carcano, pretending that he had left the gun on the sixth floor at the time of the assassination.

Vince Drain of the FBI arrived at Dallas Police Headquarters the evening of the assassination. He was given the 6.5 caliber Italian Mannlicher-Carcano and other evidence which he transported to Washington. Since Oswald had never handled that particular weapon, there were no prints of his found on the weapon when examined by the FBI.

* * *

5

OSWALD'S MARKSMANSHIP

Warren Commission. The Commission concluded that Oswald possessed the capability with a rifle that would have enabled him to commit the assassination.[64]

NCO. Oswald's NCO in the Marine Corps gave an interview to his hometown newspaper. Two days after the assassination, the NCO, who asked that his name and address not be used for the article, said that Oswald shot himself in the arm with a .22 caliber pistol. As far as Oswald's marksmanship was concerned, the NCO said, "He was a very poor shot."[65]

Nelson Delgado. Nelson Delgado was a Marine Corps buddy of Oswald's while the two were stationed in Santa Ana, California during the summer of 1959. Lee had joined the Marines on October 24, 1956 and was discharged September 11, 1959. "We went to the range at one time and he didn't show no particular aspect of being a sharpshooter at all," Delgado told the commission.[66]

Delgado was with Oswald for almost a year and, when questioned about Oswald's marksmanship, said, "No he didn't even place, he just barely got his score, which I think was about 170, just barely a sharpshooter."[67] Delgado continued: "It was a pretty big joke because he got a lot of maggie drawers, you know, a lot of misses, but he didn't give a darn."[68] Delgado told the commission that he believed Oswald's test score of 170 was erroneously reported. "Now your NCO, especially your NCO, may want to rush you or make you qualify because he doesn't want to spend another day out there on the rifle range.[69] You can't take a man that is shooting poorly and give him a 190 score. You could just give him the bare minimum, 170 or 171, to make it look good."[70]

Delgado made it clear to the commission that Oswald was a poor shot because of all the "maggie drawers" and that the NCO gave him the bare minimum so that he wouldn't have to keep bringing Oswald out to the range.[71]

* * *

6

ACCURACY OF THE RIFLE

Warren Commission. The various tests showed that the Mannlicher-Carcano was an accurate rifle and the use of the four-power scope was a substantial aid to rapid, accurate firing.[72]

The FBI Tests. Robert Frazier, the FBI firearms expert, took the assassin's rifle out to the range to determine the firing capability of the rifle. Frazier, Cortland Cunningham, and Charles Killion took their turns with the rifle. One of the things to be determined was how rapidly the rifle could be fired. All the shots fired at the President began and ended in six seconds. Three shots had been counted in those six seconds.

Charles Killion took nine seconds to pull off his three shots. Cortland Cunningham took seven seconds. Only Frazier was able to fire the rifle in six seconds.[73] When the men checked their targets, which were only 15 yards away, all three men had missed the target with all three shots. At one hundred yards, Frazier hit five inches high and five inches to the right of the target.[74] After examining the rifle, Frazier was able to determine that the scope of the rifle was defective.[75] The scope has been improperly mounted on the rifle before it was shipped to Oswald the previous spring.

Frazier told the Commission that in order to hit the President, Oswald would have had to aim six to eight inches above the President's head and give a three-inch lead.[76] He told the Commission the barrel of the gun showed the effects of wear and corrosion. The lands and grooves were worn as well as the corners. The interior surface was generally roughened from corrosion.[77] He told the Commission the scope was a very inexpensive Japanese telescope.[78] He also pointed out that normally when shooting at some object and finishing, one would not reload. Oswald's rifle was found with another bullet in the chamber ready to shoot. The Warren Commission ordered the military to set up a test to determine the accuracy of the Mannlicher-Carcano.

Ronald Simmons. Ronald Simmons, a chief of infantry weapons, evaluated the test. The first thing to note is that the three marksmen are just that—expert marksmen. They are not ordinary men with ordinary shooting skills like Oswald— even giving Oswald the benefit of the doubt.

The first thing the expert marksmen found was that they could not sight the weapon in using the telescopic site.[79] Mr. Simmons told the Commission—that they did adjust the telescope by adding two shims, one adjusting the elevation and the other adjusting the azimuth.[80] They were put in by a gunsmith in one of their mechanical shops.[81] Oswald didn't have that luxury. The Warren Commission lawyer corrected Mr. Simmons and told him it was three shims that the gunsmith placed to fix the telescope.[82]

And how did our experts fare at their exhibition? Not too bad. All hit the target on the first shot (after taking as much time as they wanted, unlike Oswald), and all three missed with the second shot. All three hit the target with their third shot. Not bad shooting for three premier rifle marksmen shooting at stationary targets, taking as much time with the first shot as they cared to, using the telescope that a gunsmith had ensured was perfect. They also had time to practice before their big day. Certainly, the three FBI men's experiment a few days after the assassination was more realistic in light of what Oswald's situation would have been in the sniper's nest.

The expert marksmen made some interesting comments about the assassin's rifle. They said much effort was needed to open the bolt and that the trigger pulled in two stages. They did not practice first with the rifle because of concern about breaking the firing pin. The conclusion was, "The pressure to open the bolt was so great that we tended to move the rifle off the target."

* * *

7

DISCOVERY OF THE CARTRIDGE CASES

Warren Commission. Deputy Sheriff Luke Mooney found three empty cartridge cases on the floor near the window at approximately 1:12 p.m.[83]

Frazier. Robert Frazier, the FBI firearms expert, testified to the Commission about the likelihood of the location of the cartridge cases. In the photograph of the cartridge cases there are two them lying side by side and a third is just out of range of the photograph. Frazier told the Commission that two cartridge cases were found against the wall. When the Commission lawyer inquired as to the likelihood of this happening, Frazier commented that ejected shells would land anywhere from eight inches to ten or fifteen feet away.[84] The bullet shells found on the sixth floor in the sniper's nest were found against the wall of the window that Oswald was allegedly firing from. Therefore, not only did these shells fail to eject backward as all shells do, they ejected forward and landed most courteously in a row.

Marvin Johnson. Homicide Detective Marvin Johnson was on the sixth floor of the book depository when the shells were discovered. He told the Warren Commission that "they were underneath a window, right near a window."[85] When the Warren Commission lawyer showed Detective Johnson a photograph of the rifle hulls as photographed by the Dallas Police Department, Detective Johnson was hesitant. The Commission lawyer asked him if the shells appeared to be in the same position as they were when he saw them. Detective Johnson answered, "There is only two that show in that photograph, that I see."[86] The Commission lawyer recovered and pointed out the two hulls lying side by side and a third bullet nearby, just out of the photograph, supposedly by a box that is pictured in the photograph.

Detective Johnson said "Yes, I see it. All I can say, at the time these hulls were mentioned, I went over there and looked. I don't remember them being that far apart."[87] It was my impression that they were all three next to the wall...I thought they were all three closer to the wall."[88]

J. W. Fritz. In his affidavit, the chief of homicide, J. W. Fritz, who was also on the sixth floor at the time the shells were discovered, said the same thing: "Three spent rifle hulls were found under the window in the southeast corner of the sixth floor of the book depository on the afternoon of November 22, 1963."[89]

Luke Mooney. Deputy Sheriff Luke Mooney was the man who found the shells. When the Warren Commission lawyer showed him the photograph of the shells that he found, taken at the time that they were discovered, Officer Mooney also questioned the positions of the shells in the photograph.[90]

What does it matter if two shells were lying side by side and a third shell discovered some distance away, or if all three were lined up neatly in a row? The importance of the shells resting at the foot of the sniper's window is that expended bullet shells are ejected away from and behind the

rifleman for his own protection. To have found rifle cartridges at the foot of the sniper's window means that someone purposely placed them there.

The reason that a photograph exists showing two bullets
together instead of three was to throw the Commission off
track. It looks too much like a set up to have three bullet
shells lying side by side like three pigs in a blanket. When the
conspirators placed the cartridges in the sniper's nest, the
first mistake was placing them against the wall. The second
mistake was lining them up all three in a row. I suggest that
when the CIA first took a look at the photographs of the
hulls before having them sent to the Warren Commission,
one of the CIA agents noticed how ridiculous it looked. The
original photograph of the hulls looked like they had been
placed there on purpose, which, of course, they had. The
CIA had the hulls rephotographed, this time having two hulls
together instead of three so as not to be so obvious. They
had to have at least two hulls together in the photograph
because too many police officers had seen those shells in
their original position. However, even with this effort, the
Agency lost out. The police officers who were shown the
photograph by the Warren Commission were not fooled by
it. By the same token, the police officers who found the rifle
did not cave into pressure to change their original impression
concerning the rifle they found. Furthermore, Secret Service
agents weren't fooled as to the origin and direction of the
shots.

* * *

8

DISCOVERY OF THE BULLET
AT PARKLAND HOSPITAL

Warren Commission. A nearly whole bullet was found on Governor Connally's stretcher at Parkland Hospital after the assassination.[91] All the evidence indicated that the bullet found on the Governor's stretcher could have caused all of his wounds.[92] On the weakness of this concept alone, without consideration of contributing evidence, the Commission's conclusions tumble like a house of cards.

The Magic Bullet. The problem confronting the Commission was that all indications seemed to point to three shots having been fired. The testimony of eye witnesses in Dealey Plaza was that three to six shots were fired. The overwhelming majority of them heard only three. In addition, only three bullet hulls were found in the sniper's nest. Furthermore, the shooting began and ended within six seconds.

The FBI tested the speed of the Zapruder camera, which recorded the assassination on film. Then the Bureau divided the film frame by frame. The President's clutching his throat until the final shot to his head represents only six seconds. We thus have three cartridges and three shots in six seconds. The first shot to ring out apparently missed the President's vehicle altogether. We know this from the abundant testimony of Secret Service agents, spectators, and the reaction of the President as he heard the first shot, recognized it as a shot, and looked frantically around for the source. A look of seriousness came over the World War II hero's face; he looked to his right and then turned rapidly to his left. As he emerged from behind the sign he began to reach for his throat while looking straight ahead toward the overpass. Obviously he had been hit by one of the other shots by this time. Seconds later he received the shot to his head.

However, the problem is that we have two men seriously wounded. The President had been hit twice and Governor Connally, sitting in front of the President, also suffered serious and multiple wounds. If the first bullet missed, that leaves only two bullets to cause all of the wounds of both men. When you subtract one of the two remaining bullets as the one which struck the President's head, only one bullet remains to cause all of the other wounds. The Commission concluded that a bullet penetrated the rear of the President's head and exited through a large wound on the right side of his head.[93]

It is also observed that another bullet wound was found near the base of the back of President Kennedy's neck, slightly to the right of his spine. It was an entrance wound.[94] The bullet exited from the front portion of the President's neck.[95] But what about Governor Connally's multiple wounds? A bullet entered Governor Connally's back, shattered his fifth rib and exited below the right nipple. Since only three bullets were fired, the Commission reasoned that the bullet that entered President Kennedy's back and exited through his throat must have then continued through Governor Connally's body, and thus was the origin of all his wounds. There could not have been four or more shots because it is impossible to fire the bolt action Mannlicher-Carcano more than three times in six seconds. Also, there were only three bullet shells found in the sniper's nest. Thus, to conclude that there were four or more shots is to imply a conspiracy of at least two men shooting simultaneously.

Most witnesses, in both their verbal testimony, as well as in their written statements on the day of the assassination, said there was one shot, then a space of a few seconds, then the second and third shots on the heels of one another. This spacing of the three shots already precludes the possibility that one man fired at the President. The equally preposterous notion that somehow the wounds of two men were made by one bullet slowly became the undoing of the conspiracy. All this brings us back to exhibit #399, the "Magic Bullet."

The bullet found on Governor Connally's stretcher was in perfect condition, nearly whole. Such a whole bullet typically weighs 161 grams. This one weighed 158 grams. Why is it that it didn't shatter and fragment? It supposedly entered the back of President Kennedy's neck and exited out his throat. Then it entered Governor Connally's back, traversed his chest, snapped off a rib, exploded out his chest, then struck (and broke) his right wrist, finally resting in his left thigh. Yet the bullet found on the stretcher at Parkland Hospital, the only bullet left that could have caused all of these wounds, was in nearly perfect condition. It's impossible to fool a layman with this bullet. What about surgeons?

James Humes. Commander Humes was the surgeon given the task of conducting the President's autopsy. At the Warren Commission hearings he was asked if exhibit #399, the "magic bullet," could have gone through President Kennedy. Humes answered in the negative. He was then asked if this bullet could have made the wound on Governor Connally's wrist. Humes answered, "I think that that is most unlikely."[96] He continued, "The reason I believe it most unlikely that this missile could have inflicted either of these wounds is that *this missile is basically intact.* I do not understand how it could possibly have left fragments in either of these locations."[97]

Humes further elaborated on Connally's wounds and why this bullet never touched the governor. "...passed through lattisimus dorsi muscle, shattered approximately ten centimeters of a lateral and anterior portion of the right fifth rib and emerged below the right nipple anterially."[98] With Commander Hume's graphic summary of why the magic bullet could not have gone through either man, comes the shattering of the conspiracy.

Robert Frazier. Once again we have Frazier, the FBI firearms expert, asked his opinion on whether exhibit #399 could have caused Governor Connally's wounds. Frazier pointed out that there was no blood on the bullet, that it was clean and in perfect condition. He pointed out to the Commission that the bullet's regular weight was 161 grams and that it now weighed 158.6 grams. Frazier said it should weighed far less.[99]

So it definitely appears to have been a plant. Tests showed that the bullet at some point had been fired from the Italian Mannlicher-Carcano that had been found in the book depository. If this bullet was indeed a plant, the fact that it had been fired from the Mannlicher-Carcano strongly hints that the Mannlicher-Carcano was a plant as well. That is, the bullet and rifle offer cross-evidence of their having been planted.

Dr. Robert Shaw. Dr. Robert Shaw was the surgeon who operated on Governor Connally. When asked at the Warren Commission hearings about the possibility that the magic bullet caused Governor Connally's wounds, Dr. Shaw answered forthrightly.

> But the examination of the wrist, both by x-ray and at the time of surgery, showed some fragments of metal that make it difficult to believe that the same missile could have caused these two wounds. There seems to be more than three grains

of metal missing as far as the—I mean in the wrist...The bullet has lost literally none of its substance.[100]...I feel that these would be more difficult in explaining all of the wounds as being inflicted by bullet #399 without causing more in the way of loss of substance to the bullet, or deformation of the bullet."[101]

Dr. Shaw explained to the Warren Commission that more metal was in the Governor's wrist, let alone anywhere else the bullet had traveled, than was missing from bullet #399. On top of this, he stated that the bullet was remarkably undeformed.

Alfred G. Olivier. The Commission, wanting to prove that bullet #399 could actually do the damage claimed for it and remain perfectly intact, conducted a study. Alfred G. Olivier, a research veterinarian, was given the job of conducting it. First, a goat was dressed up in an undershirt and given a jacket to wear. The Commission wanted the experiment to simulate Governor Connally and his wounds at the time of the assassination. The ammunition used was the same type as that of bullet #399. The same Mannlicher-Carcano that Oswald supposedly fired was used. So a goat was all dressed up with nowhere to go, and, at 70 yards, was fired at. The bullet that entered the goat was demolished. "Our particular bullet is flattened the whole length," Dr. Olivier commented to the Warren Commission.[102] Another bullet fired into a wrist of a cadaver to simulate Governor Connally's wounds was likewise demolished. "The nose of the bullet is quite flattened from striking the radius. This one is very severely flattened on the end."[103]

Despite this evidence, the Warren Commission concluded that this bullet, exhibit #399, not only broke Governor Connally's wrist but went through both men. On the other hand, if this bullet could not go have gone through both men, much less caused all the wounds suffered by them, it can only mean that more than one man fired at the President.

Equally important was the discovery of magic bullet #399 on the stretcher at the hospital. Obviously, someone had planted it there. And, because it had been fired at some point by the Mannlicher-Carcano, we have a clear framing of Lee Harvey Oswald. Consider: A rifle appeared out of nowhere on the sixth floor at the time of the assassination. Bullet hulls lying neatly in a row were found in the sniper's nest. Finally, to create a triangulation of manufactured evidence that could frame Oswald—the planting of the magic bullet. The rifle could be traced to Oswald through the mail, the bullet hulls traced to the rifle. The magic bullet was merely the icing on the cake, a whole bullet to cement Oswald's guilt once and for all. Tests showed unequivocally that this bullet had been fired from the particular rifle, to the exclusion of all others.[104]

* * *

9

THE BULLET WOUNDS

Warren Commission. The Warren Commission concluded that a bullet penetrated the rear of the President's head
and exited through a large wound on the right side of the
head.[105] Another bullet wound was observed near the base of
the back of President Kennedy's neck slightly to the right of
his spine. It is a wound of entrance.[106] The bullet exited
from the front portion of the President's neck.[107]

Overview. Unfortunately for the Warren Commission,
the evidence does not support these conclusions or even
come close to supporting these conclusions. The evidence in
the 26 volumes of testimony and exhibits points to the following:

> One shot missed the Presidential limousine. One shot hit the
> President in the back, six inches down from his collar and an
> inch to the right of his spine. This shot was fired from a po-
> sition behind the President. Another shot also fired from be-
> hind the President missed JFK and struck Governor
> Connally. Finally, a shot was fired from the front of the
> President, slightly to his right. This shot was fired from the
> bushes atop the grassy knoll, next to the overpass. This shot

hit the President in the right temple, causing a wound of entrance and exiting out the back of the President's skull. This shot proved fatal, snapping the President's head back, lifting his body and driving him violently backward against his seat.

Newspaper Reports. Newspapers throughout the country reported the following: "A single shot through the right temple took the life of the 46-year-old chief executive."[108] So many identical accounts pointed to a single source—in this case, Parkland Hospital. The men who provided the information about the shots were the surgeons who tried to save the President's life, who then talked to the press.

Seth Kantor. Seth Kantor was a reporter covering the President's trip to Dallas. He took notes of everything as well as his own personal impressions as they were occurring at the time. Kantor's notes can be found tucked away in volume 20 of the exhibits of the Warren Commission. At the hospital, Kantor and the rest of the world awaited word on President Kennedy's condition. Malcolm Kilduff, the White House press secretary, came out to give an announcement. His statement was that the President of the United States was dead from a gunshot wound. Kantor's notes, written at the time of the announcement, disclose that a bullet had "Intered (sic) right temple."[109]

Who told Seth Kantor that the bullet that killed the President had entered through his right temple? Why, naturally, that would have been Malcolm Kilduff. Where had Kilduff gotten his information? From the surgeons who operated on the President.

Dr. Kenneth Everett Salyer. Doctor Salyer in his testimony before the Warren Commission had this to say: "And, that he also had a wound of his right temporal region[110]...I came in on the left side of him and noticed that his major wound seemed to be in his *right temporal area*, at least from the point of view that I could see him, and other than that—

nothing other than he did have a gaping, scalp wound, cranial wound."[111]

Well, there we have it. The doctor clearly distinguished the wound in the temporal area from that of the "cranial wound" in the back of the head. What is the significance of the President being shot through the temple as opposed to being shot through the back of the head? As the President's vehicle was moving down Elm Street, away from the book depository, the President was looking forward toward the overpass. The school book building was almost 100 yards behind him when he received the fatal head wound. For the President to have been shot through the right temple means that the fatal bullet was fired from in front of the President, not from the building behind him. This means that someone was shooting at the President from the front while another was firing from behind. Thus, the President was in a cross-fire, and had certainly been led into an ambush.

William Newman. William Newman was standing alongside the President when the latter was shot in the head. Mr. Newman was on the sidewalk to the right of the President. He was just a few feet away from the vehicle when the shots rang out. "By this time he was directly in front of us and I was looking directly at him when he was hit *in the side of the head*."[112] Newman wrote his affidavit at the Sheriff's office the very afternoon of the assassination. The memory of the ghastly deed was still fresh in his mind. According to Newman, a bullet fired from the front hit the President in the right temple, driving him backward.

Roy Kellerman. Roy Kellerman was in charge of the Secret Service detachment from the White House accompanying the President on his trip to Dallas. He attended the President's autopsy. Kellerman stayed with the President from the time of the ambush until after the autopsy, and to just before morticians arrived to prepare the body for the funeral in Washington. Kellerman was the agent riding in the

President's vehicle. He was adamant that the shots were fired "in a flurry."

Kellerman described the skull wound to the Commission. He also described a second wound. "The other wound that I noticed was on his shoulder—right shoulder."[113] Kellerman spoke of an interesting moment during the autopsy. The surgeons wondered what happened to the bullet that struck the President in the back. "There were three gentlemen who were performing this autopsy, a Colonel Finck—during the examination of the President, from the hole that was in his shoulder, and with a probe, and we were standing right alongside of him, he is probing inside the shoulder with his instrument. And I said, "Colonel, where did it go?" He said, "*There are no lanes for an outlet of this entry in this man's shoulder.*"[114] Yet this shoulder wound, seen by Kellerman and inspected by Colonel Finck, disappeared from the Warren Report!

Kellerman informed the Commission of another interesting and devastating fact. "From all the x-rays that were taken—all the medical people who were in the morgue at the time, the two bureau agents, myself, Greer—they were looking for pieces of fragments of this bullet. There was none. Only one piece to my knowledge. That was removed from inside, above the eye."[115]

How can two bullets enter the President's body, leaving several entrance and exit wounds, as well as blowing out the back of his skull, without leaving fragments somewhere in the President's body? The answer, of course, is that it's impossible. The only explanation for there being no bullet fragments in the President's body is that persons unknown—yet with surgeon's skills—removed the fragments before the President's autopsy. That is, there was a pre-autopsy performed on the President to remove vital evidence that would have led to the conclusion that there were multiple gunmen. The pre-autopsy and the probable secret hijacking of the body, unknown to Kellerman (but for which there is evidence), will be discussed in a later chapter.

The main thing one gleans from Kellerman's testimony is that a very clear and specific back wound in the President's right shoulder was not discussed in the Warren Report. The Warren Report does speak of a bullet wound near the base of the back of the President's neck slightly to the right of his spine. The wound Kellerman was speaking of was in the President's shoulder. The surgeon, Colonel Finck, put a probe into the hole. There was no lane for an exit. The bullet that went into the shoulder never went all the way through the President's body. This means the Warren Commission's conclusion of a shot entering the back of the President's neck and exiting through his throat was untenable.

Clint Hill. Clint Hill was one of the Secret Service agents assigned to the President's back-up vehicle. This team of agents stood on the running boards of the back-up vehicle, periodically alighting and getting between the crowd and the President's car.

Clint Hill was standing on the left front running board of the vehicle when the first shot was heard. At that moment, he saw the President grab at himself and lurch forward. He jumped from the backup car and ran to the limousine. Just as he reached the limousine, he heard another shot. This was the shot which resulted in the fatal head wound.

Agent Hill described how Mrs. Kennedy jumped from her seat and reached for something coming off the right rear bumper of the car. He grabbed her and guided her back into her seat and hung onto the back seat himself for the ride to Parkland Hospital. Mr. Hill related how Mrs. Kennedy exclaimed, "My God, they have shot his head off. Jack, Jack, what have they done to you?" [116] Clint Hill was also the agent who covered the President's head and shoulders with his coat when taking the President out of the car and into the emergency room.

After the autopsy, but before the embalming, Kellerman summoned Agent Hill to the morgue to view the body and witness the damage of the gunshot wounds. Agent Hill described the wounds he saw on the President. "*I observed a wound about six inches down from the neckline, on the back, just to the right of the spinal column.* I observed another wound on the right rear portion of the skull."[117] This is the best description of the location of the President's back wound. It is specific and it is clear. It is also absent from the autopsy report as well as from the Warren Report.

The conspirators, in order to frame Lee Harvey Oswald as the President's assassin, had to show that three shots, only three shots, were fired at the motorcade from the book depository. But, with one bullet missing the vehicle altogether, another shattering the President's skull, only one bullet was left to inflict all of Governor Connally's wounds and President Kennedy's throat wound. It was only by "raising" the shoulder wounds to the base of the back of the President's neck, could it be postulated that the same bullet continued through Kennedy, exited his throat and then proceeded to strike Governor Connally.

Glen Bennett. In the Secret Service back-up car on whose running boards Clint Hill had been stationed sat agent Glen Bennett. Agent Bennett gives us one more eyewitness account of the shot that hit the President in the back. "At the moment I looked at the back of the President, I heard another firecracker noise and saw the shot hit the President about *four inches down from the right shoulder.*"[118]

* * *

9

OSWALD'S PALMPRINT ON THE RIFLE

Warren Commission. Additional evidence of ownership was given in the form of palmprint identification indicating that Oswald was possessor of the rifle he had purchased.[119]

Sebastian Latona. It was the FBI's Sebastian Latona who received the Italian Mannlicher-Carcano the day after the assassination and processed the rifle for prints. As one of the world's foremost fingerprint experts, Latona was eminently qualified to draw out any latent fingerprints left on the weapon. Latona told the Commission that he had done everything he could and had checked the whole rifle but found no identifiable prints.[120] He told the Commission, "I was not successful in developing any prints at all on the weapon." Latona added that he had processed the complete weapon—all of its parts and there were no latent prints. He had later sent the rifle back to the Dallas Police Department. Newspaper reports throughout the nation reported that the FBI had found no prints on the murder weapon and, as late as November 25, three days after the assassination, it was still being reported that the weapon had no prints on it. Latona told the Commission that on November 29, 1963 he received a palm print from the Dallas Police Department with a note saying, "Off underside of gun barrel near the end of fore grip—C2766."[121]

Was there or was there not a palm print on the rifle? The evidence overwhelmingly supports the contention that no prints were found on it by the FBI the night of the assassination. The FBI has the finest crime lab in the world. The rifle was examined by the foremost fingerprint expert in the world. He tried every technique there was to bring out any latent prints. Latona processed the whole rifle—all parts. He didn't find any prints.

This means that the rifle he examined was being used to frame Lee Harvey Oswald. The part the Mannlicher-Carcano was playing was to lay a paper trail in framing Oswald. Investigation would show that the rifle had been ordered through the mail and sent to a post office box being rented by someone using a known alias of Lee Oswald.

Additional proof as to the falsification of a palm print of Oswald's is the total silence on the part of the Dallas Police Department over the affair. Certainly, at any time after it was reported through the news media that no fingerprints were found on the rifle, the Dallas Police Department could have informed the FBI that they had recovered a palm print on the rifle. However, it wasn't until November 29, seven days after the assassination, that the Dallas Police Department contacted the FBI about the print. When you speak about the Dallas Police Department you are really speaking about one man—Lieutenant J.C. Day, head of the crime scene search section, identification bureau.

Lieutenant J.C. Day. Lieutenant Day arrived at the crime scene on the sixth floor of the book depository shortly after the assassination. He oversaw all evidence collection during the investigation. He told the Commission. "Now the gun did not leave my possession."[122] Although he testified that he'd discovered the palm print on the rifle, in doing so he violated every standard procedure for obtaining finger-prints for criminal prosecution. He also testified to taking samples of tape and a paper bag from the mail room of the book depository. These would also be used to incriminate Oswald. Actually, in Day we have one of the main players of the conspiracy.

* * *

11

OSWALD AT THE WINDOW

Paper Bag. The Commission concluded that Oswald took paper and tape from the wrapping bench of the depository and fashioned a bag large enough to carry the disassembled rifle.[123]

James Cadigan. James Cadigan was the FBI agent whose expertise lay in questioned documents. He examined a paper bag that was discovered on the sixth floor of the book depository not far from the sniper's nest. He also examined the tape that was on the bag. The theory was that Oswald carried the disassembled rifle into the building when he arrived for work the morning of the assassination. He then hid the rifle and waited for the chance to shoot the President as he passed the book depository. So far, so good. This exhibit was marked #142. Agent Cadigan then examined a replica of the paper bag and tape made by the Dallas Police Department. Our fearless "Sherlock Holmes," Lieutenant J.C. Day, told the Warren Commission that he and Detective Studebaker, his recently installed (two months) assistant took a sample of paper and tape from the mailroom of the book depository.[124] On the evening of the assassination he gave the tape and paper bag to FBI Agent Vince Drain.[125] This replica of the paper bag and tape taken from the mailroom of the book depository by Day was marked exhibit #677.

Cadigan testified that the paper bag and tape found near the sniper's nest (exhibit #142) and the paper bag and tape taken from the paper-dispensing machine in the mailroom of the book depository (exhibit #667), had the same composition under ultraviolet light.[126] Since the textures of the paper bag and tape found on the sixth floor of the book depository at the time of the assassination had the same structural characteristics as the paper and tape from the mailroom, the assumption is that Oswald took paper and tape from the mailroom where he worked and fashioned a bag to carry his rifle into the building.

Unfortunately for the CIA, the FBI did their own little test. On December 1, 1963, one week after the assassination, FBI agents went into the mailroom and removed paper and tape from the paper and tape dispensing machine, fashioning their own makeshift paper bag. When James Cadigan examined the replica of the bag put together by the FBI, this paper and tape had different characteristics than either exhibit #141 (from the sixth floor) and exhibit #677 (from the mailroom courtesy of Lieutenant Day). Theoretically, if the paper and tape are coming from the same source, all three paper bags and accompanying tape should have the same characteristics as far as composition is concerned.

Exhibit #142 (from the sixth floor) and exhibit #677 (Lieutenant Day) have the same characteristics, but exhibit #364 (FBI), is different from the other two.[127] Since exhibits #142 and #677 have the same characteristics, they had to come from the same source. It must also be true that exhibit #364 (FBI) came from a different source than the other two.

The same type of paper was in the paper dispensing machine in the mailroom on December 1, 1963 when the FBI took their samples as was there on November 22, 1963, when Lieutenant Day said he took his samples. Also, it would have been the same paper and tape that Oswald would have gotten if he had taken any paper and tape from the machine. We know this is true because James Cadigan told the Warren Commission that the book depository had received a shipment from St. Regis Paper Mills of Jacksonville, Florida on March 19, 1963. This supply lasted until January of 1964.[128] Therefore, either the FBI was lying about its replica coming from the mailroom of the book depository or Lieutenant J.C. Day was lying when he told the Commission that he obtained his sample from the School Book Depository.

The FBI had nothing to gain by such a fabrication and had only their own credibility to lose. Lieutenant J.C. Day was lying when he told the Commission he retrieved his paper bag and tape from the book depository. His paper bag and tape definitely came from the same source as that of the tape and paper bag found near the sniper's nest. However, that source was not the book depository. Instead, the source was somewhere deep within the bowels of the CIA. The two paper bags were made to frame Oswald for the assassination.

Further proof that the bags were constructed to frame Oswald is that there were no rifle marks on the inside of the bag found on the sixth floor of the depository building. James C. Cadigan explained to the Commission: "There were no marks on this bag that I could say were caused by that rifle or any other rifle."[129] How does Oswald put a disassembled rifle in a paper bag, carry the bag to work, hide the bag, then take the disassembled weapon out of the bag to shoot the President of the United States, and not have some part of his weapon leave at least a tiny scratch somewhere in the bag? For there to be an absence of any rifle marks can only mean the bag was a plant. Furthermore, to have Lieutenant J.C. Day produce a replica of that bag, and to have that replica have the same composition under ultraviolet light as the bag found near the sniper's nest, can only mean that Lieutenant Day was a member of the conspiracy.

The paper bag and tape found on the sixth floor were planted. It was to be incriminating evidence used to indict Oswald posthumously. It was apparently no problem for the CIA to get some officer to go along with the assassination and just do what he was told. The CIA would do the rest. However, Lieutenant Day was not done as far as his usefulness was concerned. A little man given a big job, to help bring down a great man, Lieutenant Day had one more scene to play.

Box. On November 27, 1963 Sebastian Latona, head of the latent fingerprint section of the identification division of the FBI, received a piece of cardboard cut from a box and sent to the FBI from Lieutenant Day of the Dallas Police Department.[130] At a glance one should start to become suspicious. One, it arrived five days after the assassination; two, a piece of cardboard had been cut out of the box; and three, it came from J.C. Day, who cut the piece from the box and took the palm print from it.[131] The piece cut out of the box was labeled exhibit #647 and the box itself was labelled exhibit #648. The box was taken from the sniper's nest and there was a right palm print on the piece of cardboard. The palm print belongs, of course, to Lee Harvey Oswald. However, we have a problem here. Latona described the print on the piece of cardboard as "fresh".[132] Latona told the Commission that on cardboard, after 24 hours, the print is gone.[133]

Arthur Mandella. Arthur Mandella, fingerprint expert of the New York Police Department, also examined the piece of cardboard cut from the box. He identified the print as belonging to Lee Harvey Oswald. Mr. Mandella said that the print was a "fresh print."[134] He explained to the Commission that cardboard was very porous and that oils and perspiration would disappear quickly. He said that prints on such surfaces would be gone within one to one-and-a-half days.

Mandella was quite specific about the print. "However, we do have an impression here with powder. That means it was quite fresh."[135] Because these prints evaporate within 24 hours, and since the print in question was fresh, it had to have been taken right after Oswald placed his palm on the box. The question is when did Oswald place his palm on the cardboard section of the box that was cut out and sent to the FBI? Latona received the cardboard cut from the box as well as the box itself on November 27, 1963. On November 27 Oswald had been dead for three days. It had been five days since he had worked at the book depository. In order for a fresh print of Oswald's to appear on the cardboard box meant that the palm print had to have come from Oswald's corpse.

Oswald was never in the sniper's nest. A palm print of Oswald could not have been taken in the opening hours of the assassination, at least not from a box from the window overlooking Elm Street. We already know that the rifle and the print on the rifle were manufactured to frame Oswald. We know the paper bag and tape left near the sniper's nest were also ingredients added to his framing for the President's murder. It is logical that the print on the cardboard cut from the box is also a part of the frame-up. But what is particularly gruesome is that the only source for a fresh palm print could have come only from the corpse of Lee Harvey Oswald.

* * *

12

PHOTOGRAPH OF OSWALD WITH THE RIFLE

Warren Commission. Oswald asked his wife to take a picture of him holding a rifle, a pistol, and issues of two newspapers later identified as the *The Worker* and *The Militant.* Two photographs were taken in different poses. The Commission has concluded that the rifle shown in these photographs is the same which was found on the sixth floor of the depository building on November 22, 1963.[136] The Commission gave great weight to these photographs of Oswald, in particular, the photograph of Oswald holding the rifle, two communist newspapers and a pistol strapped to his side. However, this photograph has a strange history.

Richard Stouval. Shortly after Oswald was arrested detectives paid a visit to the home of Ruth Paine. Oswald's wife and two children were living with Mrs. Paine when Oswald found employment at the book depository.

Oswald stayed at a boarding home in Dallas Monday through Thursday and hitched a ride with a fellow employee to the Dallas suburb of Irving, Texas and the home of Mrs.

Paine each Friday. Detective Stouval told the Commission of a conversation that Detective Rose had had with Mrs. Paine. "Ruth Paine was standing there talking to him. I could hear her talking to him and she told him that Marina suggested that he look out into the garage."[137] Detective Stouval told the Commission that they searched the house and the garage for two to two-and-a-half hours.[138]

Eddy Walthers. Deputy Sheriff Eddy (Buddy) Walthers also was at the Paine residence joining the search. The detective told the Commission how Mrs. Paine greeted them: "Come on in, we've been expecting you."[139] Detective Walthers told the Commission, "It didn't appear that they knew that Oswald had been arrested at all—the way they talked."[140] Walthers continued:

> We went into the garage there and found this—I believe it was one of those things like soap comes in, a big pasteboard barrel and it had a lot of these little leaflets in it. 'Freedom for Cuba' and they were gold color with black printing on them, and we found those and we also found a gray blanket with some red trim on it that had a string tied to one end that you could see the imprint of a gun, I mean where it had been wrapped in it.[141]

Detective Walthers also told the Commission that they found six or seven metal file cabinets that carried eight-by-ten-inch folders. He also spoke of finding a bunch of pictures and with the pictures, metal file cabinets, the soap barrel with the leaflets in it and the blanket, the detectives went downtown. "And then we took all this stuff and put it in the car and then Mrs. Paine got a phone number from Mrs. Oswald where you could call Lee Harvey Oswald in Oak Cliff.[142] They were all put in the cars and we took them to Captain Will Fritz's office."[143]

The remarkable thing is that no photograph of Lee Harvey Oswald holding a rifle and two Marxist newspapers was found that day. The question is why not? The garage to the Paine residence was very small. It was only a one-car garage. The detectives had found a blanket, file cabinets, photographs and leaflets, but had not found a photograph of Lee Harvey Oswald holding a rifle and two Marxist newspapers. If such an incriminating photograph had actually been in the garage, would not the detectives have found it? They certainly spent enough time in there. Between two and two-and-a-half hours had been spent searching the home and the garage. They rifled through all of Marina's and Oswald's possessions. They found other photographs, but not the photograph of Oswald holding a rifle.

The next day detectives were ordered back to the Paine residence to do a more thorough search.[144] Detectives Stouval, Moore, Rose and Adamchik were ordered out to the house. This time they hit the jackpot. Detective Stouval told the Warren Commission that the next day, between 1:30 p.m. and 2:00 p.m., they made a second search of the garage. Stouval testified that Detective Rose exclaimed, "Look at this!" Stouval continues: "At that time he said that— he showed us the snapshots and the negatives to me."[145] The photograph was of Lee Harvey Oswald with a rifle, two Marxist newspapers and a pistol on his hip. This photograph would help indict Oswald in the minds of the American people when they saw the photograph spread across a national news magazine.

However, why was it that detectives could search for two-and-a-half hours, find a good deal of material to cart off including photographs, but miss this one highly incriminating photograph? Yet, on the very next day, detective Rose entered the garage and went straight to it.

Will Fritz. When Captain Fritz, chief of homicide, confronted Oswald with this highly incriminating photograph during his interrogation of the prisoner, Oswald had an interesting reaction. "I know all about photography. I worked with photography for a long time. That is a picture that someone else has made. I never saw that picture before in my life...I have been through the whole deal. Someone has taken my picture and that is my face and put a different body on it."[146]

Lyndal Shaneyfelt. Lyndal Shaneyfelt was a documents expert for the FBI. He examined the photograph of Oswald posing with the rifle. The first thing we find is that the sling on the rifle in the photograph is not the same sling that was found on the Italian Mannlicher-Carcano allegedly discovered on the sixth floor of the book depository. Agent Shaneyfelt: "Commission exhibit #133b does show the sling, since it shows the bottom of the rifle, and I find it to be different from the sling that is presently on the rifle. It has the appearance of being a piece of rope that is tied to both ends."[147] Furthermore, Shaneyfelt said, "I did not find any really specific peculiarities on which I could base a positive identification.[148]

Well, either it was the same rifle or it was not, Shaneyfelt had the photograph of the rifle blown up. He compared the configuration of the rifle in the photograph with the Italian Mannlicher-Carcano. He could not conclude that they were the same rifle. If they were the same rifle, they would have had the same configuration or at least so many points of similarity that Shaneyfelt could have said in all earnestness that he felt that the rifle in the photograph of the rifle was in fact the Mannlicher-Carcano. He told the Commission that he could not make a positive identification to the exclusion of all other rifles of the same general configuration.[149] This was a polite way for the documents expert to say that the rifles were not the same.

Where, then, did Oswald acquire the rifle in the photograph? He owned one rifle only. If he didn't own an Italian Mannlicher-Carcano, then where did it come from? What happened to the rifle in the photograph? If the rifle in the photograph was not a Mannlicher-Carcano, then the Commission was faced with too many loose ends, illogical turns of fact, and unanswered questions. Therefore, the Commission decided for the sake of convenience that the rifle in the photograph was the Italian Mannlicher-Carcano. This in spite of their own expert having told them that the two rifles were not the same.

With the highly suspicious circumstance of finding the photograph in Mrs. Paine's garage during the search the second day, Oswald's claim that someone had superimposed his face on someone else's body seems wholly plausible. Given the strong evidence for shots being fired at the President from the front as well as from behind was ignored; that a bullet wound in the President's shoulder six inches down from his collarbone went unreported; the convenient discovery of three bullet hulls all lined up neatly in a row, as well as a perfectly whole bullet found on Governor Connally's stretcher; the lame suggestion that, after supposedly passing through two men, this bullet could still have no bloody residue, loss of material substance, or deformation; this doubtful information, taken together, leads one to question whether this photograph is not a sheer fabrication.

The reason why this photograph was put together by the CIA in the first place was to placate the misgivings of the populace as to Oswald's having acted alone. The American people had to be convinced of Oswald's guilt and not just the authorities. Lyndal Shaneyfelt was asked by the Commission how a fake photograph could be created. Shaneyfelt replied: "They would have had to make a picture of the background with an individual standing there, and then substitute the face, and retouch it, and then possibly rephotograph it and retouch that negative, and make a print, and then photograph it with this camera, which is Commission exhibit #750, in order to have this negative which we have identified with the camera, and is Commission exhibit #749."[150]

Summary Rebuttal to the Warren Report's Findings and Conclusions. Lee Harvey Oswald never shot anyone. The famous photograph by James Altgen, taken at the very moment JFK was first struck with a bullet, exonerates Oswald from the start. In the foreground of the photograph

JFK is clutching his throat. He has been wounded. In the background of the photograph, clear and unmistakable, is Lee Harvey Oswald standing by himself and he seems to be the only person in the photograph staring directly at the President's vehicle. The man in the photograph looks exactly like Lee Harvey Oswald and he is standing in the doorway of the place of business where Oswald worked. He is doing exactly what Lee Harvey Oswald would be doing—watching the Presidential motorcade go by.

Unless one cannot believe one's own eyes, there is abundant circumstantial evidence that exonerates Oswald. One minute after the last shot was fired, Lee Harvey Oswald had a gun pointed directly at his stomach. A police officer raced into the book depository and, following the movement of a swinging door, burst into the second-floor lunchroom. The officer testified that Oswald was at a Coke machine and did not seem nervous or out of breath. It is impossible for Lee Harvey Oswald to have shot the President from the sixth floor of the book depository, race across the sixth floor, hide the rifle and appear on the second-floor lunchroom having a Coke one minute after having shot the President of the United States. There just was not enough time.

After his confrontation with the police officer, Oswald's actions continue to clear him of having shot the President. He casually strolled out the front entrance of the book depository and hailed a cab. He politely asked the cab driver "May I have this cab?" When a little old lady stuck her head through the passenger window, he offered to let the little old lady have his cab and he reached for the door handle. These actions hardly suggest someone who is presumably fleeing from the scene of a murder he has just committed. When asked by a reporter after being arrested why he shot the President, Oswald answered, "I'm just a patsy." The question, of course, is who was he a patsy for? The President rode into an ambush. He was caught in a cross fire. The Zapruder film of the assassination shows unmistakably the movement of the President's body upon impact of the fatal head shot.

Whether the film is viewed in slow motion or at regular speed, the result is the same. Upon impact the President's head snaps back, his body is almost lifted out of his seat and is driven violently backward. Its backward projection only stops when he collides with the back seat after several feet of movement. Upon colliding with the back of the seat, his backward projection halts and he then falls forward to the floor of the automobile. Only a shot fired from the front could cause his body to be driven backward with such violence and intense rapidity of movement. Eyewitness accounts of citizens in Dealey Plaza as well as police officers pinpoint the shots as coming from the grassy knoll, in front of and to the right of the President.

Oswald was framed for the assassination, but the framing does not hold up. Dallas police officers found the real assassin's gun and the discovery of two guns was glossed over by the Warren Commission. The Italian-Carcano was tied to Oswald through his supposedly ordering the rifle through the mail. The problem is that no prints were found by the FBI lab when the gun was sent to Washington. Also, there were no prints on the paper bag that was discovered near the sniper's nest which was determined to be the same bag in which Oswald carried the rifle into the building. There were no rifle markings on the inside of the bag. One week later, the Dallas Police Department sent a fingerprint and the paper bag back to the FBI. This time, however, the FBI reported that Oswald's prints had been found on the bag and that a fingerprint of his was attached to the rifle with a note explaining where the print had been lifted from the rifle by the Dallas Police Department. By this time, Oswald was being framed posthumously.

A bullet was subsequently found on the stretcher used to carry Governor Connally. This bullet was tested and found to have been fired exclusively from the Italian

Mannlicher-Carcano. Yet the bullet had no blood on it, no substantial loss of material, and it was otherwise in pristine condition. Similar bullets fired during tests of the Italian Mannlicher-Carcano showed that such bullets were demolished after striking the wrist of a cadaver. Yet this "found" bullet, which supposedly went through President Kennedy before entering Governor Connally's back, then snapped off a rib, exited his chest, broke the Governor's right wrist, then lodged itself in Connally's left thigh—is virtually in perfect condition. The bullet was obviously a plant. Since it is known to have been fired exclusively from the Italian Mannlicher-Carcano, this means that the rifle was also a plant and part of a frame-up of Oswald.

We also have testimony that Oswald was a very poor shot and had a rifle that was in dilapidated condition. Frazier, the FBI firearms expert, told the Warren Commission that in order to shoot the President, Oswald would have had to aim six to eight inches above the President's head and three inches in front of the President's moving vehicle.

We also have a photograph of Oswald. He is standing, holding a rifle in one hand, his pistol at his side and Communist newspapers in his other hand. The suspicious way in which the photograph was discovered, and the nature of the photograph itself, suggest it was made in the CIA laboratory and was made in order to convince the public of Oswald's guilt. As we see and shall see, other parameters of the assassination will likewise identify the true assassins: the CIA.

* * *

PART II—JFK VS. BUSINESS

13

JFK VS.

THE ECONOMIC ELITE

"We are in the saddle as an administration representing business and industry."[1] (Secretary of the Interior McKay, Eisenhower Administration).

vs.

"All businessmen are sons of bitches."[2] (JFK)

* * *

"What is good for General Motors is good for the USA."[3] (Secretary of Defense Wilson, Eisenhower Administration).

vs.

"...I do not believe it is necessary to remind this audience that neither you nor I believe in the philosophy that

79

what is good for one company or one union is automatically good for the United States...I believe, instead, that what is good for the United States, for the people as a whole, is going to be good for every American company, and for every American union."[4] (JFK)

* * *

"Any President who wants to run a prosperous country depends on the corporation at least as much—probably more than—the corporation depends on him. His dependence is not unlike that of King John on the landed Barons of Runnymeade, where the Magna Carta was born."[5] (John Jessup, editorial board, Fortune Corporation).

vs.

"...The American people will find it hard, as I do, to accept a situation in which a tiny handful of steel executives, whose pursuit of private power and profit exceeds their sense of public responsibility, can show such utter contempt for the interest of 185 million Americans."[6] (JFK)

* * *

"What can I and my compatriots do through government to achieve our several goals and purposes and, above all, to protect our freedom?"[7] (Milton Freidman, economist).

vs.

"Ask not what your country can do for you; ask what you can do for your country."[8] (JFK)

With the election of John F. Kennedy as President of the United States, the country embarked on an escalated ideological battle of historic, immense proportions. A battle between the public good and private power. The outcome would hardly be resolved by the President's assassination on November 22, 1963, for this battle had been ongoing since the dawn of our Republic. JFK merely inherited the circumstances. When he assumed the mantle of the presidency in 1961, the President inherited the depth and intrigue of 200 years of American history.

We can trace the motives for President Kennedy's assassination to the founding of our republic. The circumstances and problems that Thomas Jefferson had to face during his Presidency parallel the circumstances and problems that JFK would face during his administration.

* * *

14

THOMAS JEFFERSON

Jefferson had spent the first years of the Republic as Ambassador to France and, upon completing his sojourn to Paris, he returned home. The America that he returned to was a different America than the one he left. President Washington convinced Jefferson to become Secretary of State and, in the course of his tenure, he had many conversations with President Washington which, in retrospect, gives us a glimpse of the problems faced by the young nation. Jefferson was unhappy with what had happened to his country during his stay in Paris. One of his first observations upon his return to America was "...that even in this, the birth of our government, some members were found sordid enough to bend their duty to their interests, and to look after personal, rather than public good."[9]

Jefferson did accept President Washington's plea that he become Secretary of State and, in the next few years, he discussed the evolving political structure with the President:

> That a system had there been contrived for deluging the states with paper money instead of gold and silver, for withdrawing our citizens from the pursuits of commerce, manufactures,

building, and other branches of useful industry, to occupy themselves and their capitals in a species of gambling, destructive of morality, and which had introduced its poison into the government itself.[10]

In another conversation with the President, Jefferson pointed out other deficiencies within the government:

That he must know and everybody knew there was a considerable squadron in both whose votes were devoted to the paper and stock-jobbing interests... that therefore it was a cause of just uneasiness when we saw a legislature legislating for their own interests in opposition to those of the people.[11]

Jefferson also pointed out that there were a fair number of citizens who were not terribly impressed with the new Constitution.

I told him that though the people were sound, there were a numerous sect who had monarchy in contemplation. That the Secretary of the Treasury was one of these. That I heard him say that this Constitution was a shilly shally thing of mere milk and water, which could not last, and was only good as a step to something better.[12]

Jefferson had but one desire:

My wish was to see both Houses of Congress cleansed of all persons interested in the bank or public stocks, and that a pure legislature being given us, I should always be ready to acquiesce under their determinations, even if contrary to my own opinions, for that I subscribed to the principle that the will of the majority honestly expressed should give law.[13]

Jefferson also pointed out to President Washington exactly who his enemies were (John Kennedy would be making the very same enemies 169 years later):

...the laws of society oblige me always to move exactly in the circle which I know to bear me peculiar hatred, that is to say wealthy aristocrats, the merchants connected closely with England, the new created paper fortunes; that thus surrounded my words were caught, multiplied, misconstrued, and even fabricated and spread abroad to my injury, that there was such an opposition of views between myself and other parts of the administration as to render it peculiarly un-pleasing and to destroy the necessary harmony."[14]

In later years, once Jefferson was out of office, he explained how the people took back their country: "...Until their fellow citizens could be aroused to their own danger, and rally and rescue the standard of the Constitution. This has been happily done."[15]

From Jefferson's letters there emerges a clear picture of the eternal American political struggle between the public good versus private power and greed. It is the struggle of an America controlled and run for the people versus an America controlled and run for the economic elite:

> But in the meantime two very distinct parties had formed in Congress. And before the third election, the people in general became appraised of the game which was playing for drawing over them a kind of government which they never had in contemplation. At the third election, therefore, a decided majority of Republicans were sent to the lower House of Congress. And as information spread still further among the people after the fourth election, the Anti-Republicans have become a weak minority. Two parties then do exist within the United States. They embrace respectively the following description of persons. The Anti-Republicans consist of:
>
> 1) The old refugees and Tories
>
> 2) British merchants residing among us, and composing the main body of our merchants.
>
> 3) American merchants trading on British capital
>
> 4) Speculators and holders in the banks of public funds
>
> 5) Officers of the federal government with some exceptions
>
> 6) Office hunters, willing to give up principles for places
>
> The Republican part of our union comprehends:

1) The entire body of landholders throughout the United States

2) The body of laborers not being landholders, whether in the husbanding or the arts.

The latter is to the aggregate of the former party probably 500 to 1, but their wealth is not as disproportionate, tho' it is also greatly superior, and is in truth the foundation on that of their antagonist. Trifling as are the numbers of the Anti-Republican party, there are circumstances which give them an appearance of strength and numbers. They all live in cities together, and can act in a body readily and at all time; they give chief employment to the newspapers, and therefore, have most of them under their command.[16]

And so the die was cast. The Anti-Republican party would eventually become known as the Republican party. The Republicans would be transformed into the Democratic party. The battle lines were drawn. For the next 170 years, the two ideologies would battle back and forth. One ideology, expressed in the thinking of Thomas Jefferson, places power in the majority of the citizenry with an accompanying faith in the wisdom of the common man; one ideology places power in the hands of the ruling elite who gain ascendancy by the accumulation of wealth. Thomas Jefferson believed that a natural aristocracy should govern the nation that was based on virtue and talent. He recognized that there was also an artificial aristocracy based on wealth and birth and that this aristocracy was a mischievous ingredient in the government in which provision should be made to prevent its ascendancy.[17]

* * *

15

HISTORICAL PENDULUM

During the Civil War a new phenomenon sprang up. Private men had formed corporations to help in the Northern cause and, at the same time, help themselves. Fortunes were created in the war years for those men who could use their intelligence and talents in coordinating the economic leviathan that helped the North defeat the South. Following the Civil War and the assassination of President Lincoln, these men set about to increase their wealth. Men like John D. Rockefeller, Andrew Carnegie, and Cornelius Vanderbilt amassed their fortunes by creating monopolies. Every devious means imaginable was used to wipe out competition and where there were no laws to assist them, laws were created. Where laws existed to stop them, these laws were circumvented. By the 1890s, a rival ideology arose to contest the power of big business. From the time of the American Revolution until after the Civil War, the American people had assumed that if their liberties and democracy were to be taken from them, they would be usurped by the power of a centralized state. It was the power of the federal government that people largely feared. However, after 30 years of business corruption and observing the buying and selling of their legislatures via powerful business interests, the people realized that the real threat to their democracy was coming from the men who owned the post-Civil War corporations. It was the wealth and power of this economic elite that was corrupting the democracy. The only thing powerful enough to stand up to this elite was the United States Government.

In the 1890s a nationwide reform movement came about which was responsible for the Sherman Anti-Trust Act, the Pure Food and Drug Act, and the Federal Trade Commission. The vast majority of the American people, who were not part of the nation's economic elite, began to use the political process to pressure their legislatures to enact laws that protected them from the abuse of corporate America.

Still, it wasn't until the 1920s, that decade of unbridled licentiousness and deregulation, that big business cut its own throat. With the crash of the stock market in October, 1929 the subsequent collapse of the banking system and the Great Depression, the American people knew it was time for change and a new direction. The people elected Franklin Delano Roosevelt President. FDR was not intimidated by the men of wealth. With FDR big government was invented. Now, for the first time since the Civil War, the State became more powerful than the private sector. The ideology of what was good for the majority of the people was also good for the country predominated in the land. For the previous 50 years, the ideology among the rich had been whatever was good for business was good for America. Even more importantly, a certain mind set had been ingrained into the thinking of the economic elite. To the economic elite, government had no business in business. The state had no right to set wages, regulate prices or to tell free men how and in what manner they may use their capital. The economic elite developed the concept that tied corporate freedom with individual freedom in conjunction with a reduction of state power. To the economic elite the more power the state had, the less freedom they had.

During the 1930s, the business community hated and opposed FDR as much as the people loved and supported him. In 1936, President Roosevelt referred to businessmen as "economic royalists" who were opposed to democracy. It is during the administration of President Roosevelt, against the backdrop of the depression, that we get the tremendous psychological separation between the economic elite and the vast majority of Americans. It was FDR who made the power of state superior to the power of private men of wealth. Twenty years later, the Kennedy Administration would test whether the state had the right to dictate to the economic elite or if the economic elite would dictate to the state.

Thus, we can see a historical pendulum swinging back and forth throughout American history. At times, the country was being run for and by the economic elite; at other times, for and by the people at large. Immediately after the revolution and formation of the United States as an independent country, the economic elite seized control. Thomas Jefferson related to us how the people became aware of the game and their response to it in the election of 1800, whereby the country returned back over to the majority of the population. Then, in the aftermath of the Civil War, the ascendancy of the new economic elite was assured via the growth and power of the corporations. Big Business got the upper hand and essentially destroyed the power of the state from 1890 to 1929. The state regained control from 1932 to 1952, but business grabbed it back again with the election of President Eisenhower, and kept it from 1952 to 1960.

Therefore, with the election of President Kennedy, the pendulum once again swung back from the economic elite to the people. The Kennedy Administration would once again pit the public good against private greed and power. Kennedy, like Jefferson, would make enemies of the wealthy aristocrats, the merchants, the men of the newly created paper fortunes. Kennedy's words like Jefferson's will be "caught," "multiplied", "misconstrued", and even "fabricated". The administration and the assassination of John F. Kennedy is the story of America, the last best hope of mankind. In January of 1961, Thomas Jefferson had returned to the White House.

* * *

16

PSYCHOLOGICAL STATE OF THE AMERICAN PEOPLE AT THE TIME OF THE KENNEDY ADMINISTRATION

A comfortable status quo had formed in the aftermath of the American victory against the Axis powers, along with an unprecedented prosperity for the American people. The young men who had managed to defeat both the Germans and the Japanese at the same time were now forty year old family men. The explosion into the suburbs with their tract homes symbolized the desire of American couples to attempt to carve out their own small slice of heaven on earth. The post war prosperity made for a contented people and the television programs of the day show that the people were still in an innocent stage. Howdy Doody and the Mickey Mouse Club were the standard fare for the kids. For the adults, endless supplies of westerns where the good guys and bad guys were easily identified, combined with shows that depicted what family life should ideally be like were the standard fare offered and enjoyed by the viewing public.

However, during the 1950s, a few war clouds threatened on the horizon. A black woman named Rosa Parks refused to give up her seat on a bus in Montgomery, Alabama as custom dictated, sparking the civil rights movement. Two new actors appeared on the scene, Marlon Brando and James Dean, and all of a sudden Clark Gable seemed very outdated. A new singer named Elvis Presley buried an entire generation of music by engulfing the country in rock and roll. Even still, the country was rather contented and pleased with itself and these contented people were about to be called to action by the new, young President.

At the same time there was a psychological predisposition toward rabid anti-communism. With the Bolshevik Revolution of 1917-1920 and its subsequent destruction of the business class in that country, America started to look at socialism as something very evil. With the purges of Stalin in the 1930s, the American people fully recognized the evils of communism. After WWII, the Soviets were able to force communism on Eastern Europe. Next, China was taken over and with the march of communism came its relative scientific and economic success. This combination of evil and success fueled the anti-communist fervor throughout the American populace. The fervor reached hysteria during the Eisenhower Administration. Amidst this fury, led by an economic and military elite concerned almost to the point of paranoia over communism, JFK called for a change in the status quo.

* * *

17

PHASE I

Two significant reasons led to the decision by the business community to push for the assassination of President Kennedy. The first was simply an historical swing of the pendulum, when at various times the country is run by and for the economic elite and at other times the country is being run by and for the middle class. With the election of JFK, the pendulum had swung back to control of the country by the middle class. We see support for this conclusion via the legislative proposals of JFK. These targeted the following areas:

1. Consumer protection
2. Vigorous antitrust action
3. Automatic withholding of taxes on dividends
4. End to foreign tax havens
5. Medicare
6. Campaign financing restructuring
7. Miscellaneous legislation

These legislative actions initiated the conflict between JFK and the economic elite. However, it was the second reason which actually triggered the ultimate decision to have him eliminated. The ideological concept that identified corporate freedom with individual freedom in conjunction with the reduction of state power. This ideological concept came to a climax during the administration of President Kennedy. The inseparable union between corporate and individual freedom, along with Kennedy's perceived onslaught on both, provided the intellectual armor for the assassination as far as the economic elite were concerned.

Consumer Protection. To protect consumers from the careless and unscrupulous, JFK recommended improving methods of inspection and elevating the standards that were then in effect, as well as eliminating unsafe and worthless products, correcting misleading information on labels, and cracking down on the elicit sale of habit-forming drugs. The President pointed out that the largest group in the economy was consumers. He also pointed out that they are not effectively organized, that their views were not heard, and that the government had a special obligation to be alert to their needs and to advance their common interest. He proposed a consumer's "Bill of Rights" which would mandate their rights to safety, to be informed and to be protected against fraudulent, deceitful, and grossly misleading advertising and labeling. Also, consumers would be given more reliable and truthful information in order to make better informed decisions.[18]

JFK planned to use the regulatory agencies to keep a check on pesticides, food coloring, additives, deceptive trade practices, and false advertising. The President felt that it was time to "give Americans the same protection that we have been giving hogs, sheep, and cattle since 1913." He also pointed out that the cosmetics industry was a $2 billion-a-year business, yet thousands of women had suffered burns and other injuries because of inadequate testing of product safety.[19]

The consumer legislation was clearly in the best interest of a majority of Americans and the majority of Americans make up the middle class who are wage earners who spend their income on purchasing consumer goods. The people who own the factories that produce such products as cosmetics belong to the producer class. The richest producers form the economic elite. Kennedy's proposed consumer legislation clearly placed him on the side of the middle class. The producer class resented his intrusion because, as they saw it, there was no need for any government intervention against fraudulent, deceitful and grossly misleading information advertising and there was no need to force product testing in the cosmetics industry.

In July, 1962, the President replaced the Business Advisory Council of top corporate executives, who had been advising Presidents for 29 years, with the Consumers' Advisory Council. The Business Advisory Council had broken all formal ties with government in the first year of the Kennedy Administration over orders that representatives of government must be allowed to attend all of the Council's closed meetings. This was a general rule laid down by the Attorney General which applied to all government advisory committees. One cannot help but wonder what the Business Advisory Council discussed at their closed meetings that they would not want the government to hear. In any event, they were replaced by the Consumers' Advisory Council. The President commented that, "This is a council which I hope will go through the life of this administration and other administrations, and will be a definite part of our governmental structure."[20]

How symbolic yet functional a step this was. A year before there was a Business Advisory Council. Now, in its place, was a Consumers' Advisory Council. The political and economic considerations were enormous and would not be forgotten by the economic elite.

Automatic Withholding on Interest and Dividends. The President called for legislation that would provide for the withholding of taxes on interest and dividends in the same manner that withholding is held from regular paychecks. JFK pointed out that three billion dollars of taxable interest and dividends went unreported each year, and that it was patently unfair to those who had to bear a larger share of the tax burden. Kennedy felt that the recipients of dividends and interest should pay their taxes no less than those who pay taxes derived from their wages. Kennedy suggested a twenty percent withholding rate on corporate dividends.[21] He did not get his automatic tax withholding deduction on dividends and interest payments in 1961 so he asked for it again in 1962.[22]

Who were the people who would be most affected by this legislation? Who was it that received stock dividends and interest payments? In 1949, C. Wright Mills pointed out that 42 percent of all corporate dividends going to individuals went to one-tenth of one percent of all U.S. adults.[23] We are clearly talking about an economic elite who would be affected by this legislation. Once again, the President was standing up for the middle class, seemingly at the expense of the economic elite.

Vigorous Anti-Trust Enforcement. JFK asked Congress to go along with him in the strengthening of the regulatory agencies in order to uphold the right of collective bargaining and to achieve a safer and sounder outflow of savings into investments. The Federal Trade Commission would concentrate on the banning of monopolistic and unfair trade practices which Kennedy felt was necessary for the promotion of our system of competitive private enterprise.[24]

Kennedy also set up legislation pertaining to the Federal Trade Commission. He wanted the FTC to have the authority to issue temporary cease and desist orders against the continuance of unfair practices while such cases were pending in the courts. The President felt that small businessmen were being destroyed long before the lengthy process of adjudication had been completed. He felt such legislation would strengthen competition throughout the nation's economy.[25]

Once again, the President was taking action that would be perceived by the economic elite as an assault against their entrenched power and monied interests. If one is a member of the economic elite, and is bent on swallowing up the competition through legal maneuvering, this proposed legislation would be an obstacle to such an end. The strengthening of the regulatory agencies would be something the ecnomic elite would fight tooth and nail. The weaker government is in regard to regulating business, the more apt the economic elite are to abuse the free enterprise system.

In 1961, the business community was very concerned about the attitude of government toward business. They were concerned about the appointment of men to key regulatory positions who were unfriendly to investor owned utility enterprises and of the wide variety of investigations of business aimed at everything from stock market operation to price and labeling practices in the food industry.[26]

The business community, led by the economic elite, was becoming estranged from the Kennedy Administration. There was clearly a different perception of what was going on in the country between the economic elite and the American middle class. From the economic elite's point of view, the Kennedy Administration was government by regulation and not the least bit desirable. President Kennedy's point of view was expressed in an article from *U.S. News and World Report* toward the end of his first year in office. The Administration's viewpoint in strongly stated in regard to vigorous antitrust enforcement. Robert Kennedy, the Attorney General, spoke out in defense of such policy: "When possible, I believe that we should not only take action against the corporation or companies involved but against the individuals who have participated in these frauds. I am against granting immunity to the individuals with the result that the cases end with their companies paying a fine."[27]

In effect, Bobby Kennedy was saying that he believed that corporate presidents and vice-presidents should be sent to jail just like any other thief. The economic elite understood and were concerned about it. It is hard to administer hundreds of millions of dollars from the inside of a jail cell.

This marked an important change in the nature and execution of government regulation of business. Until the Kennedy Administration, if corporate presidents and their associates got caught with their hands in the cookie jar, all that would happen to them would be wrist slapping and fines to be paid. Now, with the Kennedy Administration, the economic elite were faced with both an Attorney General and a President who are talking about prison terms for economic crimes.

Medical Aid for the Aged. The President called for a new concept in medical care for the aged. His plan was to have it tied to the Social Security program.[28] The President pointed out that medical costs represented the greatest threat to economic security in old age. He felt that only the Social Security system could furnish satisfactory protection against the costs of illness.[29] The President also turned out a bill for the development of out-of-hospital health care facilities, particularly for the aged and chronically ill. He wanted them to be spared the high cost of hospital care.[30]

When Congress failed to pass his medical care legislation for the aged, he again asked for it the following year. He once again pointed out to the Congress and to the nation during his State of the Union speech that the aged have longer and more frequent illnesses, higher hospitalization and medical bills, and too little income to pay for them. Kennedy said that private health insurance helps very few; its cost is high and its coverage is limited. He pointed out that Social Security had long helped to meet the hardships of retirement, death and disability and urged that its coverage be extended without delay.[31]

Once again we see that Kennedy was looking out for that segment of American society that had the least amount of power—senior citizens. This legislation was fiercely opposed by both the American Medical Association and those special interest lawyers who represented the owners of hospitals.[32] The question once again arises, to which class do members of the American Medical Association belong? The answer is—the economic elite.

Campaign Funding Restructuring. The President put out a statement on the establishment of a presidential commission on campaign costs. He felt the present system was detrimental to the welfare of the nation. We have his own words on the subject: "To have Presidential candidates dependent on large financial contributions of those with special interests is highly undesirable. It is not healthy for the government to keep our national candidate in this condition of dependence."[33]

This was an indirect threat to the economic elite. C. Wright Mills points out that, after World War II, Texas millionaires started contributing sizable amounts of money toward political campaigns in Texas and in out-of-state political contests as well. Politicians in 30 states were receiving contributions from Texas millionaires and from millionaires elsewhere across the nation. In 1952, the Rockefellers gave $94,000 in campaign contributions, the Duponts gave $74,000 and the Mellons gave $54,000. One must keep in mind the purchasing ability of the 1952 dollar. Mr. Mills also pointed out in his book another important observation: "As the corporate world has become more intimately involved in the political order, these associated executives have become intimately associated with the politicians and especially with the key politicians who form the political directorate of the United States."[34] The economic elite knew that if Kennedy had his way on campaign reform then a major tool of theirs used to control the political structure, would be broken. The present regulations concerning the amount of money an individual can donate to political candidates derives directly from this proposed Kennedy legislation.

Miscellaneous Legislation. The President called for a 10-year program of matching grants for the construction of new medical and dental schools and for the provisions of four-year scholarships and cost of education grants for a quarter of the entering students in each medical and dental school. The rationale behind this request was that over forty percent of all medical students (1962) came from twelve percent of those families with incomes over $10,000 or more a year. We have JFK's own words on the subject: "This is unfair and unreasonable. A student's ability, not his parent's income, should determine whether he has the opportunity to enter medicine or dentistry."[35]

Once again the President was sticking up for the American middle class. JFK wanted the federal government to have a role in controlling the pollution of our country's rivers and streams, so he signed the Federal Water Pollution Act.[36] In trying to get American companies to invest in America and not in overseas tax shelters, he proposed action that would eliminate such tax havens.[37]

However, Kennedy's actions during his initial conflict with the economic elite did not provoke his murder. It brought antagonism between JFK and the economic elite, but not a decision by the economic elite to have him eliminated altogether.

* * *

18

PHASE II

During 1962 and 1963, the conflict between JFK and the economic elite escalated in regard to state power and its relationship with corporate freedom. The escalation of the conflict between President Kennedy and the economic elite centered upon the power of the state which, in a democracy, means the power of the people as embodied in the President, versus the ideology that equated corporate freedom with individual freedom and a reduction of state power, embodied in the persona of the economic elite.

Business's Attitude Toward JFK at the End of his First Year in Office. In November and December of 1961, the theme of antisocialism was starting to become a rallying cry to stop Kennedy. In December, 1961, Donald Hardenbrook, the new president of the National Association of Manufacturers, addressed its convention. He had this warning to deliver:

> I would not be surprised if future historians writing about this period we are living in would call it a return to the age of intervention—intervention by government into the lives and

rights of the citizens. How do bills which are unsound and collectivist in principle become law?

But tonight I want to say that deep down below the surface, another tide is forming—a tide of revulsion against unsound and false economic government and social doctrines. We don't have to run scared anymore. We can save our children, their children, and their children's children.[38]

One wonders just what Mr. Hardenbrook had in mind as to the steps that they were going to take to save their children and their children's children from the death throes of Kennedy style socialism. Also, at the end of 1961, we have another businessman's observation. Gerald S. Kennedy, Chairman of the Executive Committee, General Mills Corporation had this to say: "Government is working its way towards what might be called crippling controls over business, and is being held back only by not having the power that it would like over Congress."[39]

It is particularly disturbing that these observations are not coming from what one would imagine to be right-wing extremists. These observations are coming from responsible businessmen who have reached the pinnacle of success in their business careers. The membership of the National Association of Manufacturers reads like a who's who of the top corporate world. Here are some examples:

Division Vice-Presidents
1. P.S. Dupont—Secretary, E.I. Dupont de Nemours and Company
2. J. Robert Flur—Executive Vice-President of the Flur Company
3. Russel L. Peters—Vice President of Finance and Chairman Finance Company of Inland Steel Company.

Regional Vice Presidents
1. David Graham—Financial Vice President, Standard Oil Company of Indiana

2.   Raymond Rowland—President, Ralston-Purina
3.   R.O. Hunt—President, Crown Zellerbach[40]

And so, at the end of 1961, with Robert Kennedy, the Attorney General, wanting to put the economic elite who commit economic crimes in prison, and Donald Hardenbrook, the President of NAM, calling for a war to save his children and their children's children's trust funds, 1962 promised to be catastrophic.

The Steel Crisis. On April 11, 1962 JFK and the business community reached a turning point in their relationship which seriously escalated their conflict. The President, up until this point, had been very bothersome to the economic elite. However, after this date, the president's actions seemed to threaten their very financial existence, at least from their own point of view. A class unto themselves with a fanatical belief in the relationship between corporate freedom and individual freedom was about to have its corporate freedom shattered.

For eight months the President had been meeting with the steel workers union representative. JFK wanted the unions to refrain from asking for substantial salary increases and he also wanted the steel companies to refrain from raising their prices. The President had managed to get inflation under control and he wanted to keep it that way. The steel workers settled for a contract that got them very little, mostly in deference to the President's requests that the union think of the good of the country in containing inflation. Hardly longer than it took for the ink to dry on the contract, U.S. Steel announced that it was raising the price of steel six dollars a ton. Kennedy was furious. He felt double-crossed which, in fact, he was. United States Steel had used him to get an excellent contract from labor and then, as a direct affront to the President, had raised their prices as if to put him in his place.

On April 11, 1962, the President held a televised news conference. In cold fury he expressed his feelings on the action that had been taken by the steel industry:

> Simultaneous and identical actions of United States Steel and other leading steel corporations increasing steel prices by six dollars a ton, constitute a wholly unjustifiable and irresponsible defiance of the public interest. In this serious hour of our Nation's history, when we are confronted with grave crises in Berlin and Southeast Asia, when we are devoting our energies to economic recovery and stability, when we are asking reservists to leave their homes and families for months on end and servicemen to risk their lives—four were killed in the last two days in Vietnam...the American people will find it hard, as I do, to accept a situation in which a tiny handful of *steel executives, whose pursuit of private power and profit exceeds their sense of public responsibility, can show such utter contempt for the interests of 185 million Americans.*
>
> The industry's cash dividends have exceeded $600 million in each of the last five years, and its earnings in the first quarter of this year were estimated in the February 28th, Wall Street Journal to be among the highest in history.
>
> Some time ago, I asked each American to consider what they would do for his country and I asked the steel companies. In the last 24 hours we had their answer.[41]

Almost two hundred years of American history culminated in his speech. Clearly it is once again Thomas Jefferson versus the merchant and stock-jobbing class. Clearly it is the "entire body of landholders throughout the United States; the body of laborers not being landholders, whether in husbanding or the arts," as Jefferson put it so many years ago versus British and American merchants trading on British capital.

In Kennedy's age the antagonists had changed their names, but not their class. To Kennedy, it was American servicemen dying in Vietnam, steel workers, union workers, the public interest, the sacrifice of every American citizen versus a "tiny handful of steel executives, private power and profit, a few gigantic corporations, and the utter contempt of the interest of 185 million Americans."

However, it was actions, and not just words, that truly killed JFK. Following his speech, President Kennedy ordered the Department of Defense to place orders for steel only with those companies that had not raised their prices. This action effectively cut U.S. Steel out of any more government contracts. At the same time Robert Kennedy, as Attorney General, ordered the FBI to investigate U.S. Steel for anti-trust violations since several steel companies had raised their prices at the same time and to the same level.

After a few days of thinking it over, U.S. Steel re-scinded its price increase. The President had won the battle, but in doing so, he had lost the war. It is here, in the after-math of the steel controversy, that American business, led by the economic elite, started to ponder of the necessity of rid-ding the nation of the President. As we shall see, the day be-fore JFK's assassination, H.L. Hunt, the richest man in the world was meeting with Jack Ruby who three days later would go on to kill Lee Harvey Oswald. The day after JFK was buried the stock market staged its biggest rally in his-tory.

Business Reacts. The business community did not react to Kennedy's actions lying down. The economic elite lost no time in launching a counter offensive against the President. "This is a sustained attack on the free enterprise system. It may be an all out war," said Avery Adams, Chairman, Jones and Loughlin Steel Corporation.[42]

Also, from the *American Banker* magazine we get an interesting excerpt from an editorial:

> The quick marshaling of the forces of government by the Kennedy administration to counteract the steel action is dis-turbing to those of us who still believe the United States is a democracy and not a police state ... In just this way we arrive at a super, planned economy, *the next thing to socialism. It is just around the corner. It may even have rounded the cor-*

ner.....First, standby controls over prices, wages, profits, then full-fledged controls, then an actual veto over prices, wages, profits, under the third man's rule. This is the pattern of how socialism enters the government of a democratic state. The next step is profit control.[43]

Once again the specter of socialism is seen to be materializing and hovering ever so near. This *American Banker* editorial hearkens back to Roger Blough, Chairman of the Board of United States Steel, in his statement a year earlier. Back then he warned of a sinister Washington which may try to eliminate profits and, by doing so, create Russian socialism in the United States.[44]

More business reaction to Kennedy's actions are found in the *Journal of Commerce* magazine. Mr. Richard Wagner, the retiring national president of the Chamber of Commerce and the head of the Champlain Oil Company, said that some of the constitutional curbs on the power of the federal executive had eroded over the past years and pointedly warned that further erosion could lead to a dictatorship or personal government.[45] Mr. Wagner's fear is a classic case of a member of the economic elite equating corporate freedom with individual freedom tied to the reduction of state power. When he spoke about the federal executive, he was speaking about JFK. In effect, he was saying that if JFK acquired any more power, this would lead to a dictatorship.

Henry Ford II, at an annual Ford Motor Company stockholder's meeting, said the administration's intervention in wage and price decisions had "dangerous implications."[46] Ray P. Dinsmore, retired Vice-President of Goodyear Tire and Rubber Company had this to say, "Lip service to free enterprise in the United States is belied by the steady march to socialism."[47] Most steel executives said they warmly endorsed the views of a Mr. Maxwell when he gave a speech in their company:

"Utter disregard for the constitutional principle on which this country was founded...the power of regimentation we are seeking to defeat abroad is now threatening our very way of life at home. These tactics are not only anti-business but anti-individual rights."[48]

Here in Mr. Maxwell's speech we find the crux of the problem. There is the paranoid fear that socialism is going to be victorious over capitalism even in the United States and there is also that ideology of corporate freedom being tied to individual freedom. In effect, the Kennedy Administration was a double whammy to the economic elite; the permeation of socialism and a direct attack upon corporate freedom.

From another business publication, *Business Week*, we get more corporate reaction to Kennedy's handling of the steel controversy. Most executives felt that everlasting injury had been inflicted on business's most sacred area of freedom—pricing. Many felt that a precedent had been set for government control over decisions in almost any area.[49]

"Business confidence has been shaken by the naked exercise of federal power against a company that acted within its legal rights."[50]

The central question in the conflict between JFK and the business community, in particular with the economic elite, is one of power. In the eyes of the economic elite, the more power the federal government has, the less power business has. If the federal government can take power away from the economic elite, then how much easier it would be to subsequently take power away from the masses? This is the ideological basis that equates corporate freedom with individual freedom. In their minds Kennedy is King George III and they are the brave Americans who are intent on seeing their freedoms preserved, even if it means removing the king.

The height of bad taste and anti-Kennedy fervor on the part of the business community can be found in the April 30, 1962 issue of *U.S. News and World Report*. The article is a thinly disguised comparison of the Kennedy Administration and the Soviet Politburo. Kennedy was made to look like he was on the verge of instituting a planned economy, much like the Soviets have. It would be a system complete with police powers to regulate business through the anti-trust laws, the Federal Trade Commission and the power to approve and disapprove mergers in industry, banking, railroads, and airlines.[51]

There is real concern on the part of the economic elite that Kennedy may actually be leading the country toward socialism. He is not, but sometimes one's perception of what is happening is more important than what may actually be happening. The real central issue though is power. JFK was constantly trying to take from them their customary power and they resented it with a passion. Part of the problem is ego on both sides. Kennedy is also too rich to be bought off and he is too brave to be scared off. He also had the intellectual capacity and the personality to make great changes in the status quo. There was only one alternative which they felt they had open to them. JFK had to be removed from office. This was the only way the threat to themselves, as well as to the country at large, could be eliminated. But this would not happen for awhile. In the meantime, Kennedy fought like a tiger.

JFK Fights Back. In May of 1962, the President began to defend his administration from the attack of the business community. He began with an address before the United Auto Workers at their convention in Atlantic City. Sorenson points out in his book how the Chamber of Commerce had given him an icy reception the week before and how they refused to stand when he entered the room. This time he had a rousing reception when he entered the room full of workers.

> Last week, after speaking to the Chamber of Commerce and the Presidents of the American Medical Association, I began to wonder how I got elected. And now I remember.

> I said last week to the Chamber that I thought I was the second choice for President of a majority of the members of the Chamber; anyone else was first choice. Harry Truman once

said, there are 14 or 15 million Americans who have the resources to have representatives in Washington to protect their interest, and that the interests of the great masses of other people, the hundred and fifty or sixty million is the responsibility of the President of the United States. And I propose to fulfill it...then I believe it is the business of the President of the United States to concern himself with the general welfare and the public interest. And if the people feel that it is not, then they should secure the services of a new President of the United States...for I do not believe it necessary to remind this audience that neither you nor I believe in the philosophy that what is good for one company, or one union is automatically good for the United States. I believe, instead, that what is good for the United States, for the people as a whole, is going to be good for every American company and for every American union.[52]

It is clear that the steel company executives and that class of Americans who own large tracts of stock have a different psychological and intellectual bearing from John F. Kennedy and the great majority of Americans. The majority of Americans love their country and are willing to make sacrifices toward forming a more perfect union. Thus, we had the steel workers agree to a contract that did not give them very much in the way of concessions in order to help the President keep inflation down. Yet, when U.S. Steel had the first opportunity, it had raised its price six dollars a ton, even while knowing that inflation was tied to the price of steel. The stockholders had also been given plump dividends in each of the previous five years. Also, there was quite a difference between the reception that was given to the President by the economic elite during his address to the Chamber of Commerce and the reception given him by the auto workers a week later. The problem was simply this: which group of Americans was going to hold political power? Would it be Jefferson's landholders and laborers or would it be the American merchants?

Kennedy continued his counterattack. He still had not been able to get his legislation passed that would have pro vided for the automatic deduction from interest and dividend payments. Clarifying his position on the subject while in the midst of a propaganda campaign launched by the savings and loan companies that were using scare tactics to defeat his legislation, JFK pointed out that the only ones affected by his proposed legislation would be those individuals who were not paying the taxes they owed on this income.

"That is tax evasion, tax evasion of $800 million a year which must be made up by other taxpayers who pay their taxes. And it should be remembered that about 80 percent of dividends income goes to fewer than 7 percent of the taxpayers whose income exceeds $10,000."[53]

Who was President Kennedy speaking about when he referred to those citizens who were getting away with not paying their taxes on corporate dividends? He was talking about the economic elite. Their response to the Kennedy legislation was not to go along with the plan and pay their fair share of taxes, but instead, to launch a campaign to discredit Kennedy and convince the majority of citizens that this plan of his would be detrimental to their own well-being.

President Eisenhower was brought into the act by the economic elite in May of 1962. At a press conference a question involving statements by President Eisenhower was brought up: Question: "Former President Eisenhower charged that many bills you support would put too much power in the presidency, and that is the real threat to liberty in this country?"[54]

Kennedy's answer is not important. It is the question that was important. If one reads the question backward it reads like this: The real threat in this country is the power the presidency is deriving from the many bills that Kennedy is proposing. Therefore, Kennedy was the real threat to the country. This is very dangerous. The economic elite were trying to gain some legitimacy for their views by getting an ex-president to voice them. Before Caesar can be struck down, legitimacy for such action must be created.

After the steel episode and the rancor shown toward Kennedy's Administration by the business community, the President understood full well which sector of the American people was for him and which sector was against him. It was after the steel controversy that he decided to take off his kid gloves and push against those interests that opposed his legislation.

At a New York rally in support of the President's program for medical care for the aged, he had these words to say:

> The AMA is against it. This is not a campaign against doctors. This is a campaign to help people meet their responsibilities. There are doctors in New Jersey who say they will not treat any patient who receives it. They are engaged in an effort to stop the bill. It is as if I took out someone's appendix. The point is that the AMA is doing very well in their effort to stop this bill.... This bill serves the public interest. It involves the government because it involves the public welfare.... And then I read that this bill will sap the individual self reliance of Americans. I can't imagine anything worse, or anything better, to sap someone's self reliance, than to be sick, alone, broke—or to have saved for a lifetime and put it out in a week, two weeks, a month, two months.... Because what we are now talking about, in our children's day will seem to be the ordinary business of government.[55]

We have much of JFK's presidency in this address. First, we have JFK sticking his neck out for those Americans who do not have a battery of lawyers watching out for their special interests. Senior citizens living on social security checks do not have a lot of pull. JFK is also working on something that will be for the public good. His opponent, on the other hand, is a special interest group that is part of the economic elite—the American Medical Association. The AMA was very successful in stopping his legislation, so Kennedy went directly to the people to get them involved. In this way they would act as a counterbalance to the special interest groups and force their congressmen to pass his legislation. Finally, we see Kennedy the visionary. "Because what we are talking about, in our children's day, will seem to be the ordinary business of government."

JFK continued his attack on the economic elite and their grip upon the American people. The President felt that public policy should enable presidential candidates to free themselves of dependence on large contributions from those with special interests. "An effective system of disclosure and publicity to reveal where money comes from and goes in such campaigns has been proposed. Full and effective disclosure is the best way to control both excessive contributions and unlimited expenditures."[56]

With this legislation, JFK was trying to break the power of the economic elite over the political structure by the obligatory prostrations of congressmen to those who financed their campaigns. He also wanted to expose those politicians who sold out to special interests. One would be able to deduce who they sold out to by effective disclosure of campaign funding. One is reminded once again of Thomas Jefferson and his conversations with President Washington. "...There was a considerable squadron in both whose votes were devoted to the paper and stock-jobbing interest, that the names of weighty number were known and several others suspected on good grounds."

Kennedy was tired of having such men in Congress who are helping to defeat his legislation and, in the fall, he would try to rid himself of such men. However, in the summer of 1962 he was still busy defending himself, as well as his policies. While the business attacks against his administration reached an hysterical high, Kennedy gave a speech at Yale University defending his economic innovations.

> As every past generation has had to disenthrall itself from an inheritance of truisms and stereotypes, so in our own time we must move on from the reassuring repetition of stale phrases to a new, difficult, but essential confrontation with reality.... What is at stake in our economic decisions today is not some

grand warfare of rival ideologies which will sweep the country with passion but the practical management of a modern economy.... They [economic problems] cannot be solved from incantations from the forgotten past. If there is any current trend toward meeting present problems with old clichés, this is the moment to stop it before it lands us all in a bog of sterile acrimony.[57]

However, the business community did not see Kennedy's actions or proposed legislation quite in this manner. Many of the top executives of the corporate world felt that Kennedy was leading the country toward socialism. The rest of the economic elite resented their power and customary fringe benefits being taken away from them.

All through the spring and summer of 1962, Kennedy had to endure the onslaught of the economic elite as they twisted his words and concepts and continually harangued him. Kennedy decided to fight back in the way that he had learned was the most effective for him. By appealing directly to the people, and especially with his expert use of the camera, JFK realized that he could take his programs directly to the people. By convincing them, they would, in turn, put pressure on their elected representatives to pass the Kennedy legislation. The economic elite understood this concept as well. Thus, it was in August of 1962, when Kennedy started taking his legislation to the people and not just to Congress, that the economic elite of the business community decided, once and for all, to have JFK removed from office via extra legal means.

In the meantime, Kennedy continued to push. In a televised address to the American people, he said:

I know that there are those who oppose all these moves as they opposed social security, much as they opposed minimum wage, much as they opposed a ban on child labor, and more recently in the Senate, medical care for the elderly. This country would still be in the dark ages economically if we permitted these opponents of progress and defenders of special privileges and interest to veto every forward move.... To close tax loopholes enjoyed by a comparative few that will otherwise cost the taxpayers of the United States a billion dollars annually.[58]

The President was now identifying to the majority of Americans just who it was that opposed his legislation and, as in Thomas Jefferson's time, the people began to catch on to the game that was being played. It was the economic elite who were opposed to Kennedy's legislation. It was the American Medical Association that was blocking the medical aid for the elderly. It was the top seven percent of all stockholders who earn eighty percent of all stock dividends who opposed the legislation that would provide an automatic deduction on all corporate dividends. It was the stockholders and owners of corporations with overseas branches who did not want an end to overseas tax havens. In short, it was the economic elite of the business community versus the American people, as embodied in the President of the United States, who were holding back progress.

In Cincinnati, President Kennedy had these words for the American people:

> Eighty percent of the Republicans in the house voted against the minimum wage of $1.25 an hour. These Republicans do not agree with our view of the necessity for the passage of this kind of legislation. They are joined by a few Democrats who oppose progress also, and this combination, this coalition, prevents us on issue after issue from securing the passage of important legislation. They have opposed it for thirty years. This summer we lost health care for the aged, which affects not only the aged, but their sons and daughters who are about forty or forty-five years old, who must support their fathers or mothers and also must educate their children. A change of one vote in the United States Senate would have secured the passage of this piece of legislation.[59]

In every state Kennedy visited, he pointed out how the Republicans had failed to vote for medical aid for the aged, education for their children, housing at lower interest rates and the minimum wage. At the University of Pittsburgh, he said:

> I'm sure that they will be proud to run on this record, and let me describe it to you.[60]...Can you tell me one single piece of progressive legislation of benefit to the people of this country that the Republican party has sponsored in thirty years? There are a hundred pieces of legislation that they've opposed. The right of labor to organize, social security and minimum wage, housing legislation.[61]

Kennedy was having fun now. All spring and summer he endured their abuse and now he is giving it back, for the economic elite's tool in the political structure of the United States is the Republican party. He went after those congressmen and senators who had faulted him on his foreign policy:

> But those self-appointed generals and admirals who want to send someone else's son to war, and who consistently vote against the instrument of peace, ought to be kept at home by the voters and replaced in Washington by someone who understands what the twentieth century is all about.[62]

During his Congressional campaigning in the fall of 1962, Kennedy had also found the key to the 1964 presidential election. He was going to take his case to the people and the people were going to give him loyal Democrats, and with the loyal Democrats he was going to be able to get his legislation passed. By the looks of things he also was going to be given a tremendous mandate by the people in the 1964 election.

The problem is that the economic elite had figured out the very same thing. They probably figured it out before Kennedy did. By the fall of 1962, the economic elite believed that Kennedy was leading the country toward socialism and was trying to destroy corporate freedom. This Kennedy concept of corporations being subservient to law and government struck terror in the hearts of the business community. It struck terror and deep animal animosity in the business community because it is corporate freedom that is the source of their wealth. And it is their wealth that is the source of their power. As we shall see, a traitorous combination between the economic elite and the CIA, along with the military's decision to go along with the assassination, doomed JFK.

Let us leave JFK and the economic elite with one last thought. This impression sums up the conflict between the public good versus the private power and the greed of the economic elite. A summary that describes 200 years of American history and the see-saw battle between the people and a tiny handful of the wealthy. The battle between good and evil. Kennedy's remarks at Vanderbilt University sum it up:

> "For we can have only one form of aristocracy in this country," as Jefferson wrote long ago in rejecting John Adam's suggestion of an artificial aristocracy of wealth and birth. It is, he wrote, "the natural Aristocracy of character and talent, " and the best form of government, he added, was "that which selected these men for positions of responsibility. "[63]

* * *

PART III—JFK VS. THE MILITARY

19

JFK, COMMUNISM AND THE CONFLICT WITH THE MILITARY

During the preceding administration, the Chairman of the Joint Chiefs of Staff, Admiral Radford, appeared before a Congressional committee. He told the committee that Red China had to be destroyed, even if it required a fifty year war. He also argued for the use of five hundred planes to drop tactical atomic bombs on Vietnamese troops before the fall of Dien Bien Phu, and, if China then came into the picture, they would get the same treatment.[1]

With the administration of JFK we have a somewhat different philosophical approach: "But we shall do our part to build a world of peace where the weak are safe and the strong are just. We are not helpless before that task or hopeless of its success. Confident and unafraid, we labor on—not toward a strategy of annihilation but toward a strategy of peace."[2]

With the coming of the Kennedy Administration, there was a change in foreign policy that reflected a different

119

philosophical way of thinking toward the Cold War. This philosophical difference between JFK and his military would manifest in five areas of conflict.

1. Kennedy's own views toward Communism in general
2. Disarmament efforts and his desire for an end of the Cold War
3. Reorganization of the armed forces
4. Cuba
5. Vietnam

* * *

20

KENNEDY'S ATTITUDE TOWARD COMMUNISM IN GENERAL

First, let us focus on Kennedy's attitude toward communism. In October of 1962, Kennedy signed a bill modifying the anti-communist oath requirements for student loans.

"...It is highly unlikely that the affidavit requirement kept any communist out of the programs. It did, however, keep out those who considered the disclaimer affidavit a bridle upon freedom of thought. I am glad to approve the legislation."[3]

He also defended two men in the state department who were accused of being communists. When asked about a proposed House amendment that would prohibit the post office from distributing mail labeled as communist propaganda, he answered with a question of his own. What should be considered communist propaganda: Newspapers? speeches? He thought Congress should take a careful look at the proposed amendment.[4]

At this time there was a strong anti-United Nations movement in the United States. This was mainly due to the fact that most emerging nations usually voted against United States interests. In addition, the Soviet Union also exercised a strong influence on that body. Kennedy opposed such a movement by saying: "I see little merit in the impatience of those who would abandon this imperfect world instrument because they dislike our imperfect world."[5]

What is evident is that President Kennedy is not inflamed with anti-communist venom and he is clearly not checking under his bed each night looking for communists. His philosophical reasoning also colors his thinking on foreign policy. Starting with his inaugural address we have an indication of where he will be leading the country with regard to relations with the Soviet Union.

> So let us begin anew—remembering on both sides that civility is not a sign of weakness, and sincerity is always subject to proof. Let us never negotiate out of fear. But let us never fear to negotiate...and a new world of law, where the strong are just and the weak secure and the peace preserved.[6]

There is not much talk in his inaugural speech about 50 year wars or dropping tactical nuclear bombs on the enemy. He does have a novel view of the times he is living in: "It is easy to dismiss as communist-inspired every anti-government, anti-American riot, every overthrow of a corrupt regime. These are not all communist inspired. Communists move in to exploit them. Communists did not create the conditions which caused them."[7]

Kennedy also had the genius of being able to step in the other fellow's shoes and look back. Toward Latin America, the Far East, and for the Soviet Union he is able to stand in each position and see what they see. For an example of this ability, note: "We recognize the Soviet Union's historical concern about their security in central and eastern Europe."[8]

This is an interesting idea which is also a very dangerous one for Kennedy. The standard line at the time was that the communists were evil and were holding the eastern European nations in communist slavery. This concept is only partly true of JFK. He sees there are other reasons involved for the Soviet domination of eastern Europe, such as their fear of invasion from the west. Kennedy also felt that we should not try to alienate Yugoslavia or Poland and that there were varying degrees of socialism.[9] JFK did not see the communist world as one giant monolithic structure.

The problem is that in this same time period there is a strong anti-communist feeling throughout the United States and for good reason. After WW II the Soviets had cast an iron curtain over eastern Europe. They took control of all the eastern European countries they conquered from the Nazis and established communist dictatorships. When Hungary tried to revolt against Soviet domination in 1956, the Soviets sent their troops in. During these post-WW II years, the communist Chinese were able to drive their Nationalist rivals off the mainland. The communists were pushing hard in southeast Asia and in the newly-formed states on the continent of Africa. A communist beachhead had been established in the Americas with Fidel Castro and Cuba. Along with feeling like they were being surrounded by communism, the American people watched as the Soviets continued to make great strides in science and space travel. The Soviets also had "The Bomb" and nuclear missiles and Khrushchev, the leader of the Soviet Union, was bullying his way across the planet, especially in Berlin. He was threatening to cut off West Berlin from the rest of the Free World which could only precipitate a war. Into this atmosphere of mutual distrust and mutual disdain between the United States and the Soviet Union walked John F. Kennedy. There was much talk during Kennedy's administration that the "U.S. is afraid of Russia."[10] Kennedy's tart reply to his critics was this: "If someone thinks we should have a nuclear war in order to win, I can inform them that there will not be winners in the next nuclear war."[11]

21

ANTI-COEXISTENCE THOUGHT DURING THE KENNEDY ADMINISTRATION

Another line of thought was prevalent throughout much of the country during the Kennedy years. It expressed the idea that there could be no co-existence with the communists. That the United States was in a life and death struggle with communism and that the eventual outcome of the contest was uncertain. Senator Barry M. Goldwater of Arizona best summarized the thoughts of many Americans:

> Neutralism, coexistence, appeasement, pacifism, unilateral disarmament and suspension of nuclear testing are all products of the enervating fog of fear that smothers the Free World.[12]

General Lemnitzer, a member of the Joint Chiefs of Staff had this to say:

> It boils down to this: Are we going to continue to permit areas of the Free World to be dragged behind the Iron Curtain and have the Free World get smaller and smaller and the communist controlled areas of the world get larger?[13]

And J. Edgar Hoover expressed his viewpoint:

Unfortunately, we are plagued with some Soviet apologist....
We also have in our midst some timid souls who have so little
faith in the strength of democracy that they would have our
country yield to international threats and intimidation. As for
me, I would rather be dead than red.[14]

The Kennedy philosophy is the exact opposite:

The old policies and old complacencies are gone...equating
negotiation with appeasement, substituting rigidity for firm-
ness.... It is a curious fact that each of these extreme
opposites resemble each other. Each believes that we only
have two choices: appeasement or war, suicide or surrender,
humiliation or holocaust, to be either red or dead.[15]

Kennedy was caught in the middle. Not wanting appeasement or war, he wanted a normalization of relations
with the Soviet Union—the communists. However, there
was a very strong faction in the government and throughout
the military who felt that we were in a life and death struggle
with communism. The fact that Kennedy did not share this
view was the reason for the first fissure between JFK and
the military.

* * *

22

MUZZLING THE MILITARY

A furor developed in 1961 over Kennedy's muzzling of the military. Kennedy wanted the Defense Department to back what the State Department wanted implemented. The State Department was trying to see if there were mutual concerns that would be of interest to both the Soviet Union and the United States. At the same time though, the military was indoctrinating the troops with fervent anti-communist propaganda, as well as individual military brass giving anti-communist speeches to the general public. Kennedy wanted it stopped. He had McNamara, the Secretary of Defense muzzle the military. Orders were given that all public speeches by military officers were to be limited to military subjects, be non-partisan and non-political, and be in accordance with established policy. From this point forward, all public speeches had to be cleared in advance for review by the Defense Department.[16]

For example, Admiral Arleigh Burke had to rewrite a speech because of its tough tone about the Soviets. General Trudeau, Chief of Army Research, and Rear Admiral Samuel B. Frankel, Chief of Naval Intelligence, had their speeches changed to soften or leave out references to Russia and communist activities.[17] Kennedy also relieved General Walker of his command in Europe for accusing former President Harry S. Truman of being "pink."[18]

Kennedy ordered two Army anti-communist films banned and Senator J.W. Fulbright, chairman of the Senate Foreign Relations Committee, fully backed the President's orders. Fulbright accused the military of sponsoring "radical right wing speakers" and programs around the country with overtones of domestic politics. "If the military is infected with the virus of right wing radicalism, the danger is worth the attention."[19]

The military complained so strongly about their being muzzled that a Senate Select Committee looked into the matter.[20] The press wanted to know why it was national policy to delete from speeches of admirals and generals such phrases as "emerge victorious" and "beat the Communists." Kennedy replied that the purpose was to make sure that the government "speaks with one voice."[21] The muzzling of the military and their resistance to it, along with Kennedy's laissez-faire attitude toward communism was just a warm-up for events that followed.

* * *

23

REORGANIZATION
OF THE MILITARY

Rejection of Nuclear War in Europe. The second fissure that erupted between JFK and the military was over Kennedy's reorganizational plans for the armed forces. In JFK's special message to Congress in March of 1961, he made a request for an expanded defense budget. He wanted to improve our missile deterrent and develop hidden, moving, invulnerable bases which would not be wiped out by a surprise attack. He wanted an enlargement of the Polaris submarine program in order to have this moving strike force and he wanted more Minuteman missiles. He wanted a flexible response to a war in Europe developed so as not to rely on nuclear war as the only course of action should Soviet troops invade western Europe.[22]

The new direction in military thinking caused a great deal of concern in the military quarters of the country. Soviet troops greatly outnumbered NATO forces and, to make up for this numerical superiority, our policy was, and still is today, to use nuclear weapons should Soviet armies invade western Europe. Also, the United States made it clear to the Soviets that if they did invade Western Europe, Moscow would be attacked by American nuclear missiles. This policy was developed by John Foster Dulles in the 1950s.

Kennedy, on the other hand, rejected the use of nuclear weapons under these circumstances. Thus, part of his re-organizational plans for the Armed Forces was to develop a new plan of action against the Soviets in Europe, short of n-clear war. In effect, JFK had reversed the nuclear blackmail deterrent policy of John Foster Dulles and the American military was not amused.

The military also endorsed the concepts of stationary nuclear missiles and the use of bombers to carry nuclear bombs. Kennedy did not like either idea and in 1963 would cancel a multimillion dollar bomber program. He felt the grounded, stationary nuclear missile made the bomber obsolete.

A New Kind of Warfare. Kennedy envisioned a new kind of warfare on the horizon. He did not think the next war would be another world war with tremendous movements of troops across the world stage. He spoke of the new type of warfare he was anticipating while giving an address to the graduating class of West Point.

> This is another type of war, new in its intensity, ancient in its origin—war by guerrillas, subversives, insurgents, assassins, war by ambush instead of by combat, by infiltration, instead of aggression, seeking victory by eroding and exhausting the enemy instead of engaging him.[23]

The problem was that the military brass was still thinking along World War II lines. The enemy is the Soviet Union and Europe will be the next battleground. The enemy is China with with a population of 500 million, making it necessary to employ nuclear weapons in any engagement with the Chinese. Kennedy's views on warfare seemed unrealistic and unwarranted.

Changes in the Defense of Western Europe. Not only did the President refuse to go along with the concept of using nuclear weapons in Europe as a response to Soviet invasion, he also wanted a major change in overall policy toward western Europe. JFK wanted western European nations to carry their own weight in containing the Soviets. The United States was paying for thirty percent of NATO's total cost and the President wanted the other member nations to pay their fair share of the burden.[24] By early 1963, the President had withdrawn 15,000 U.S. troops from Europe.[25] On the other hand, the military felt it was imperative to keep up troop strength in Europe since the Soviets already outnumbered the NATO forces. Kennedy did not see things this way so his actions concerning the defense of western Europe caused yet another rift between himself and the military.

Loss of Faith in the Military High Command. The Bay of Pigs changed Kennedy's thinking in regard to the military high command. Paul Fay was a friend of JFK's during World War II who remained good friends with the President for the following 20 years. He was appointed by Kennedy as Undersecretary of the Navy. He had an interesting conversation with JFK soon after the Bay of Pigs debacle. Kennedy expressed doubts about the wisdom of his military advisors:

> Looking back on the whole Cuban mess, one of the things that appalled me the most was the lack of broad judgment by some of the heads of the military services. They wanted to fight and probably calculated that if we committed ourselves part way and started to lose, I would probably give the OK to pour in whatever else was needed. I found out among other things that when it comes to making decisions I want facts more than advice.[26]

Unhappy with the Bay of Pigs fiasco, he started to take steps to make sure the mistake was never repeated. Kennedy formed his own private "National Security Council. " First, General Maxwell Taylor was asked to come out of retirement and investigate the Bay of Pigs mishap. After analyzing Taylor's report and being impressed with his work, the President appointed him special assistant. He was given four aides to assist him, one each coming from the Army, Navy and Air Force, with the fourth from the civilian sector. This staff worked for the White House and concentrated on the problems of Laos, Berlin, and overall intelligence.[27] Every morning General Taylor, along with Brigadier General Chester Clifton, the President's Army aide, would brief the President on world developments.[28]

The President's new military advisor had also worked out a second "little national security council" made up of Taylor, Defense Secretary Robert McNamara, Secretary of State Dean Rusk, Treasury Secretary Douglas Dillon, and White House Advisor McGeorge Bundy. This group dealt with overall policy matters.[29]

What the President did was quite innovative and astounding. He had insulated himself from the Joint Chiefs of Staff and was relying instead on General Taylor as his intermediary. More important, the three top military officers from the three services became subservient to the one military leader. Kennedy had in effect instituted the concept of a single military service composed of three subsidiary, interdependent branches.

He also all but did away with the regular National Security Council, which included the nation's top military leaders, the Director of Central Intelligence, other professional intelligence personnel. He replaced them, briefing daily with General Taylor and his staff, as well as with the meetings with his own inner group.

These steps, though innovative, would have been seen as highly threatening and might have caused some bitterness. At this point, the President didn't trust the judgment of his senior career military advisors. By these innovations, he had cut himself off from the military elite. This separation of the President from his military elite would cause a breakdown in communications between the President and the military, and this would in turn lead to his assassination. But that was for the future. For now, let us look at a further cause in the conflict between JFK and the military—the civilian secretariat.

The Civilian Secretariat. When McNamara first became Defense Secretary he held a meeting with the Joint Chiefs. He asked many questions but received few answers. He then wrote out a list of more than one hundred questions and demanded detailed answers in writing.

With these answers in mind, he started reorganizing the Department of Defense. He organized a new agency that was responsible for the purchase of food, clothing, gasoline, and medical supplies that were used in common by the three services. McNamara believed that Defense could save two billion dollars a year with this program.[30] What McNamara was trying to do was end duplication in the Armed Forces. Coming from the corporate world, he understood that duplication meant waste and waste meant unnecessary expenditure.

Kennedy and McNamara brought computers and cost-benefits analysis into all military decisions. They tried to unify and simplify command. What JFK and McNamara were, in effect, trying to do was to reform the Armed Services based on a private corporate model. By so reforming the Armed Forces, they hoped to increase its effectiveness.

From the April 23, 1962 issue of *U.S. News and World Report*, one gets an insight into just how resentful the military elite may have been of these innovations:

> Military men no longer call the tunes, make strategy decisions and choose weapons. In years past, defense of the U.S. was run mainly by military men—suddenly all that has changed. In the Pentagon, military men say they are being forced to the sidelines by top civilians, their advice either ignored or not given proper hearing in many vital military matters."

...It is claimed influence over decisions on U.S. Defense is now passing away from military men and into the hands of a "scientific elite. " In one officer's words, they represent the height of intellectual arrogance.

Many military men at all levels of command were found to be clearly upset by the trend. Such a course, many of them insist, will lead to great danger.[31]

McNamara set up two directorates. One was for systems planning and the other was for weapons systems analysis. McNamara was going to use civilian "whiz kids" to determine which weapons of war would be built. This had always been strictly the military's responsibility. McNamara also shut down or curtailed growth at 50 bases overseas to avoid wasteful expenditures. He also created three new civilian planning offices.[32] He instituted the censoring of military speeches. The friction caused by putting civilians in higher authority over military men in military matters would, indeed, reach a boiling point as the Kennedy Administration unfolded.

Morale reached an especially low point in 1963 among the military at the Pentagon due to their heavy-handed treatment by McNamara and his civilian secretariat. By April 1963, the animosity between the civilian secretariat and the military had spilled over into Congress. A Senate subcommittee investigated the Secretary of Defense to determine if he had gone too far in overruling the top brass in the choice of one new plane prototype over another.[33]

Retirement of Top Military Personnel. The President also contributed to the tension with his liberal use of the tactic of retiring top military personnel. General Norstad was in charge of NATO forces in Europe and had been wildly popular with the Europeans. But he was retired because Kennedy wanted a man who was not in favor of using tactical nuclear weapons in Europe and would go along with Kennedy's desire for Europe to take more responsibility for its own defense. Kennedy put in his place General Lemnitzer. By removing General Lemnitzer as Chairman of the Joint Chiefs of

Staff, he created an opening for his friend, General Maxwell D. Taylor.

General Decker, chief of staff of the Army and a member of the Joint Chiefs of Staff from October 1, 1960 until September 30, 1962, was retired upon expiration of his term. Admiral Burke, Chief of the Navy and also member of the Joint Chiefs of Staff was also retired.

By the fall of 1963, President Kennedy had cleaned the decks of those military men who were opposed to his foreign policy. It was too late, though. The assassination plans as we shall see had been underway for a year at this point. The military had already given the go-ahead for the CIA to proceed with them.

The reorganization of the Armed Forces was very innovative. From the military's point of view, however, it was dangerous. With computers run by civilians and civilians having authority over military men, especially over matters that traditionally were the prerogative of the military to make, the situation was exasperating. Kennedy's new ideas on warfare and his apparent softness on communism further antagonized them. The muzzling of the military followed by Kennedy's cutting them out of decisions upon which they would have liked and expected to be consulted, as well as the civilian secretariat and other innovations that Kennedy created, all contributed to set the stage for the last 12 months of his administration. In these last 12 months, four actions Kennedy took convinced the military that Kennedy's term in office had to be abbreviated, if necessary by terminating Kennedy.

* * *

24

CUBA

Kennedy's reorganization of the Armed Forces; the preparation for a new type of warfare not yet anticipated by the majority of the military elite; the muzzling of the military; the installation of a civilian secretariat with authority over generals and admirals; the rethinking of the use of tactical nuclear weapons in Europe and the loss of prestige and power of the top military brass; all these were of course more than minor irritants to the military. Of course, they are hardly reasons enough to have the President assassinated.

Cuba, on the other hand, was a different story. Kennedy's actions toward Cuba and his final disposition of it led to the decision on the part of the military to become a party to his assassination.

After the Bay of Pigs debacle and the Cuban Missile Crisis, it was clear that Cuba was becoming a Soviet satellite. Kennedy, in the fall of 1963, began to reassess U.S.-Cuban relations. He decided to see if a rapprochement with Castro could be made. Kennedy saw no sense in pushing Castro any further into the arms of the Soviets. It was this decision that helped solidify a consensus that JFK was a national security threat and had to be removed from office for the good of the country.

After Castro seized power in 1959, one of the things he did was seize American property on the island—$750 million in assets were initially seized. Not surprisingly, as of 1960, the CIA was actively trying to assassinate him.[34]

In April, 1961, Kennedy was asked what he intended to do militarily to Cuba in defense of American property and citizens. Kennedy answered that he did not intend to take any action with respect to property or other economic interests which American citizens formerly held in Cuba, other than through diplomatic negotiations.[35] Of course, Kennedy was hoping that the CIA-Cuban invasion would be a success. If so, it would be one big headache out of the way. The expropriation of American property would be a thing of the past.

But Kennedy had reservations about the invasion after finally being informed that the U.S. was about to send anti-Castro Cubans onto the island. He was also told that simultaneous internal uprisings by anti-Castro Cubans would occur.[36] He was told that if anything went wrong with the invasion, the anti-Castro Cubans could fade into the mountains.[37] Still, after being assured of the success of the mission by the CIA and after getting a reserved assurance by the Joint Chiefs of Staff, who feared the lack of air support, JFK gave the go-ahead.

Unfortunately, Castro and his troops were waiting for the invaders. Also, it turned out that the mountains that the invaders were supposed to fade into were many miles away from them, across swampland. There were no simultaneous uprisings. The logistics were so bad that the invaders ran out of ammunition while on the beach. The Joint Chiefs screamed for U.S. air support, but Kennedy refused. Brave men died, the rest were captured and imprisoned, and Kennedy was handed the worst political defeat of his career.

Never again would Kennedy trust the CIA. Never again would he trust the Joint Chiefs of Staff for, although they had expressed misgivings, in the end they supported the plan. An investigation into why the plan failed showed gross mistakes that should have been caught in the planning stages. At this point, Kennedy's faith in the military had truly evaporated. It was at this point, too, that Kennedy brought in his brother to assist him in all major decisions. Also, he simply decided to start doing things his own way. If he was to have any more political defeats, he concluded, he was going to be the one responsible for them. At a press conference in January 1963, JFK explained why there was no air cover during the Bay of Pigs invasion:

> There was no United States air cover planned...obviously, if you're going to have United States air cover, you might as well have a complete United States commitment—which was not the policy of the United States in April of 1961.[38]

After the Bay of Pigs, the Soviets solidified their hold on Castro and Cuba. Soviet "advisors" came to Cuba. Castro found that he had jumped from the frying pan into the fire. For the next year and a half, Kennedy did not take any direct military action against Castro. Then, in late August 1962, the Cuban Missile Crisis began heating up. A question from a reporter quoted Senator Capeheart of Indiana to the effect that the communists were sending in troops, not technicians. Capeheart called for an invasion of Cuba to stop the flow of troops and supplies.[39] This demand was being made throughout the country and especially among the Armed Forces.

In October, the President received hard evidence that the Soviets were building missile sites in Cuba and the Joint Chiefs were adamant about mounting an invasion by U.S. troops. It was the only way they believed that the U.S. could be sure the missile sites would be dismantled. Still, Kennedy once again refused to invade Cuba, even though the Soviets were in the process of installing nuclear missiles on the island. Instead, Kennedy decided on a quarantine. The Soviets turned back the ships that were carrying the nuclear missiles and the crisis was resolved.

But the military was furious at Kennedy for not sending the troops in. We get an indication of the depth of their anger by the comments of David M. Shoup, Marine Corps Commandant, during this period:

> Only by the grace of God and an aerial photograph is it possible to make these remarks to many of you in person rather than to your spirits. The invasion force was one of the greatest assault teams in American history. Tucked away in scores of ships were thousands of Marines, with their aircraft and ground weapons ready, teamed up with the Navy in this getting ashore and staying ashore. The 45,000 Marines awaiting their government's decision on invasion, and the one hundred thousand more ready to back them up, knew all the answers. I saw it in their eyes.[40]

At this point in Kennedy's administration, the military became concerned that the President might be a national security risk. He had failed to invade Cuba not once but twice. If the Soviet Union's installing nuclear weapons 90 miles off the coast of Florida wasn't enough to get Kennedy to respond militarily, what would be? Also, the missiles had been a perfect excuse to invade Cuba and get rid of Castro once and for all.

The missiles of October had brought the U.S. and the Soviet Union to the brink of nuclear war. From the military's point of view, this would never have happened if Kennedy had done the job in April 1961. Kennedy himself traced the origins of the Missile Crisis even further back:

> Had the needs of the people of Cuba been met in the pre-Castro period—their need for housing, education, jobs and above all, for a democratic responsibility in the fulfillment of their own hopes, there would have been no Castro, no missiles in Cuba.[41]

In any event, something had to be done about Cuba. The military was calling for an end to Communist rule in this hemisphere. Cuba had become a Soviet satellite and Castro a Soviet agent. Senator Stennis of Mississippi had concerns which typified those of many other Americans: "What concerns me is whether we intend to permit a Communist government to exist in Cuba or other Latin American countries.... Sooner or later, the entire Western Hemisphere may be lost to us."[42]

While Senator Stennis wanted to eradicate all Communist influence in this hemisphere, Kennedy was actually using government action to discourage the hit-and-run raids that were being run against Cuba by the anti-Castro Cubans based in Miami. JFK stopped the hit-and-run tactics because they were escalating tension in the area and because they were also not effective, controlled, and they gave an incentive for Soviet troops to remain on the island. He had these words to say: "We distinguish between those actions which we feel advance the cause of freedom and these hit-and-run raids which we do not feel advance the cause of freedom."[43]

By the summer of 1963, Kennedy was truly reassessing what U.S. policy should be toward Cuba. Making use of spokesmen in the Senate, faint feelers were put out by the White House to test the waters for some sort of a dialogue between Cuba and the United States.[44]

In September, Kennedy instructed his diplomatic corps to contact Cuba's U.N. delegation to see if such a dialogue could be established. On October 24, 1963, President Kennedy met with Jean Daniels, a French writer who was about to embark on a trip to Cuba to interview Castro. Kennedy wanted Daniels to speak on his behalf to Castro. Apparently Kennedy desired rapprochement. During the conversation with Daniels, Kennedy said:

> I believe that we created, built and manufactured the Castro movement out of whole cloth and without realizing it. I approved the proclamation which Fidel Castro made in the

Sierra Maestra when he justifiably called for justice and especially yearned to rid Cuba of corruption. I will go further.

To some extent it is as though Batista was the incarnation of a number of sins on the part of the United States. Now we shall have to pay for those sins. In the matter of the Batista regime, I am in agreement with the first Cuban revolutionaries. That's perfectly clear.[45]

William Atwood, special adviser to the U.S. delegation to the United Nations, under orders from JFK, initiated a series of talks to discuss opening negotiations or effecting accomodations between Castro and the United States. This series of talks started in September 1963 and lasted until the President's assassination two months later. Atwood stated that President Kennedy was in favor of pushing an opening toward Cuba to take Castro out of the Soviet fold and establish normal diplomatic relations.

So, it was clear that by the fall of 1963, Kennedy had decided to patch things up with Castro. Since he wasn't going to invade the island and since Castro wasn't going to disappear (at least voluntarily), Kennedy, being a realist, decided to work with him. By moving to establish diplomatic relations, Kennedy hoped to wean Castro from Soviet influence and at the very least end the unnecessary tension between the two countries.

But the military was not in such a gracious state of mind. The military was not interested in such rapprochement. It was not interested in having a communist country 90 miles off the coast of Florida spreading Marxism throughout Central and South America. The military was not interested in having Soviet troops and Soviet intelligence personnel stationed indefinitely in Cuba.

To the military, Kennedy, in moving at all to establish diplomatic relations with Cuba, was accepting the presence of a communist state in the Western Hemisphere. To Kennedy, it wasn't so much accepting a communist nation in the Western Hemisphere—for it did not matter if he accepted it—in that it already existed. Kennedy, being a realist, had merely faced up to the fact. By doing so, however, his status as a national security threat was reaffirmed.

By summer, both the CIA and military intelligence were monitoring Kennedy's actions and speeches in order to figure out his next move. When they realized Kennedy was close to reestablishing relations with communist Cuba, this became another factor in the decision to remove Kennedy from office.

Khrushchev leaves us with an interesting image from his memoirs, which were smuggled out of the Soviet Union in 1970. He was speaking about the Cuban Missile Crisis. A certain climax was reached, he wrote, when the Soviet Ambassador to Washington, Anatoly Dobrinin, reported a conversation he had had with Robert Kennedy, the President's brother.

> The President is in a grave situation, RFK said, and he does not know how to get out of it. We are under very severe stress. In fact, we are under pressure from our military to use force against Cuba. Probably at this very moment the President is sitting down to write a message to Chairman Khrushchev.
>
> We want to ask you, Mr. Dobrinin, to pass President Kennedy's message to Chairman Khrushchev through unofficial channels. President Kennedy implores Chairman Khrushchev to accept this offer and to take into consideration the peculiarities of the American system. Even though the President is very much against starting a war over Cuba, an irreversible chain of events could occur against his will. *That is why the president is not sure that the military will not overthrow him and seize power. The American Army could get out of control.*[46]

* * *

25

DISARMAMENT AND THE
CALL FOR AN END
TO THE COLD WAR

Cuba then, was one of four conflicts that culminated in a drastic change in foreign policy which led, in turn, to the decision to have JFK assassinated, as he was a national security risk. The decision to attempt a rapprochement with Castro was made in the fall of 1963. Another fateful impasse was reached in the fall of 1963. This impasse had to do with disarmament.

Over the summer, Kennedy had started to make progress on his plan for disarmament. By fall, he was able to convince the Senate and the American people that the Nuclear Test Ban Treaty was in the best interests of the United States. But the Nuclear Test Ban Treaty was fiercely opposed by the military establishment. The military establishment realized that the test ban treaty was only the first step in Kennedy's campaign for disarmament and that the next steps were even more extreme. Kennedy's disarmament policy was seen as a grave national security risk. That the military was unable to convince the leaders of the political directorate of the country was one more reason to justify Kennedy's assassination.

Like Cuba, disarmament had been an ongoing special interest of the President for three years. As with Cuba, his actions and disposition of the problem had come to a head in September 1963.

Early in President Kennedy's administration he announced that a conference on a limited test ban treaty would be held. His goal was to halt the proliferation of nuclear weapons.[47] On June 29, 1961, JFK proposed the establishment of the United States Disarmament Agency. The agency was to make an intensified effort to develop acceptable political and technical alternatives to the arms race.[48]

From the start then, Kennedy wanted constructive action toward disarmament, but his military advisors were equally opposed to such action. Keep in mind that, at this point in history, the Communists were on the move. They had taken Eastern Europe, Red China had forced Nationalist China to occupy an island, North Korea had invaded South Korea, Laos was on the verge of being forced into the Communist camp, and South Vietnam was equally threatened by the Communists. The Congo was ablaze with Communist activity. Even in our own hemisphere, Cuba was now a Communist beachhead only 90 miles offshore.

The last thing the U.S. military wanted was nuclear disarmament The last thing it wanted was to stop atmospheric testing of bigger atomic bombs or to stop nuclear missile production. But in the fall of 1961, JFK had proposed that the U.S. do all these things. In a speech to the United Nations, Kennedy had these words to say: "Mankind must put an end to war or war will put an end to mankind. Let us call a truce to terror."[49] The President then outlined his plan for peace. It's major points were:
1) an end to nuclear tests of all kinds,
2) a mutual ban of atmospheric testing,

3)   a prohibition on nuclear weapons in outer space,
4)   a halt to the testing and production of, and the
      eventual destruction of, strategic nuclear delivery
      vehicles

Kennedy finished his address at the United Nations by adding, "Together we shall save our planet, or together we shall perish in its flames. Save it we can and save it we must—and then shall we earn the eternal thanks of mankind and, as peacemakers, the eternal blessing of God."[50] Kennedy's plan for peace was very idealistic but from the military's point of view, it was not practical—especially with Khrushchev in charge across the sea.

To understand how wide the gulf was between Kennedy and his military chiefs, one need only look at the request by the military to develop the neutron bomb. The military wanted to develop a new bomb that would kill people but leave the buildings standing. Kennedy thought this was preposterous and vetoed development of such a weapon.

Kennedy could not even talk to these men. It was as if he and they were on different planets. The gulf widened between Kennedy and the military over the course of his administration. By June of 1963, the beginning of the end of JFK had commenced—with his speech at the American University that month, the military elite were convinced of the absolute need to remove him from office. The military had already seen the President refuse to invade Cuba—not once, but twice. Because of JFK's inaction in Cuba, there was now a virtual Soviet base in the Western Hemisphere. Kennedy had also refused to give the Soviets a thumping over Berlin when Khrushchev had threatened to cut off the city to the west. By 1963, Kennedy was taking thousands of American troops out of Europe and he had rejected the concept of ever using tactical nuclear weapons to stop Soviet aggression in Western Europe. JFK also refused to use American combat troops in Laos to stop Communist aggression as had been recommended by the Joint Chiefs of Staff. President

Sukarno of Indonesia was receiving millions of dollars in military aid from the Soviet Union and all of Latin America was falling apart. Leftists in Latin America were calling for the takeover of American businesses in Brazil,[51] to be followed by takeovers in Peru, Venezuela, and Argentina.[52] Many leftist governments actually succeeded in stealing American businesses without having to pay compensation. It was in this atmosphere of world revolution and Communist aggression that Kennedy nonetheless said the following:

> But surely the acquisition of such idle stockpiles—which can only destroy and never create—is not the only, much less the most efficient, means of peace.
>
> ...No Government or social system is so evil that its people must be considered as lacking in virtue. As Americans, we find Communism profoundly repugnant by a negation of personal freedom and dignity. But we can still hail the Russian people for their many achievements in science and space, in economic and industrial growth, in culture and acts of courage.
>
> ...For we are both devoting massive sums of money to weapons that could be better devoted to combating ignorance, poverty and disease.
>
> The United States, as the world knows, will never start a war. We do not want a war, we do not now expect a war. This generation of Americans has already had enough, more than enough of war, and hate, and oppression. We shall be prepared if others wish it. We shall be alert to try and stop it. But we shall also do our part to build a world of peace, where the weak are safe and the strong are just. We are not helpless before that task or hopeless of its success. Confident and unafraid we labor on—not toward a strategy of annihilation, but toward a strategy of peace.[53]

With his speech at American University in June, 1963, came the beginning of the end of JFK. This is when the military started in earnest to consider his removal from the Presidency. Kennedy's speech was a great and bold call but its timing could not have been worse. It came eight months after the Soviets had tried to put nuclear weapons only 90 miles off the coast of Florida—not the best timing for such a call. At least not from the perspective of the military. If anything, now was the time to step up missile production. We find how the military was struck by Kennedy's American University speech in the July 15, 1963 issue of *U.S. News and World Report:*

> High officers in the Armed Forces are deeply concerned over what they say is an apparent trend in U.S. Defense policy to "disarm by example." They insist the present policies are weakening the U.S. position relative to Russia and will go on weakening it until a shift in the balance of power will threaten.[54]

Nevertheless, after reading a translation of Kennedy's speech, Khrushchev immediately contacted the American Embassy in Moscow and joked that he was ready to sign the test ban treaty unseen. Kennedy had been working on the Russians to get them to sign such a treaty since his first month in office.

Kennedy jumped at the change in Soviet policy and sent his team to Moscow in July to sign and work out the treaty. The treaty was returned to the United States for ratification by the Senate. The *U.S. News and World Report* of August 5, 1963 gives us insight into how the highest military officers really felt toward the treaty:

> It was over the unanimous opposition of the chiefs of the country's military services, reportedly withdrawn at the last moment, that the U.S. government negotiated with Russia on a nuclear test ban treaty.... The Joint Chiefs of Staff, on at least two occasions, filed written, formal dissents to the administration's proposal for such a ban.... Last spring the chiefs of the Air Force, Army, Navy and Marines told the Senate Armed Services Committee that testing in the atmosphere was absolutely vital.[55]

A showdown between the President and his military chiefs was around the corner.

26

NUCLEAR TEST
BAN TREATY

The Secretary of State was called to appear before a Congressional committee which was investigating the feasibility of President Kennedy's proposed Nuclear Test Ban Treaty. The committee was trying to discern whether the treaty was in the best interests of the country. Secretary of State Rusk was asked by committee members why no military advisors were taken to Moscow in the consultations with the Soviets over the treaty. Secretary Rusk answered that he did not consider their presence necessary, because the negotiators were operating on instructions directly from the President.

"Did the State Department and the White House consult the members of the Joint Chiefs of Staff prior to our participating in the negotiations in Moscow?," one committee member asked. Rusk replied there was a "Committee of Principals" who met to develop the principles of disarmament.[56]

Also questioned by the committee was Robert McNamara, Secretary of Defense. His answers were so evasive that Senator Goldwater, in exasperation, told him: "Mr. Secretary, this is a hearing on the Test Ban Treaty, not the school system, not anything else but this Test Ban Treaty."[57]

The Joint Chiefs were brought in. As it turned out none of them had been consulted on the treaty.[58] The truth is that Kennedy did not check with the Joint Chiefs of Staff during the formative period of the Nuclear Test Ban Treaty. Why? He didn't have to check with them to get their opinions. He knew that every one of them was dead set against it. Their testimony in March to the Armed Forces Committee was evidence enough of their feelings on the subject. Just six months before the treaty was signed, the Joint Chiefs had expressed their vehement opposition to it.

Kennedy, in effect, negotiated the Nuclear Test Ban Treaty through his own intermediaries in the State Department. After the Soviets signed it in Moscow, he smoothed things over with the Joint Chiefs of Staff. They agreed to support it if underground testing was continued. But they remained fundamentally opposed to it.

After the treaty was signed in Moscow, JFK could still lose it if the Senate would not ratify it. To prevent this from happening, he appealed directly to the people by television. The battle for ratification had begun.

Late in July, just before the Senate Foreign Relations Committee's hearings on ratification of the treaty commenced, JFK addressed the American people: "Negotiations were concluded in Moscow on a treaty to ban all nuclear tests in the atmosphere, outer space, and underwater."[59]

The President continued, pointing out that if the U.S. had a nuclear war with the Soviets, three hundred million people would be killed and that the survivors would envy the dead. He also pointed out that our grandchildren would have cancer in their bones, poison in their lungs, and that our children and grandchildren were not merely statistics toward which we could be indifferent.[60] "This debate will involve military, scientific, and political experts, but it must not be left to them alone. The right and responsibility are yours."[61]

Kennedy was, in effect, once again taking an issue to the people, just as he had the year before when he was fighting back against the economic elite by going to the people with the legislation he wanted passed. He was hoping his fellow Americans would, in turn, pressure their legislators to approve the treaty.

Significance of the Test Ban Treaty in Relation to the Assassination. The American University speech, which called for an end to the Cold War, and the subsequent signing of the Test Ban Treaty, led to the conclusion that JFK was a national security threat. What concerned the military even more than the Test Ban Treaty was the realization of what was to come next. In his first appearance before the General Assembly of the United Nations the President outlined his program for peace. It included:

1) an end to nuclear testing of all kinds,
2) a mutual ban on atmospheric testing,
3) a ban on nuclear weapons in outer space,
4) a halt to testing-production of strategic nuclear delivery vehicles, and their eventual destruction.[62]

Thus, by the fall of 1963, Kennedy had in one fell swoop pushed through both a mutual ban on atmospheric testing and an agreement that there would be no nuclear weapons in space. Points two and three were accomplished. This left Kennedy to work on points one and four—an end to all nuclear testing and a halt to the production of strategic nuclear delivery vehicles, along with their destruction. If the military objected vehemently to the cessation of atmospheric testing, it was also opposed to the gradual destruction of the current arsenal of nuclear warhead delivery systems. Pursuit of this type of logic, the chiefs thought, would lead to the destruction of the nuclear weapons themselves.

Kennedy was killed not just for jeopardizing the country with the Nuclear Test Ban Treaty, but for what he might do in a subsequent year should he be re-elected. Robert and Ted Kennedy were also on the horizon as future political candidates. The prospect of 16 years of the Kennedy occupation of the White House was seen as a national security threat and the military decided to nip things in the bud.

* * *

27

BILL OF INDICTMENT

Let the military speak for itself. The August 5, 1963 issue of *U.S. News and World Report* reads like an attorney's brief in defense of the military in their decision to support the President's assassination. It is an indictment against JFK's policies. The article is very similar in tone to the article from the summer of 1962, which made a parallel between Kennedy and his cabinet and the Soviet Politburo. The hysteria of the time screams out to the reader:

> A major upheaval in U.S. Defense is now taking place. A vast arsenal is being canceled or dismantled. The Kennedy Administration is responsible. The military establishment feels that the new strategy adds up to a type of intentional, one-sided disarmament.
>
> Heads of the Armed Services simply do not buy the slogan "The more we arm, the less secure we get." Instead, the Joint Chiefs of Staff, often with unanimity, have opposed almost all of the arms cutbacks now being considered:
>
> 1) B-58 bomber—carries 15 megaton bomb at supersonic speed-scrapped.

2) RS-70 bomber—Air Force plan for the 1970s scrapped.

3) Thor missile—from bases in England, 60 medium-range missiles that can easily reach Russia—ordered dismantled shortly after Soviet Union withdrew its missiles from Cuba.

4) Jupiter missile—bases in Turkey and Italy, 45 missiles ordered abandoned.

5) Skybolt—eliminated, Britain complained.

6) Nike Zeus—"missile killer," Army requested to put this anti-missile around U.S. cities. Requests refused over strong protest of General Maxwell D. Taylor, Chairman, Joint Chiefs of Staff.

7) Midas spy satellite killed.

8) Signposts indicating a cut of one-third of the Navy's 15 attack carriers.

9) Overseas bases, flying bases in England, Morocco, Spain, France, Guam—shut down.

10) Atomic production—shut down half of 14 major plants manufacturing nuclear materials for weapons. The administration feels that the present stockpile is bigger than any demand can foresee.

11) Nuclear Test Ban Treaty. Military requests to continue testing were set aside.[63]

With this indictment against Kennedy's policies, we see how the military felt about him and his administration. From the military's point of view, JFK was a grave national security risk. The choice in their minds was either to sacrifice the life of one man or to continue to risk the lives of 180 million Americans. Their choice was made easier by one more action that Kennedy took in September of 1963. The decision for a rapprochement with Castro, which would have signaled an acceptance on the part of Kennedy of a Communist nation in our hemisphere, combined with a call for an end to the

Cold War at its very height, caused tremendous anxiety in the men who were at the top in the military establishment. Then, with the signing of the Nuclear Test Ban Treaty (which, apparently, was only the beginning of Kennedy's disarmament program), only one more ingredient was needed in order to push the military into committing treason. That ingredient was Vietnam.

* * *

28

VIETNAM

For Kennedy, Vietnam started back in the early 1950s. He had traveled to the Far East and, in his 14 years as a congressman and senator, he had kept abreast of foreign affairs, ultimately serving as a member of the Senate Foreign Relations Committee. Senator Kennedy gave a speech to Congress on April 6, 1954. The subject was Indochina and Vietnam:

> In Indochina we have allied ourselves to the desperate effort of a French regime to hang on to the remnants of Empire. There is no broad, general support of the native Vietnam Government among the people of the area.
>
> To check the southern drive of Communism makes sense but not only through reliance on the force of arms. The task is rather to build strong native noncommunist sentiment within these areas and rely on that as a spearhead of defense, rather than upon the legions of General de Tassigny. To do this apart from and in defiance of innately nationalistic aims spells foredoomed failure.
>
> The hard truth of the matter is, first, that without the wholehearted support of the people of the associated states, with-

out a reliable crusading native army with a dependable officer corps, *A military victory even with American support in the area is difficult if not impossible to achieve* (author's emphasis).[64]

This was a brilliantly foresighted analysis of the conflict in Indochina and Vietnam. In this speech, Kennedy showed a rare wisdom and deep insight into the conflict going on in Indochina. Kennedy realized that the communists were the main problem but he was able to look beneath the surface of the problem to see the root cause was nationalism. The Indochinese wanted the Europeans out. Communism, interacting with nationalism, would be doubly hard to defeat—it would be that much harder to get the noncommunist countrymen to mount a counterattack. He remembered this analysis after he became President, when he was handed the same problem that the French had confronted ten years before.

While President, Kennedy was forever trying to end the corruption of the South Vietnamese government. He continually pressured the South Vietnamese government into reforms that would persuade their own people to get behind the war effort. By 1963, the President stared to reassess U.S. foreign policy in Vietnam. In the spring, Kennedy sent a delegation led by Senator Mike Mansfield to Vietnam for the purpose of making an independent assessment of the situation. In March, Mansfield reported back to Kennedy.

Mansfield reported that since his prior trip to South Vietnam "a year and two billion dollars ago," substantially the same difficulties remained and, indeed, the situation had become more complicated. In 1961, South Vietnam was on the verge of collapse. After a joint reevaluation the U.S. enlarged its role and sent in ten thousand men as advisors, then spent four hundred million dollars annually to prop up the government. As of 1963, 50 American soldiers had died. Mansfield reported that, as early as 1955, there was great corruption, repression and divisiveness in the country.

It's most disturbing to find that after seven years, Vietnam appears less, not more, stable than it was at the outset, that it appears more removed from, rather than closer to, the achievement of popularly responsible and responsive government. Intensification to the point of conflict in Vietnam could become of greater concern and greater responsibility to the United States than it is to the government and people of South Vietnam.

If we are to avoid that course it must be clear to ourselves as well as to the Vietnamese where the primary responsibility lies in this situation. It must rest, as it has rested, with the Vietnamese Government and people. What further effort may be needed for the survival of the Republic of Vietnam in present circumstances must come from that source. If it is not forthcoming, the United States can reduce its commitment or abandon it entirely, *but there is no interest of the United States in Vietnam, which would justify, in present circumstances, the conversion of the war in that country primarily into an American war* (author's emphasis)."[65]

Senator Mansfield was a respected friend of Kennedy. That was why JFK picked him to lead the delegation to Vietnam—he trusted his judgment.

During his administration, Kennedy had previously asked for the advice of General MacArthur, President Eisenhower, and David M. Shoup, the Commandant of the Marine Corps, on Vietnam. All three men told him it would be a mistake to send in combat troops. Now, in the spring of 1963, he received the Mansfield report on the situation in Vietnam. Mansfield's analysis must have sounded very familiar. In many respects, the report echoed his own analysis of events in Indochina ten years before.

President Kennedy was already unhappy with the lack of success in the war in Vietnam. President Diem had not made a real effort toward ending the corruption and implementing the political reforms that had been the strings attached to President Kennedy sending aid to South Vietnam.

In May, Diem's brother made the comment that there were too many American soldiers in South Vietnam. Kennedy, with American soldiers dying and millions of dollars being wasted, was in no mood to hear such criticism coming from the government that we were supporting. He tersely replied:

> We would withdraw the troops, any number of troops, anytime the government of South Vietnam would suggest it. The day after it was suggested, we would have some troops on their way home. But I would say, if requested to, we will do it immediately.[66]

Kennedy was beginning to see what the end of the tunnel looked like and he didn't like what he saw—endless men and material going down a big hole. But he weighed against this vision the possibility that all of Southeast Asia would be falling to the communists. The summer of 1963 came and Vietnam exploded. The South Vietnamese government began a savage repression of Buddhist monks. They, in turn, self-immolated in protest. Madame Nhu, Diem's sister-in-law, joked about having a barbecue over the burning monks and these problems, combined with the Mansfield report, in addition to Kennedy's own thinking of the last ten years toward events in Southeast Asia, were with him during a September 2, 1963, televised interview with Walter Cronkite. In this interview on national television we get Kennedy's final thoughts on the subject of Vietnam, for two-and-a-half months later he would be dead.

> Question: "Do you think the government still has time to regain the support of the people?"
>
> Kennedy: "I do, with changes in policy and perhaps with personnel, I think it can. If it doesn't make those changes, I would think that chances of winning it would not be very good. In the final analysis, it is their war. They are the ones who have to win it or lose it. We can help them, we can give them equipment, we can send our men out there as advisors,

but they have to win it, the people of Vietnam against the communists."[67]

This interview gives us the best insight yet into President Kennedy's thinking on the course of the war. He had clearly drawn the line at advisors. He would not be sending American combat troops to fight the war for the Vietnamese. If the military establishment hadn't figured that out yet, they certainly would have after this interview.

At a press conference on November 14, Kennedy was asked about the purpose of the Honolulu Conference, which was being attended by General Harkins, Ambassador Lodge, Secretary McNamara and other administration officials. The meeting was called to assess the situation in Vietnam. Questions to be discussed were on the topics of aid policy, what American policy should be, and if there should be an intensification of the struggle. Kennedy brought home the following point: "Now that is our object, to bring Americans home, permit the South Vietnamese to maintain themselves as a free and independent country, so the purpose of the meeting in Honolulu is how to pursue these objectives."[68]

Four days later, on November 18, the withdrawal of one thousand troops from Vietnam was announced. Kennedy was pulling out.

Summary of the Conflict Between JFK and the Military and the Decision to Allow the Central Intelligence Agency to Proceed with the Assassination. Kennedy's conflict with the military began soon after he took office. The military was upset with Kennedy because he refused to authorize air cover during the Bay of Pigs invasion. Kennedy was upset with the military because after the report came in by the Commission headed by Maxwell Taylor, Kennedy learned how ill-conceived the entire plan was in the first place. After the Bay of Pigs, Kennedy never again trusted the military elite or the CIA. Kennedy proceeded to set up his own national security staff made up of his own inner circle. He also made General Maxwell Taylor his military advisor and in this capacity Taylor acted as the President's intermediary with the Joint Chiefs of Staff. Kennedy in many ways isolated himself from his own military chiefs.

With McNamara, Kennedy formed a civilian secretariat that had power over the military and was staffed by civilian whiz kids whose opinions on military matters carried more weight than those of the professional soldiers. Where the professional soldiers relied on instincts and experience, the whiz kids relied on computers and statistics and cost-benefit analysis. So, a basic restructuring of the military services was initiated. JFK was preparing the military for the last half of the 20th century with basic changes in doctrine such as resisting the use of nuclear weapons in case of Soviet aggression in Western Europe, preparing for guerrilla warfare, and limited warfare. Other changes were instituted as well, such as making nuclear missiles portable under the Polaris submarine program, eliminating the nuclear weapon carrying bomber as a military mainstay, and ending the duplication of services and products by commerce for the three different services, when one prototype would work for all of them.

The structural changes Kennedy was making caused consternation and anxiety among nearly all of the military elite. These men, after all, had fought both the Japanese and the Germans at the same time and defeated them both. They also were the men who had fought in Korea and held back the Red tide. Certainly they felt they knew what was best for the country. They greatly resented being left out of the decision-making process. Adding the backdrop of the Cold War and anti-communist hysteria, when Kennedy failed to invade Cuba in the face of proof that the Soviets were building nuclear missile sites on the island, he was regarded as a national security risk by the military.

However, it was actions taken in the last 12 months of his term of office which led directly to his death. Kennedy made four major moves that resulted in his assassination.

These four major policy changes were viewed as grave national security risks. They center on the following:

1) Cuba.
2) Disarmament.
3) Ending of the Cold War.
4) Vietnam.

When Kennedy refused to order a U.S. military invasion of Cuba during the Cuban Missile Crisis, it was the turning point in the military's thinking toward the President. No longer merely a nuisance, JFK was now regarded as a national security threat. In the summer of 1963 when Kennedy decided on a rapprochement with Castro, this was merely a-other nail in his coffin. Acceptance of the Castro regime meant that a communist beachhead had been formed in the Americas. This was abhorrent to the military.

The President's disarmament program was viewed as dangerous by the military right from the beginning. With the signing of the Nuclear Test Ban Treaty and the realization that Kennedy was going to get the other tenets of his program passed, including not only the elimination of nuclear weapons but nuclear delivery systems, the military became further convinced that JFK was a national security risk. In their eyes, he was jeopardizing the entire nation.

JFK's call for an end to the Cold War at the height of the Cold War was a bold move. But the timing was bad. The country was still in its anticommunist hysteria stage. The man was 50 years ahead of his time; but he was about to pay the price that visionaries often pay.

The last step that the President took concerned Vietnam. JFK knew that the nation was heading into quicksand and decided to extricate it while it could still get out. The military figured this out also, and because of the current thinking toward communism and the Domino Theory it became essential to eliminate the man who was going to permit communists to overrun Southeast Asia.

Before we turn to JFK and his conflict with the CIA, let us take one last look at JFK and his feelings about the military elite. Kennedy actually wrote his own epitaph during the summer of 1962. While sailing on "The Honey Fitz," the Presidential yacht, JFK had a conversation with his old friend, Paul Fay, Undersecretary of the Navy. He discussed the possibility of such a military takeover very calmly:

It's possible. It could happen in this country, but the conditions would have to be just right. If, for example, the country had a young President, and he had a "Bay of Pigs," there would be a certain uneasiness. Maybe the military would do a little criticizing behind his back, but this would be written off as the usual military dissatisfaction with civilian control. Then, if there were another "Bay of Pigs," the reaction of the country would be "Is he too young and inexperienced?" The military would almost feel that it was their patriotic obligation to stand ready to preserve the integrity of the nation, and only God knows just what segment of democracy they would be defending if they overthrew the elected establishment. Then, if there were a third "Bay of Pigs," it could happen.[69]

* * *

PART IV—JFK VS. CIA

26

JFK, THE STRUGGLE FOR CONTROL OVER THE CIA AND ITS ASSASSINATION OF THE PRESIDENT

The central conflict that JFK had with the CIA was over the concept of autonomy. The mandate given the CIA during its creation by Congress in 1947 centered around intelligence gathering. It quickly became an intelligence gathering agency but with a higher purpose—to fight Communism. Soon, the major part of the CIA's budget was being allocated to the covert section of the Agency. Because it was a secret agency, many of its men, as well as its structure, were insulated from outside interference. By the time Kennedy took office, the agency had become a god unto itself. Its top executives had decided on their own that the use of assassination for political purposes could serve the interests of the country. Being an autonomous entity, the top executives did not have to get approval from the political directorate. Neither Congress nor three Presidents ever guessed at the dark direction upon which the agency had embarked.

Kennedy, in his first months in office, had been approached by Allen Dulles, Director of the CIA (DCI), who asked for permission to use assassination in conjunction with the Bay of Pigs invasion. Kennedy, throughout his first year in office, repeatedly rejected the CIA's assassination plans. Albeit the targets were communists and dictators, Kennedy rejected assassination as something too foreign to American ideology. Although concerned that the CIA would even contemplate such plans, he decided to do a little intelligence gathering on his own. Using two Mafia bosses that the CIA was using in their Castro assassination plots, Kennedy learned just how deeply the CIA was involved in assassinating foreign leaders. He used the information furnished him by the two Mafia men to clean house at CIA.

With documented evidence of CIA's Mafia assassination plans, he demanded the resignation of Dulles. Then, in the next few months fired Richard Bissell, Deputy Director for Plans, as well as General Cabell, the Deputy Director of the agency. These were the three men most involved in plotting assassinations against foreign leaders.

In the fall of 1962, once again the CIA, this time at the direction of Richard Helms, the new Deputy Director for Plans, initiated another assassination plot to get rid of Castro. Kennedy then realized that the problem was structural. With that realization, Kennedy was going to take care of the problem in 1964, once assured of reelection. He would make structural changes by going to Congress with his accumulated proof of the CIA's wrongdoing and willful disobedience of Presidential orders. With proof of CIA assassinations and assassination attempts, President Kennedy planned to ask Congress for legislation that would have reorganized the CIA, taking away its covert ability, putting it on an information-gathering footing only.

The CIA realized this and decided that JFK had to be assassinated before the 1964 election. Unfortunately for JFK, the CIA had already organized an "Executive Action" (execution) squad that was being used on foreign leaders. The CIA merely turned the squad inward on Kennedy.

30

CIA'S PREDISPOSITION TOWARD ASSASSINATION

On December 11, 1959, J. C. King, head of the Western Hemisphere division of the CIA, sent a memo to Allen Dulles, DCI. The King memorandum pointed out that a "far left" dictatorship now existed in Cuba which, "if permitted to stand, would encourage similar actions against U.S. holdings in other Latin American countries." One of King's four "Recommended Actions" was that "Thorough consideration be given to the elimination of Fidel Castro. None of those close to Fidel, such as his brother Raul or his companion Che Guevara, have the same mesmeric appeal to the masses. Many informed people believe that the disappearance of Fidel would greatly accelerate the fall of the present government."[1]

Allen Dulles approved of the recommendation.[2] As JFK was preparing to take the oath of office as President of the United States, the CIA was already adding assassination to its arsenal for the implementation of foreign policy.

John Kennedy was not about to violate the morality on which this country was founded. The CIA was violating every one of those principles. A major clash was on the horizon between the President of the United States and an intelligence agency that was running wild like a "rogue elephant out of control. "

To understand the psychology of the Agency at the time the Kennedy Administration took over, one needs only look at its action immediately preceding the President's tenure. We turn to Africa and Patrice Lumumba, the charismatic pro-Soviet leader of the Congo. By mid-September 1960, Lumumba had lost a power struggle for the leadership of the government to his rival, President Kasavubu. Lumumba was facing another enemy as well, Joseph Mobutu, chief of staff of the Congolese Armed Forces. Lumumba sought the protection of the United Nations peacekeeping forces in Leopoldville.

From the Senate Select Committee to Study Governmental Operations with Respect to Intelligence Activities and its investigation of the CIA in 1975, we learn what was going on behind the scenes in regard to Lumumba's assassination. The Agency was worried that Lumumba's fall from power might be temporary, so while Lumumba was under the protection of U.N. troops in Leopoldville, Allen Dulles ordered his assassination.[3]

Joseph Scheider, a CIA scientist, was ordered to deliver toxic material to the station officer in Leopoldville. Scheider instructed the station officer to assassinate Lumumba. This order had been given him by Richard Bissell, Deputy Director for Plans, who was responsible for covert operations. Joseph Scheider was falsely told that President Eisenhower had approved of the plan.[4]

The toxic material had to be used within a specific time to be effective. Agents intended to get it into Lumumba's food supply, including his toothpaste but the time limit had expired, so the toxic material was disposed of.[5]

So a plan B direct action went into effect. Agent QJ/WIN was sent to Africa. QJ/WIN arrived in Leopoldville on November 21, 1960 and returned to Europe in late December 1960. It was during this time period that Lumumba was captured by his enemies. QJ/WIN began to implement a plan to "pierce" both the Congolese and U.N. guards protecting Lumumba, then "To enter Lumumba's residence and provide escort out of residence." The Agency had been expecting and hoping that Lumumba might try to make a run for it and was preparing for such a possibility. When Lumumba made his move, he broke out of protective custody of the U.N. troops and tried to reach his own stronghold in another part of the country. A CIA cable was sent from Leopoldville to Washington that relayed the CIA was working with the Congolese Armed Forces to get the roads blocked and the troops alerted. The escape routes were blocked off and Lumumba was captured. On January 17, 1961, authorities in Leopoldville placed Lumumba and two of his followers aboard an airplane bound for Bakwanga Province. But their airplane was redirected in mid-flight to Elizabethville in Katanga Province "when it was learned that United Nations troops were at Bakwanga airport." Two days later, the CIA station chief in Elizabethville sent an unusual message to headquarters: THANKS FOR PATRICE. IF WE HAD KNOWN HE WAS COMING WE WOULD HAVE BAKED A SNAKE.[6] After the plane was diverted to Elizabethville, Lumumba was tortured and executed.

The Lumumba assassination, as well as the beginning of the many attempts on Castro's life by the CIA, show that the Agency had embarked on a worldwide campaign of assassination just as President Kennedy was taking office. The mentality for assassination already pervaded the Agency and the mechanism for carrying it out was in place.

* * *

31

"EXECUTIVE ACTION"
EXECUTION SQUAD

An even more ominous arm of the CIA was being formed during the same time period. The "executive action" assassination team was being formed even as President Kennedy was giving his Inaugural Address. A Senate subcommittee investigating alleged assassination attempts of foreign leaders by the CIA learned that sometime in early 1961, Richard Bissell instructed William Harvey, chief of the CIA's foreign intelligence staff, to establish an "executive action capability." This "capability" was research into various ways to assassinate foreign leaders.[7] "Executive action" was a CIA euphemism for a project to develop means for overthrowing foreign political leaders, including a "capability to perform assassination." The project was given the code name ZR/RIFLE.[8]

A single agent ("asset") was given the cryptonym QJ/WIN and placed under William Harvey's supervision for the ZR/RIFLE project. Harvey used QJ/WIN to spot "individuals with criminal and underworld connections in Europe for possible multipurpose use." QJ/WIN reported that one potential asset in the Middle East was "the leader of a gambling syndicate with an available pool of assassins."[9]

In December 1960, in Africa, while plotting how best to go about the assassination of Lumumba, QJ/WIN was approached by another CIA asset with the code name WI/ROGUE. QJ/WIN reported to the station chief that WI/ROGUE had offered him $300 per month to participate in an intelligence network and be a member of an "execution squad." Under questioning WI/ROGUE later said he was working for an American intelligence service.[10] In effect, by December, 1960, the CIA was forming an execution squad, sometimes called "the International Team." The team was made up of foreign nationals who were professional assassins employed and directed by the Agency. The reason that foreign nationals were being used was the "cut out" concept. If a target were to be executed by the squad the trail would lead and end in Europe, cutting out any hint of CIA involvement.

This execution squad remained secret until the Senate's intensive investigation into CIA abuses in 1975. I suggest that the men who were firing at the President in Dealy Plaza were most likely members of this assassination team. Because the men fired at the President from several different locations in Dealy Plaza, in all likelihood the President's assassination was in reality just another job for the CIA professional assassination team.

* * *

32

JFK AND THE
CONFLICT WITH CIA

The basic conflict between the CIA and President Kennedy was over the concept of autonomy. The CIA had become its own autonomous creation. In President Kennedy's quest to bring CIA under control, he learned that not only was the CIA too autonomous, but that it was doing things that were contrary to the ideology that underlay American civilization. When he found out that the CIA was assassinating foreign leaders, he was doubly upset. Not only were they taking such action, but they did so in direct violation of Presidential orders. After gaining evidence of the CIA's transgressions, he confronted CIA Director Allen Dulles and demanded his resignation. After JFK fired the men who were most responsible for the assassination concept, Richard Helms, Deputy Director for Plans, once again activated the assassination mechanism. Kennedy then realized that the answer was a restructuring of CIA. The CIA in turn decided to assassinate the President before he could effect his reorganizational plans.

33

CONVERSATION WITH SENATOR SMATHERS

An interesting conversation took place between Senator George Smathers and the President barely two months after JFK assumed the Presidency. The President asked Senator Smathers what the reaction would be throughout Latin America if Fidel Castro were assassinated. Smathers told him that the U.S. would be blamed no matter who was actually responsible and he personally disapproved of assassination. The President agreed. Smathers felt that the President raised the subject of assassination because someone else "had apparently discussed this and other possibilities with respect to Cuba with the President." [11]

* * *

34

CONVERSATION WITH TAD SZULC

In early November, 1961, President Kennedy invited a *New York Times* reporter based in Washington to meet with him in the Oval Office. The reporter was Tad Szulc and the President was interested in his views on Cuba. Szulc was familiar with current conditions in Cuba, having paid a visit to the island in May and June. He had had a series of long conversations with Castro. Kennedy asked him a number of questions about Castro, including what the United States could do to establish some kind of dialogue with the Cuban leader.

The President also asked Szulc, "What would you think if I ordered Castro to be assassinated?" Based on Szulc's notes, which Szulc held in the intervening years, he replied that the United States should not be a party to murder or political assassination. Szulc said that the President's response was "I agree with you completely." President Kennedy then went on for a few minutes to indicate how strongly he and his brother felt that the United States for moral reasons should never resort to assassination.

According to Szulc's notes, JFK said he raised the question because he was under terrific pressure from advisers ("think he said intelligence people, but not positive") to okay a Castro murder. The President said that he was resisting the pressure. [12]

Richard Goodwin, special assistant to the President and in attendance at the meeting between JFK and Szulc, testified that Kennedy also said, "Well, that's the kind of thing I'm never going to do." Goodwin also told the Senate Select Committee that, several days later, the President told him, "We can't get into that kind of thing, or we would all be targets." [13] Seven days after his conversation with Tad Szulc, the President gave a speech at the University of Washington where he said, "We cannot, as a free nation, compete with our adversaries in the tactics of terror, assassination, false promises, counterfeit mobs, and crisis." [14] Two weeks after this speech, Allen Dulles was replaced by John McCone as DCI. Then, in February 1962, Richard Bissell was fired as Deputy Director for Plans. In April, General Cabell was fired as the Deputy Director.

Kennedy biographers have always contended that Kennedy fired Allen Dulles because of Kennedy's unhappiness over the Bay of Pigs incident. This was not so. Allen Dulles, then Richard Bissell, and then General Cabell were all fired for trying to assassinate foreign leaders against Kennedy's specific orders not to do so.

From the testimony of Senator Smathers we learn that, shortly after entering office, the President was queried about the viability of assassination as a political tool. Senator Smathers testified that he felt the subject of assassination had been brought to the President's attention by someone else— in regard to the Cuba problem. Eight months later, Tad Szulc was being asked his views on the subject of assassination. According to Szulc's notes, he felt rather certain that the

President was under terrific pressure from his advisers to murder Castro. Although Allen Dulles had asked for presidential permission to initiate assassinations, he had already been proceeding on his own. He was assassinating foreign leaders without regard to higher authority. Just as he had failed to inform President Eisenhower of the assassination plans against Patrice Lumumba and Castro, he was acting now on his own authority in direct violation of a Presidential directive.

* * *

35

CIA-MAFIA ASSASSINATION PLOTS AGAINST CASTRO

At the time that QJ/WIN was dispatched to take care of Patrice Lumumba, a CIA support chief was sitting down with Johnny Rosselli, a West Coast gangster. Their discussion concerned the best way to assassinate Fidel Castro.[15] With Castro out of the way, the CIA would be rid of a Soviet agent in the Western Hemisphere. And, its officials hoped, any leftist tendencies to take over American businesses would be squelched in Latin America. The Mafia would gain by regaining control of the casinos on Cuba. It was a match made in hell. The CIA was hoping to use Mafia connections still on the island in order to effect Castro's death. Again using the "cut out" concept, if Castro's assassination was traced anywhere it would lead to the Mafia and not the CIA. The CIA would use the same concept with President Kennedy's murder. By employing Jack Ruby and other Mafia elements in the President 's assassination, if the public failed to buy Oswald as the lone gunman, the CIA would be able to direct blame for the President's assassination on the Mafia.

John Rosselli then brought in Sam Giancana as well as an old friend, Santo Trafficante, the Mafia boss of Miami. In March 1961, poison pills were passed from the CIA to Johnny Rosselli, who then passed them to a Cuban who had access to Castro. It was Trafficante who set up the meeting between the Cuban and the CIA via Rosselli.

Since the following month brought the Bay of Pigs invasion, it is likely that Allen Dulles was trying to effect Castro's murder as a prelude. For Castro to die immediately preceding the invasion would clearly have helped the invasion's chances of success. Dulles was meeting with the President in March, trying to get his permission to assassinate Castro. Kennedy denied him permission, so he went ahead and had the poison pills delivered anyway. Senator Smathers testified that it was in March that he had the assassination conversation with the President.

Another assassination attempt was made in the Caribbean on May 30, 1961. This time it was successful. Trujillo, the dictator of the Dominican Republic, was assassinated.[16] The plot to assassinate Trujillo went back to July 1, 1960. During the Eisenhower Administration, General Cabell, the CIA's Deputy Director, as well as Richard Helms, the acting Deputy Director for Plans, approved an arms shipment of twelve sterile (untraceable) rifles with telescopic sights together with five hundred rounds of ammunition to a dissident group in the Dominican Republic. The expressed goal was to assassinate Trujillo. The initial plan fell through, but the CIA kept plotting with the Dominican dissidents until the assassination was effected.

On April 19, 1961, machine guns arrived on the island via diplomatic pouch courtesy of the CIA. Then, on May 5, 1961, the President voiced disapproval of the United States initiating the overthrow of the Trujillo government.[17] But Trujillo was nonetheless assassinated on May 30. Trujillo was killed with carbines that had earlier been passed by the CIA to the dissident group that claimed responsibility.[18]

The CIA was clearly out of control. Dulles not only continued with the Castro-Mafia assassination plots, but was instrumental in the Trujillo murder. The Trujillo assassination took place two months after Kennedy had his conversation with Senator Smathers and three weeks after Kennedy voiced disapproval of participation in the overthrow of Trujillo. The struggle between JFK and CIA over who would be in control of foreign policy was on.

* * *

36

PRESIDENT KENNEDY GATHERS INTELLIGENCE ON THE CIA

The President, concerned over the direction in which the CIA was moving, started gathering information on the Agency via the aforementioned gangsters Rosselli and Giancana. The development of the CIA-Mafia plots during the spring and summer of 1961 was reported back to JFK through a female courier who shuttled between JFK and the Mafia chieftains. With this information, Kennedy was able to confront Allen Dulles and demand his resignation.

The Select Committee found evidence that President Kennedy had been seeing a woman who was also a close friend of Rosselli and Giancana. This woman was in contact with the President from the end of 1960 through mid-1962. She was also in frequent contact with the gangsters during this time. A White House log shows 70 instances of phone contact between the White House and the President's friend in this period.[19]

We learn more about this woman and what was happening from the February 19, 1988 issue of *People* magazine. Judith Exner stated that the President asked her to fly to Las Vegas and pick up an envelope from Rosselli and then fly to Chicago and give the envelope to Giancana. This was a few days after the Bay of Pigs invasion on April 17, 1961. On April 28, 1961, she arranged a meeting between the President and the Mafia boss, Giancana, who had greeted the President as "Jack." On April 29, 1961, she flew to Florida at Kennedy's request, had drinks with Giancana and Rosselli, who were there for a meeting, and returned to Washington with an envelope for the President. For days, and sometimes weeks, throughout the spring and summer, she crisscrossed the country carrying plain 9" x 12" manila envelopes from Kennedy to Giancana and Rosselli and back again. "I knew that the contents were very important to Jack," she said.[20] On August 8, 1961, Giancana met with the President in the Oval Office. She then delivered one more envelope from Giancana and Rosselli to Kennedy on August 24, 1961.[21]

The significance of the intimate correspondence between the President and the Mafia chieftains is overwhelming. On the one hand, we know that Johnny Rosselli and Sam Giancana were plotting the murder of Fidel Castro in association with the CIA. We know that the idea to use the Mafia to assassinate Castro originated with the CIA. We know that the Agency had been working with these two gangsters since the fall of 1960 and we know that the CIA passed poison pills to these men for use against Castro in March of 1961, shortly before the Bay of Pigs invasion. We know that the plans to assassinate Castro continued after the Bay of Pigs invasion failed.

We also know that President Kennedy had been approached by Allen Dulles with the proposal to use assassination as a tool for foreign policy. We know this because of the testimony of Senator Smathers and his conversation with the President in March shortly before the Bay of Pigs invasion. This conversation coincided with the passing of poison pills to the Mafia chieftains in Florida. We also have the conversation with Tad Szulc in November of 1961 and the President's own aversion to the concept of the United States using assassination as a political tool. Szulc also said the President mentioned that he had been under terrific pressure to go along with the assassination concept and that the pressure was coming from the intelligence community, but that he was resisting. Finally, we have the President's own speech at the University of Washington in which he said, "We cannot, as a free nation, compete with our adversaries in tactics of terror, assassination, false promise, counterfeit mobs, and crises." The very thing that the President was saying that we should not do were the very things that Allen Dulles and the CIA were doing. After the speech at the University of Washington, Allen Dulles was relieved of command of CIA and Richard Bissell and General Cabell followed in his wake. All three men were the CIA executives involved in the assassination of foreign leaders.

The reason all three men were fired by Kennedy was because he found out about their traitorous activities. I suggest that Kennedy was using his relationship with the two mobsters to spy on the CIA. It was less than two weeks after the Bay of Pigs invasion when Kennedy met with Sam Giancana. Kennedy's lady friend also said that she had flown to Florida to receive an envelope from the Mafia men for President Kennedy. It was in Miami that the CIA was meeting with both Rosselli and Giancana going over final plans to assassinate Castro. It was also the summer of 1961 when the CIA and the two Mafia men plotted Castro's murder. Also, during this time all the envelopes were passed between the mobsters and Kennedy. Finally, the lady friend delivered one last envelope from Giancana and Rosselli to the President on August 24, 1961. It is after this envelope reached the President that he then asked Allen Dulles to step down. In effect, Kennedy had the goods on the current DCI and there was nothing Dulles could say or do. After the August 24, 1961 envelope reached the President, communication between the President and the Mafia chieftains ceased. The cessation of the relationship coincided with the termination of Allen Dulles as CIA Director.

Every move throughout the spring and summer of 1961 between the CIA and the Mafia was being reported back to Kennedy. The envelopes that passed between the men contained questions that Kennedy wanted the Mafia men to ask the CIA. Kennedy wanted to know just how deeply the CIA was involved in violating the Constitution. He also wanted to know the specific players involved within the CIA. He was holding the information in those envelopes until such time as he could go to Congress with evidence and demand a reorganization of the CIA. By August 24, 1961, he had accumulated enough evidence that he was able to confront Allen Dulles and demand his resignation. He was also able to get the names of Richard Bissell and General Cabell from Giancana and Rosselli. This is why Kennedy promptly fired them, too. The Agency was confounded by Kennedy's discovery of their assassination plots. After all, only a handful of personnel had been made aware of this new direction.

* * *

37

REALIZATION OF THE NEED FOR STRUCTURAL REORGANIZATION OF CIA

After he fired the terrible trio, Kennedy was hopeful that he had managed to get CIA under control. But in 1962, the President once again found himself confronted with the CIA's autonomy. Earlier, in April of 1962, William Harvey, acting on "explicit orders" from Richard Helms, requested Sheffield Edwards, the CIA's Director of Security, to put him in touch with Johnny Rosselli. Under instructions from Richard Helms, William Harvey reactivated the plot to assassinate Castro.[22] Weapons and equipment were passed to Rosselli. He then passed them on to Cubans in Miami who were to take the weapons to Cuba and assassinate Castro.

After the Cuban Missile Crisis, William Harvey was, in effect, exiled to Rome as station chief. Finding out that once again the CIA was countermanding his orders made Kennedy understand the absolute need to reorganize the agency. Evidently, getting rid of a few bad apples did not do the trick. The CIA's autonomy and evil were structural. A case in point was Richard Helms. Although Kennedy had gotten rid of the top three bad apples, in Richard Helms he had a man who was worse than the other three put together. A year later, Helms would be playing the key part in the President's assassination.

In order to preserve CIA autonomy, the decision was made to assassinate the President. No doubt there were other factors of a national security nature that contributed to the decision, such as Kennedy's refusal to subvert the Latin American democracies in order to protect American businesses, but the main point was preserving the CIA's autonomy. By September 1962, the CIA was determined that the President was to be assassinated. By the same time, the business community, for their own specific reasons, had also determined that Kennedy must be removed from office. This left only the military to agree to the assassination. Its assent was granted in the summer of 1963 when it appeared to them once and for all that Kennedy was a national security risk.

* * *

PART V—THE PLAYERS

38

LEE HARVEY OSWALD

The first thing one notices is how young Lee Harvey Oswald was when he was arrested for the murders of the President and Dallas police officer J. D. Tippit. Lee had just turned 24. With his receding hairline and calm demeanor while in custody, he appeared to be a decade older. Indeed, in his 24 years, he had packed a lot of living. Growing up in New Orleans, Lee had had two older brothers, John Pic and Robert Oswald. Because of the age differences among the three, Lee was raised somewhat as an only child. His relationship with his mother was strained throughout adolescence mostly because of his mother's neurosis. John Pic suggested to the Warren Commission that Lee joined the armed forces straight out of high school in order to get away from their mother, Marguerite. At least that was the reason the two older boys had fled the nest.

Lee is described as a loner by his childhood pals and the adults who watched him grow up. Lee had a higher than average IQ and was often truant. His probation officer asked him why he never wanted to attend classes and Lee told him that he preferred to stay home and watch television or read. At 17, he escaped into the Marine Corps and began the adventure that, just a few years later, would find him arrested and being interrogated for the murder of the President of the United States.

The Warren Commission fiction is that Lee joined the Marine Corps, where he became enamored of Marxism, received an early out based on a hardship pertaining to his mother, and then left for the Soviet Union immediately following his discharge. While in the Soviet Union he defected, giving up his U.S. citizenship while releasing state secrets he learned concerning his military specialty, radar. After a few years in the Soviet Union, Lee decided to return home. Through a legal technicality, he was able to get a passport and return to the United States. On June 14, 1962, Lee arrived in New York City, accompanied by his beautiful, Russian-born wife, Marina, and their first-born child, June. The following day Lee arrived in Fort Worth, Texas, where his mother lived. Shortly thereafter, Lee moved his family to Dallas. After a succession of low-paying jobs, he moved once again, this time to New Orleans. The family remained there through the spring and summer of 1963. Ruth Paine, a family friend, convinced Marina to come and live with her in the fall in Irving, Texas, a suburb of Dallas, in order to have a less stressful birth of the Oswald's second child. Lee soon followed the family to Irving, Texas, arriving in October, having secured a job as an order filler at the book depository on October 4, 1963. When the President's visit to Dallas was announced, Lee got it into his head that he would take the opportunity to shoot the President.

So, the Warren Commission never discovered a motive for Lee's killing of the President. It suggested that perhaps Lee assassinated the President in order to become famous. Under this theory, Lee as an unknown person with a persecution complex shot JFK in order to improve his self-esteem. This theory, of course, conflicts with Lee's stringent protests while in custody that he didn't shoot the President or anybody else. If he killed the President in order to become famous, why did he adamantly deny shooting anyone? So much for motive.

When one examines the 26 volumes of hearings and exhibits produced by the Warren Commission, one learns who the real Lee Harvey Oswald was. We learn that, as a teenager growing up in New Orleans, he joined the Civil Air Patrol, a civilian cadre affiliated with the United States Air Force. Sidney Voebel, a teenage friend of Lee's, joined the group and asked Lee if he, too, wanted to join. Lee bought a uniform and attended meetings as a member. What is most interesting is that the captain of the Civil Air Patrol was David Ferrie. Not too many years later David Ferrie would be a central character in New Orleans District Attorney Jim Garrison's case implicating the CIA in the assassination. Voebel told the Warren Commission that Lee attended a party at the home of David Ferrie and that Ferrie was quite a "character," in that he rode a motorcycle and had several degrees.[1] Garrison believed that Ferrie was a CIA agent or, at the very least, flew missions for the CIA as an expert pilot. My question is this: Did Ferrie recruit Lee into the CIA? In just a few years Lee would be "defecting" to the Soviet Union as a Marxist Marine. But was he? One of the keys to understanding whether Lee was an undercover intelligence agent is his learning the Russian language. Lee went straight from high school into the Marines. After his discharge from the Marines, he appeared in Moscow, speaking fluent Russian. He had to have learned the Russian language while he was in the Marines. He also had to have studied the language intensively for three years to have such comprehensive language skills as he displayed in Russia. Just how good were these skills?

When Marina and Lee arrived in Dallas from the Soviet Union, she told her Russian émigré friends that his Russian was so good she originally thought he was from one of the

Soviet provinces, perhaps one of the Baltic states. The Russian émigré citizens of Dallas who appeared before the Warren Commission also pointed to Lee's language abilities. Evidently, Lee arrived in the Soviet Union speaking fluent Russian. Yet he was only 20 years old and had spent the previous three years in the Marine Corps so he had to have learned the language during this time. But what is of paramount importance is *where* he learned it.

Shortly after Lee appeared at the American Embassy in Moscow and renounced his citizenship, he gave an interview to a reporter based in Moscow named Priscilla Johnson. Throughout the long interview, she asked, among other things, where he had learned to speak Russian so fluently. In her Warren Commission testimony, she said, "Well, how did you teach yourself to read and write—from Berlitz? Did you just get a textbook or did you go to some city nearby for lessons at a school?" And he wouldn't answer and that struck me as being one hell of a—I mean, a strange thing to be elusive."[2]

Lee's refusal to say where he learned to speak Russian, in retrospect, may not have been so strange. It was merely something Lee wanted to keep secret. But in keeping it private, he may have tipped off the KGB as to his true identity. In volume 9, page 304, of the *Hearings and Exhibits* produced for the Warren Commission, a memo indicates that on February 15, 1959, Lee Harvey Oswald had taken a Russian language examination.[3]

Evidently, Lee was being taught the Russian language by the Marine Corps. The Marine Corps doesn't do anything without having a specific objective. Lee's being given the opportunity to learn the Russian language would have been the result of a conscious decision on the part of his superiors. But the problem is that Lee had already declared himself a Marxist. This was widely known by both officers and fellow corpsmen. His fellow Marines would address him as "comrade" and "Comrade Oswaldovitch." Why would the

Marine Corps be teaching a self-proclaimed Marxist the Russian language? And even more incriminating, why did Lee want to keep this fact a secret?

After Lee spent two years in the Soviet Union, he decided to come back to the United States. The State Department gave him back his passport, paving the way for his return. Not only was this unusual, it was extraordinary. Lee's affidavit at the time of his defection speaks for itself: "My request for revoking of my American citizenship is made only after the longest and most serious consideration. I affirm my allegiance is to the Soviet Socialist Republic."[4] And Lee didn't merely give up his American citizenship. He actually defected. Another action on the part of Lee shows that he didn't merely switch nationality, but actually committed treason.

The FBI did a security check on Lee when it became known that he had indeed defected to the Soviet Union: "The FBI learned through an unnamed Soviet official that an American born Marine radar operator would make available information about his Marine Corps specialty when he becomes a Soviet citizen."[5] Richard Snyder was the American consul at the embassy when Lee arrived to renounce his citizenship. Snyder tried to get Lee to take more time with the decision but Snyder eventually did report what was, in effect, Lee's treason: "He would make available to the Soviet Union any knowledge as he had acquired while in the Marine Corps concerning his specialty."[6]

So Lee was not merely giving up his U.S. citizenship and taking up Soviet citizenship. He was defecting and giving up state secrets that could endanger his fellow Americans back home. This could have gotten him a prison term at Leavenworth had he been stopped and captured before arriving in Moscow. Yet, when Lee decided to return to the U.S., he breezed back with the greatest of ease. He was treated almost as though he had gone to the Soviet Union as a tourist.

Abraham Chayes and other State Department officials were grilled incessantly by the Warren Commission lawyers on their having allowed Lee Harvey Oswald to return to the United States. The Immigration and Naturalization Service flatly denied Lee's entrance back into the country—they were overridden by the State Department.[7] The State Department officials gave various reasons why they overrode the immigration authorities. The bottom line was expressed by Congressman Gerald Ford in response to State's explanations: "This isn't a question of freedom of speech. This is a question of giving away government secrets."[8]

This special treatment of Lee happened one more time—a year after his readmittance to the United States. In June 1963, Lee decided he wanted to visit Cuba. The State Department had travel restrictions for Americans wanting to go to Cuba. Cuba was, in fact, off limits to Americans. But one could go to Cuba via Mexico. Lee applied for a passport on June 24, 1963. Within 24 hours, he was issued one. Once again, a government action throws doubt on Lee being just another guy, as the Warren Commission would have us believe. Lee was a Marxist. Not only was he a Marxist but he had defected to the Soviet Union. Throughout the 1950s and in the early 1960s, the passports of American communists were rigidly scrutinized. But not Lee Oswald's, apparently. Someone—somewhere in the State Department or CIA—was watching out for him. I believe the CIA pressured the State Department both to let Lee return to the U.S. and to issue his passport this second time.

There are other strong indications that Lee was an intelligence operative. While he was in the Soviet Union, Oswald's mother, Marguerite, paid a visit to the State Department in Washington, D.C. on January 26, 1961. John Fain, the FBI agent in charge of investigating Lee Oswald's defection wrote the following report:

> Mrs. Marguerite Oswald appeared at the U.S. Department of State in Washington D.C. to see what could be done to help

her son, the subject. She expressed the thought that her son had gone to the Soviet Union as a "secret agent" and that the State Department was not doing enough to help him.[9]

Curiously, three weeks after this contact at the State Department, Lee requested to return to the United States. One can assume he had blown his cover, perhaps as early as his interview with Priscilla Johnson, in which he refused to say where he learned to speak Russian. The KGB was not sitting idly by during Lee's defection. A Marxist who nevertheless joins the Marines, who is secretive of where and how he learned the Russian language, and whose mother professes her son to be a secret agent might have alerted the KGB.

We get an interesting look into the psychology of the mother of the accused assassin in the State Department's own report of the incident. "She said her son had gone to the Soviet Union as a U.S. secret agent, and if it were true she wished the appropriate authorities to know that she was destitute and should receive some compensation."[10] Mommy dearest was trying to shake down the State Department.

When Lee arrived back in the States, his actions suggest, that just as his mother claimed, he was an intelligence agent. Just as he used his cover as a Marxist Marine to facilitate a defection to the Soviet Union, he now had unimpeachable credentials to infiltrate the left wing of his homeland. A Marxist ex-defector who had actually lived in the Promised Land would have easy access to left wing organizations.

Despite this, Lee began to intimate his deep cover role as an intelligence agent on several occasions. Immediately after his return in June 1962, Lee contacted Pauline Bates, a professional typist. He had smuggled out notes that he wanted her to type up. He was very secretive about the notes and would insist on remaining in the office while she typed them. Mrs. Bates told the Warren Commission that, based on his writings, he was actually very bitter toward Russia. He described how the Russians were forced to go to the annual

May Day parade and how they had to work from sun-up to sundown. There were no vacations and propaganda was everywhere and continuous. There was always a party member around ready to inform on citizens. People couldn't talk freely. He also wrote at length on Communist Party cells, their organization as well as where their various buildings were located and what type of administrative offices occupied the buildings. Mind you, these are the observations of a supposedly Marxist fanatic whose allegiances were intact after returning from the Soviet Union.

But this reads like a CIA report. Could Lee have been so naïve as to hand over his CIA report to an unknown professional typist? He was only twenty three years old; at this age there's inevitably naiveté. In any case, after only two sessions, Lee stopped going to Mrs. Bates's office. Another CIA agent, perhaps his handler, probably told him what a fool he was being. Or perhaps he figured it out for himself. In any event, his writings show us that he was clearly not merely an avowed Marxist ideologue. But if he was not a true Marxist, then what was he? Who was he? Pauline Bates told the Warren Commission that Lee had given her the impression that he had gone to Russia under the auspices of the State Department.[11]

Lee gave further hints as to his intelligence background while working at Jaggers-Stiles, a mapmaking company that had the U.S. Army as one of its customers. At the company, Lee worked with Dennis Offstein, who had some interesting remarks for the Warren Commission about Lee's observations in the Soviet Union:

> He mentioned about the disbursement of military units, saying that they didn't intermingle their armored divisions and infantry divisions and various units the way we do in the United States. That they would have all of their aircraft in one geographical location and their tanks in another geographical location. He mentioned that aircraft in Minsk—he never saw a vapor trail, indicating the lack of aircraft in the area. [12]

Lee had also explained to Offstein what microdots were and their use in espionage. Offstein finished his testimony with the following: "My assumption was that he was an agent of the U.S. at first."

I believe Offstein's assumption to be correct. A true defector would never have noticed the things Lee noticed while in the Soviet Union. His familiarity with the tools of espionage; his learning the Russian language in the service; trying to cover it up; his ease in returning to the U.S. when anyone else having done such things would have been imprisoned; all of these point to Lee Harvey Oswald as an intelligence agent.

In the summer of 1963, Lee did one more thing that indicated he was something other than what he pretended to be. Living in New Orleans, Lee paid a visit to the store of a Cuban leader of the anti-Castro faction that was demanding Castro's ouster from power. His name was Carlos Bringuir. Lee first encountered a young man in the store named Phillip Geraci. Lee told the young man that he was against Fidel Castro and wanted to lend his Marine Corps expertise to the cause. Geraci tells us that Lee said how he knew how to blow up bridges and derail trains. Lee also said he could make homemade guns and gunpowder.[13] As Lee was talking, Carlos Bringuir walked in. Bringuir told the Warren Commission that he and Lee shared the same view of Castro.

> He told me he was against Castro and that he was against Communism. After that Oswald told me he had been in the Marine Corps and that he had training in guerrilla warfare and that he was willing to train Cubans to fight against Castro. Even more, he told me that he was willing to go himself to fight against Castro.[14]

The next day Lee returned to the store and dropped off a "guidebook for Marines." Lee's visit to the store raises an obvious question: What was a Marxist, pro-Soviet, pro-Fidel Castro leftist doing cozying up to a supremely anti-Castro Cuban? What game was Lee playing? He seems to have been playing the role of an agent provocateur.

Three days after leaving his guidebook with Carlos Bringuir, Lee's actions revealed the purpose behind the charade. Bringuir told the Warren Commission that a man named Hernandez rushed into the store saying that another young man was carrying a sign saying "Viva Fidel" down on Canal Street. Bringuir hurried out of his store in search of the young man. Much to his surprise, the man carrying the "Viva Fidel" and "Hands off Cuba" sign was none other than Lee Harvey Oswald. Bringuir became angry and a shouting match ensued. According to Bringuir, Lee told him, "Ok Carlos, if you want to hit me, hit me."[15]

Obviously, Lee had set up Carlos Bringuir. Lt. Martello of the New Orleans Police Department felt the same way: "He seemed to have set them up, so to speak, to create an incident."[16] Lee was arrested and the event was covered by the news media. Afterward, Lee appeared on local television espousing his Marxist views.

I believe that the CIA ordered Lee to create this disturbance. Its purpose was tied to the President's planned assassination. By the summer of 1963 the assassination of the President was speeding to its climax. This incident was going to be used to instill in the minds of the American people Lee's lone guilt once the assasination took place. Now the agency had film footage of the President's soon-to-be-accused assassin carrying pro-Castro leaflets and a sign, as well as film of Lee debating the merits of Marxism on television.

Are there any other indications that Lee was an intelligence agent for the U.S. government? Henry Wade, the Dallas district attorney who prosecuted Jack Ruby for the murder of Lee, told the Warren Commission of the many citizens who had seen Jack Ruby and Lee Oswald together in Dallas. He also mentioned that a voucher had been found indicating Lee was working for either the CIA or the FBI. Henry Wade should know. Prior to his becoming a district attorney, Henry Wade had been an FBI agent.

Before we turn to Lee's arrest for the shooting of the President and Dallas police officer J.D. Tippit and his denials of the allegations, let's take a look at one more fact. After Lee had been arrested for allegedly shooting Officer Tippit, his personal belongings were searched and recorded. One of Lee's possessions, taken from the room he rented at the boarding house was an "unknown electronic device" in a paper case.[17] I suggest the unknown electronic device was part of a spy's paraphernalia. Lee Harvey Oswald, at the very least, was a much more complicated man than the Warren Commission would have us believe.

* * *

39

THE INTERROGATION OF
LEE HARVEY OSWALD

The President was gunned down at 12:30 p.m. Lee left
the book depository and between 12:30 p.m. and 12:45 p.m.,
entered the cab of William Whalley, who drove him a few
blocks past his boarding house. Lee left his boarding room a
few minutes past 1:00 p.m. Dallas Police Officer J.D. Tippit
was shot at approximately 1:15 p.m. At 1:40 p.m., Lee was
arrested at the Texas Theater for the murder of Officer
Tippit.

When we take a more in depth look at what was happening between 12:30 p.m., when the President was assassinated, and 1:40 p.m., when Lee was taken into custody, we
see a lot of action taking place. Equally important, Lee's defense, in his own words, is available.

After a scuffle with police officers, Lee was led out of
the Texas Theater and placed in a patrol car. In the car on
the way down to police headquarters, Dallas police officer
Walker spoke to Lee. Officer Walker tells us how the ex-

change went. Officer Walker asked Lee, "Why did you kill the officer? Did you kill the officer because you were afraid of being arrested for something?" Lee replied, "I am not scared of anything. Do I look like I am scared now?"[18]

Officer Walker told the Warren Commission that Lee didn't look like he was scared. "He was calm, and not a bit nervous." Gerald Hill was another Dallas police officer who responded to the Tippit shooting. Officer Hill told the Warren Commission that, on the way to headquarters, Lee said, "I don't know why you are treating me like this. The only thing I have done is carry a pistol into a movie."[19] As Lee was being taken out of the police vehicle in the basement of the police garage, he was asked if he wanted to cover his face. Lee responded, "Why should I hide my face. I haven't done anything to be ashamed of."[20]

Lee was taken to the third floor into the homicide office where Captain Will Fritz, chief of homicide, began interrogating him. He asked Lee if he had in fact shot Officer Tippit. Lee denied shooting Officer Tippit. According to Captain Fritz, Lee told him, "The only law I violated was in the show. I hit the officer in the show, he hit me in the eye and I guess I deserved it. That is the only law I violated. That is the only thing I have done wrong."[21] The interrogation turned to the President's assassination. Lee denied killing the President. Lee told Captain Fritz that he admired JFK and said he had a nice family. He also told Detective Leavelle the following, "Well, I think the Vice President has about the same views as the President has and probably will do about the same thing Kennedy has done."[22] Once again, so much for motivation. Captain Fritz next asked Lee why he left the book depository. Lee's response was the following: "I didn't think there would be any more work done that afternoon and we don't punch a time clock and they don't keep very close tabs on your work, so I left."[23]

Detective Elmer Boyd was also in on the interrogation of Lee throughout the day. Detective Boyd told the Warren Commission that he asked Lee about the mark above his eye. Lee responded, "Well, I struck an officer and the officer struck me back, which he should have done."[24] Detective Boyd told the Commission those were his exact words. Stuart Stern, the Warren Commission lawyer who was questioning Detective Boyd, made a summary statement that, in effect, offered a glimpse of Lee's true identity: "This is quite unnatural—really rather exceptional. A man is accused of killing two people, one of them the President of the United States and at the end of the day he is pretty well in command."[25] The fact is Lee was just too cool throughout this ordeal to be an ordinary citizen who either had just assassinated the President or, conversely, was entirely innocent of the act.

Detective Leaville was in on part of the interrogation of Lee and in response to his questioning Lee said, "If you want me to "cop" out to hitting or pleading [*sic*] guilty to hitting a cop in the mouth when I was arrested," he said, "yeah, I plead guilty to that."[26] Eventually Lee's precarious situation began to dawn on him as evidence began to pile up throughout the day pointing toward Lee as the President's assassin. Lee asked in all seriousness, "I am filed on the President's murder, is that right?"[27]

Along with gathering evidence that Lee had assassinated the President, the Dallas Police Department was gathering evidence in the murder of Officer Tippit. Sergeant W.E. Barnes, of the crime scene search section of the identification bureau of the Dallas Police Department, performed a paraffin test on Lee. The paraffin test shows if nitrate, a component of gunpowder, is on the suspect's hands. Sgt. Barnes explains the process; "When you put the paraffin on your hands, the nitrate that might be on your hands will stick to the paraffin as it cools; and when you remove the paraffin, then this nitrate or powder residue which might be on the hands will be hardened into the paraffin and will slip off with the paraffin."[28]

While W.E. Barnes was administering the paraffin test, Lee asked him, "What are you trying to do, prove that I fired a gun?"[29] What the test did prove, inadvertently, was that Lee never fired a rifle. The paraffin test was positive as far as there being nitrate on Lee's hands. But, the test was negative as far as there being nitrate on Lee's cheeks. If Lee had been in the sniper's nest looking down the barrel of a rifle as he fired three times at the President, then nitrate from the gunpowder would have descended on his cheeks. The absence of nitrate on his cheeks indicates he was never in the sniper's nest and any substance Lee may have come in contact with that contained nitrate while on the job that morning would have stuck to his hands.

The FBI also examined the paraffin cast. John Gallagher, the FBI agent who specialized in physics and chemistry found the following: "The deposits found on the paraffin casts from the hands and cheek of Oswald could not be specifically associated with the rifle cartridges."[30]

* * *

204   JFK VS. CIA

40

LEE AND THE KILLING
OF OFFICER J. D. TIPPIT

At approximately 1:15 p.m., Officer J.D. Tippit was shot and killed in the Oak Cliff section of Dallas. This was 45 minutes after the President was struck down. The Warren Commission tried valiantly to prove Lee Harvey Oswald murdered Officer Tippit. By proving Lee had killed Officer Tippit then, by extension, Lee must have assassinated the President and must have been trying to avoid capture when Officer Tippit came upon him. The murder of Tippit would show, at the very least, that Lee was capable of committing murder. But let's take a look at police radio activity. At 12:27 p.m., Dallas police channel I became inoperable. Three minutes later, the President was fired upon. Dallas police channel I went back on the air at 12:34 p.m., over four minutes after the President was slain. At 12:40 p.m., the dispatcher broadcast a description of the suspect. The description was of a white male, about thirty, 5'10" tall and 165 pounds. Although this description could have fitted about half the white males in the city of Dallas, the Warren Commission wanted the public to believe that Officer Tippit, upon seeing Lee walking down the street in another section of the city, immediately recognized him as the suspected assassin and attempted to arrest him. At 12:45 p.m. the dispatcher ordered "all squads [to] report to the downtown area, code 3, Elm and Houston; with caution." At 12:46 p.m. Officer Tippit was told to move into the Oak Cliff section. There was no response from Officer Tippit. At 12:54 p.m., Officer Tippit radioed in his location as Lancaster and Eighth. At 1:00 p.m. dispatch tried to reach Officer Tippit. There was no response.

Also at 1:00 p.m., there was another strange occurrence. Earlene Roberts, the housekeeper at Lee's boarding home, saw a police car parked in front of the house. The police car honked twice, waited a short while, then departed. Earlene Roberts told the Warren Commission that Lee waited until the police car departed and then hurried out the door.[31] At 1:18 p.m. police dispatch was trying to be raised by a civilian. Dispatch: "Go ahead citizen using the police radio." Citizen: "We've had a shooting here." There had indeed been a shooting. Officer Tippit lay dead on the ground beside his patrol car. All this movement of Officer Tippit from different sectors and his lack of response to the calls dispatch was making to him irked the Warren Commission lawyers.

Lt. Rio Pierce was asked the following by the Warren Commission lawyer interviewing him on this subject:

> Can you explain why, subsequent to the shooting of the President, Officer Tippit would be in the district marked 109, specifically at the corner of Lancaster and Eighth at 12:54 p.m., and then would later have proceeded into district 91, which is the area in which he was shot and killed?[32]

The Warren Commission lawyer was pointing out that Officer Tippit starting in district 78, went over to district 109 and finally got himself killed in district 91. Lt. Pierce didn't have an answer. The acting lieutenant at the Oak Cliff station, Bud Owens, was also questioned on these movements. The lieutenant pointed out that, according to the map, Tippit had zigzagged quite a lot but this was actually good police work.[33]

Officer Tippit's movements after the President was assassinated and leading up to his own murder are suspicious. The questions I have are these: Was it Officer Tippit who was parked outside Lee Harvey Oswald's boarding room; and was Tippit's zigzagging an effort to locate Lee? Officer Tippit did locate someone, and that someone killed him, but the killer wasn't Lee Oswald.

Detectives and officers raced to the scene. Gerald Hill was one of the first officers there. He received the following description of the suspect who killed Officer Tippit: "The man that shot him was a white male about 5'10", weighing 160-170 pounds, had on a jacket and a pair of dark trousers and brown bushy hair."[34]

This description given to Officer Hill right off the bat excludes Lee from being the suspect—he was balding, although only 24 years old. The suspect's estimated weight was 30 pounds more than Lee's; the suspect's physique suggests a more muscular build than that of the rail thin Lee Oswald.

Another police officer at the Tippit murder scene jumped on the radio. He said he had an "eyeball" witness to the shooting. The new description of the suspect was the following: "White male, 27, 5'11", 165 pounds, black wavy hair, fair complexion, was apparently armed with a .32, dark finish, automatic pistol which he had in his right hand."[35] This second description by another witness to the shooting is very similar to the first citizen's description. In seconds, another detective had interjected with more information: "The shells at the scene indicate that the suspect is armed with an automatic .38 rather than a pistol."

With this broadcast, we know for sure that it wasn't Lee shooting Officer Tippit. The bullet shells at the scene were the type used with automatic weapons. Lee's handgun was a revolver.

For the next 20 minutes, officers were sent to various places on tips that were pouring into dispatch of a suspect running from the crime scene. Finally, on a tip from a shoe salesman, Johnny Brewer, that a man acting suspiciously had sneaked into the Texas Theater without paying, the Dallas police surrounded the building. The lights were turned on inside the theater and the nonpaying customer was pointed out and arrested. But not without a skirmish—Lee slugged one of the arresting officers. At 1:57 p.m., the officers radioed into dispatch that the suspect was apprehended and en route to the station.

Several citizens told the Warren Commission they saw Lee running in the general vicinity of Officer Tippit's murder. Other witnesses could not identify Lee as the man they saw fleeing the scene. The first indication to the Warren Commission lawyers that something was up was the fact that Domingo Benavides, the person who had "eyeballed" the shooting of the officer and had spoken on the police radio, was never brought down to the lineup to identify Lee as Officer Tippit's killer. David Belin, a Warren Commission lawyer, asked this question of Detective L.C. Graves: "Ted Calloway and Sam Guinyard gave affidavits, but Domingo Benavides did not. Is there any particular reason that you know of why Benavides did not come down or give an affidavit or view a lineup?"[36] When Mr. Benavides finally made his appearance before the Warren Commission, it became clear why Domingo Benavides had not been brought down to view the line up or asked to sign an affidavit the afternoon of the assassination. Domingo Benavides told the Warren Commission that he had been driving down the street close to Officer Tippit's car. He saw Tippit's assailant shoot the officer and pause to unload his shells. The assailant started to trot around a corner of a house and stopped to reload. Benavides explained what he saw: "As I saw him, I really, I mean I really got a good view of the man after the bullets were fired. He had just turned. He was just turning away. He put the shells in a cigarette package."[37]

Benavides described Officer Tippit's assailant as 5'10" tall, dark trousers, dark shirt, and dark bushy hair. But I suggest that Domingo Benavides was never brought down to the lineup or asked to sign an affidavit because he saw someone other than Lee Harvey Oswald kill J.D. Tippit. Benavides told the Warren Commission Tippit's assailant was standing on the sidewalk and shot Officer Tippit three times. Benavides continued: "The policeman I believe was dead when he hit the ground, because he didn't put his hand out or nothing. The gun was in his hand and he was partially lying on his gun in his right hand."[38] Benavides gives us another fact. Officer Tippit, coming out of his patrol car, was attempting an arrest. Not only was he trying to arrest the assailant, he felt the assailant was dangerous enough that he had lifted his police revolver out of its holster. Unfortunately for Officer Tippit, the gunman was faster on the draw. What else can we determine about the gunman? Lt. Calvin Owens gave a description of Officer Tippit's wounds. One bullet had entered his right chest above the pocket; another entered the center of his chest, and another entered the right temple.[39] So we have Officer Tippit out of his car, with his gun drawn, but before he can fire the gunman is able to shoot Tippit twice in the chest. With the officer down on the ground, the gunman walked around the police vehicle and administered the coup de grace, firing into the officer's head. The assailant's taking the time to walk around the patrol vehicle and deliberately shoot the officer in the head suggests to me that he was a professional killer. I suggest the man who shot Officer Tippit was not Lee Harvey Oswald but a coconspirator in the assassination of the President. Most probably, he was working for the CIA.

What about the bullets left in Officer Tippit? All one would have to do is match the bullets found in Officer Tippit with the handgun that Lee owned, and he could be posthumously convicted for Tippit's murder. That shouldn't be too difficult. Cortland Cunningham of the FBI testified before the Warren Commission. He told the Warren Commission lawyer that four bullets were recovered from Tippit's body. Three bullets were Winchester Western in manufacture. But one was a Remington Peters in manufacture.[40] Thus, something was wrong right from the start.

Question: "Were you able to determine whether those bullets had been fired in the weapon?" Cortland Cunningham replied,

> No, I was not.... Three bullets were Winchester Western and one bullet was a Remington Peters but two cartridge cases were Remington Peters and two cartridge cases were Winchester Western. There was one more recovered cartridge case than there was recovered bullets. There was also one more Winchester Western bullet than there is Winchester cartridge.

Question: "Are you able to match the bullet with the cartridge case?" Cortland Cunningham: "It is not possible."

Congressman Hale Boggs piped in:

> You cannot having [*sic*] the cartridge case and the bullet—you cannot match them up? So that while you can establish the fact the cartridge case—the four that we have here, were fired in that gun, but you cannot establish the fact that the bullets were fired in that gun.[41]

Lee walks on this one as well. No wonder that Warren Commission member and Congressman Hale Boggs' airplane disappeared over Alaska a few years later. In the end, the Warren Commission couldn't prove Lee killed Officer Tippit anymore than it could prove Lee killed the President. But if Lee didn't kill Officer Tippit, who did? And what was Tippit's role in the President's assassination? Perhaps Officer Tippit's role in the conspiracy was to meet and subsequently kill Lee Harvey Oswald. In this way, the fall guy would be silenced. The weight of the circumstantial evidence would convict him posthumously. Whatever Tippit's motive was, it went horribly awry.

On Sunday morning, Lee's last Sunday morning, he was interviewed one last time. Inspector Kelley of the Secret Service wanted to know about a map of Dallas they had recovered, specifically about the marking on the map. Lee's response was, "My God, don't tell me there is a mark near where this thing happened."[42] As the detectives and Lee were getting ready to take the elevator from the third floor homicide office to the basement to transfer Lee to the county jail, Detective L.C. Graves remembers Lee saying, "If it is all the same to you, I'd rather wear the black sweater." Detective Graves assisted Lee in putting on the sweater. As Lee and the detectives were descending in the elevator to the basement, one of the detectives handcuffed to Lee joked, "I hope if someone tries to shoot you, they are as good a shot as you are." Lee replied, "Don't be so dramatic. Nobody is going to shoot me."

The door of the elevator opened up and the detectives and Lee proceeded to walk the corridor toward the waiting vehicle, set to whisk Lee off to the county jail. Then several camera lights flashed on partially blinding the detectives and Lee. A shot rang out. Lee grimaced as Jack Ruby was wrestled to the ground. Lee was dragged across the pavement to a nearby office. Detective B.H. Combest, sensing this might be the end tried to let Lee know that if he was going to say anything, that he would have to say it now. Detective Combest asked Lee if he was part of a conspiracy. Lee shook his head no. Lee was asked this question a second time while the ambulance raced to Parkland Hospital. He was too far gone by this time to answer verbally or otherwise.

Malcolm Perry, the surgeon who tried to save President Kennedy's life, was waiting for Lee in the operating room. Dr. Perry told the Warren Commission that Lee's wound needn't have been fatal, that he would have survived, except that it took 12 minutes for Lee to be transferred from the trauma room to the operating room—usually it took three to four minutes. The extra eight minutes cost Lee his life. Apparently, Lee Harvey Oswald was not fated to leave Parkland Hospital anymore than JFK was supposed to. Lee died at 1:07 p.m., almost 48 hours to the minute after President Kennedy's death. Undoubtedly, a collective sigh of relief came from the bowels of the CIA headquarters.

I think the real Lee Harvey Oswald showed himself in the last 48 hours of his life. Not the wimp as some described him, nor the moron others depicted. Nor the man of low self-esteem and lower intelligence. An entirely different picture emerges. In fact, he was a man of immense courage under fire, of quick intelligence and aplomb, of a coolest-of-the-cool demeanor. Lee Harvey Oswald, in his final hours proved his mettle. He actually turned out to be quite a man—Lee Harvey Oswald of the Central Intelligence Agency.

* * *

41

JACK RUBY

If anyone is deserving of sympathy in this tragic play it is Jack Ruby. He seems to have been involuntarily volunteered into becoming a party to the assassination of President Kennedy. Jack also proved the old adage of every mother's warning to their sons: be careful who you choose for your friends.

The Warren Commission fiction has painted Jack Ruby as a strip joint owner who, in the heat of passion, murdered Lee Harvey Oswald so as to save Jackie Kennedy the horror of returning to Dallas for the accused assassin's trial. How quaint. And how unbelievable. When one delves into the 26 volumes of *Hearings and Exhibits* produced for the Warren Commission, we learn of a much more complicated man, with a more complicated life, being tossed about by the winds of fate.

Jack's bad choices began in Chicago as a kid, running errands for the Capone mob. In the late 1930s, he formed the Junk Handler's Union with his friend and business partner, Leon Cook. The union was an immediate success. Like many successful businesses in Chicago, it attracted the attention of the mob. Like the smell of blood to sharks, the smell of money brought the interest of the Mafia. The mob attempted to take over the new union. But Jack and his partner resisted. As a result of this resistance, Jack was left with a lifelong impression. This impression would encourage him to participate in the assassination of the President 25 years later. We find out about Jack through his friend John Jackson, who was Ruby's roommate for a few years until 1958. Ruby had told him the following:

While in Chicago after forming the Junk Handler's Union, Ruby and his partner were contacted by the syndicate and informed that the organization of the union would go more smoothly if they would permit the syndicate to furnish the secretary. They agreed but were soon forced out. Ruby and his partner fought back and as a result the partner was shot to death. Ruby got out of the picture for fear of receiving the same treatment.[43]

Robert Shorman, the operator of the Peppermint Pike in Long Beach, who played in a band at Ruby's establishment in 1961, was told that Ruby had been dumped in a garbage can and left for dead in Chicago.[44]

Having your friend and business partner murdered by the Mafia and being dumped in a garbage can after a severe beating might just leave you with an impression of gangland sincerity. I believe that is why in 1963, when the mob came calling on Jack in Dallas to participate in the Kennedy assassination, and when he was subsequently ordered to shoot Lee, Ruby knew he had no choice. If the police didn't get him, the mob would.

After the murder of his business partner, having been muscled out of his own union by the mob, Jack left for the West Coast. He spent a couple of years in San Francisco working as a salesman. Slowly, he made his way back to Chicago. Ruby may even have wanted to stay on the West Coast. At one time, after he settled in Dallas, he told busi-

214 JFK VS. CIA

nessman Giles Milles that he had been expelled from Chicago. He wanted to go to California, but had been directed to go to Dallas. Paul Rowland Jones, a convicted gangster, told the FBI the real reason for Ruby's arrival in Dallas. Jones stated that Rubenstein (Ruby) had been run out of Chicago by Lenny Patrick and that Ruby left the union after it was taken over by Paul Dorfman.[45] According to the FBI, Paul Rowland Jones was the boyfriend of Eva Grant, Jack Ruby's sister. Jones arrived in Dallas in 1946 with the specific objective to open Dallas to syndicate control.[46]

The FBI report is backed by the statement of ex-Dallas Sheriff Steve Guthrie. Guthrie was elected sheriff in 1947 and served through 1948. He stated that, shortly after his election, Paul Rowland Jones contacted him on a Dallas golf course and asked him how he would like to make some money. Dallas was a wide open town and the Chicago syndicate was coming to control vice operations. Paul Rowland Jones told Sheriff-elect Guthrie that, between the two of them, they could make $40,000 a month. Guthrie informed the Texas Rangers and they put a wire on him and in his home. Ex-Sheriff Guthrie told the FBI that Jack Ruby at that time was a "small-time peanut" among the group that was going to bribe Guthrie. According to Guthrie, Jack Ruby would be taking over a fabulous restaurant at Industry and Commerce where the upper floor would be used for gambling. Ruby was to run the club. Guthrie said that if the recordings can still be heard, Ruby's name will be heard on numerous occasions. Ex-Sheriff Guthrie told the FBI that Ruby also ran some prostitution activity and other vices at his club.[47]

Lt. George Butler of the Dallas Police Department backs up ex-Sheriff Guthrie's account of Jack Ruby's appearance in Dallas. Lt. Butler told the FBI that after Paul Rowland Jones's conviction but before his appeals ran out, Jones used to hang out at Ruby's club.[48]

So it does appear that Jack Ruby was sent to Dallas by the Chicago syndicate as a front man for organized crime. Things didn't work out as expected. After the debacle, with Paul Rowland Jones sent off to prison for attempted bribery, Jack Ruby decided to stay in his newly adopted city. For the next decade, Ruby opened and closed various night clubs and courted the police establishment. On occasion, he would act as an informant for the Dallas Police Department. He was always coming up with some new money-making scheme that only a dreamer could imagine would ever get off the ground. Occasionally, he would make a few extra bucks from prostitution and perhaps smuggling, but the main portion of his income seemed to be legal, derived from the various clubs he owned and managed. At the time of the assassination, however, he didn't even own the Carousel Club. It was owned by his good friend and business partner, Ralph Paul. This is not to say that Jack didn't keep up his contacts with the underworld. One of his best friends throughout this period was Lewis McWillie, manager of the Tropicana Hotel in Havana during the heyday of the mob's control of vice in Cuba. The Tropicana belonged to Santos Trafficante, the mob boss of Florida, who, as we will learn, had prior knowledge of the Kennedy assassination a year before it took place. When Fidel Castro marched victoriously into Havana after vanquishing the Cuban dictator, Fulgencio Batista, he closed down the Mafia controlled casinos and arrested Santos Trafficante. In 1959, Ruby visited Cuba with Lewis McWillie. This visit may have had something to do with getting Santos Trafficante released from confinement on the Island.

But by 1963, Ruby's world was about to fall apart. By the fall of 1962, the CIA had decided to assassinate the President. In this endeavor, the agency enlisted the aid of the Mafia. By April 1963, Dallas had been picked as one of several sitting sites for the assassination. Dallas was under the jurisdiction of the Chicago syndicate, run by Sam Giancana.

Sam's boy in Dallas was none other than Jack Ruby. In the summer of 1963, FBI records show a marked increase in phone calls from Jack Ruby to known mob figures. As we continue into September, October and November, those phone calls increased dramatically. Ruby's travels also included a trip to California and, two months before the assassination, a trip to New York City.

The FBI did a background check on Ruby. In the days and weeks leading up to the assassination, the FBI discovered, he had met with two interesting gentlemen. The day before the assassination, at noon, Jack Ruby paid a visit to H.L. Hunt, the right-wing Dallas oil man and, at the time, the richest man in the world. The obvious question is, what was the richest man in the world doing meeting with a strip joint owner and mob associate? What did they have in common? This was a very ominous meeting. Especially with Jack going on to shoot Lee Harvey Oswald, the accused assassin of the President of the United States. Why, if one didn't know any better, one might start to think H.L. Hunt was involved in the President's assassination. What a terrific alliance had been formed. The Central Intelligence Agency, the Mafia and the economic elite teaming up with one another to knock off the President of the United States. Kennedy didn't stand a chance.

Jack had another meeting on the evening before the President's assassination. Lawrence Myers of Chicago dined with Jack. Later that evening, at midnight, Ruby paid a second visit to Myers in his room at the Cabana Hotel.[49]

If it can be proved that Lawrence Myers was in the Mafia, then I suggest the following scenario. Lawrence Myers flew down from Chicago to Dallas to give Jack verbal instructions directly from Sam Giancana. The instructions pertained to the assassination of President Kennedy. Lawrence Myers also went to Dallas to babysit Jack and make sure he followed orders. But first, what was Jack's role in the assassination?

Jean Hill, the schoolteacher who was standing to the left of the President when he received his fatal head wound, was adamant about the shots coming from the grassy knoll in front of and to the right of the President. But she also had something else to say.

> I saw a man up there running, or getting away. He was right up there by the school depository, just not at the corner where they say the shots came from, at the other end, right up the slope, at the top of the slope. I saw him go toward the railroad tracks, toward the tracks to the west. I just thought at the time, that's the man that did it."[50]

J.C. Price also saw this running man. Price was on the roof of the terminal annex building at the time of the assassination. He watched the President's motorcade make its turn in front of the book depository and proceed west on Elm Street. After hearing a volley of shots, Price said he saw a man run toward the passenger cars at the railroad siding. He said the man was carrying something in his hand—it may have been a headpiece. But we'll never know everything about what Price saw of the assassination because the Warren Commission never called him as a witness. All we have is his affidavit written the afternoon of the assassination.[51]

Finally, however, we find out what happened to the running man when the House Select Committee on Assassinations reopened the inquiry into JFK's assassination in 1978. The Committee interviewed Tom Tilson. Tilson stated that on November 22, 1963, he was an off-duty Dallas Police Department patrolman. At the time of the assassination, he was traveling east from Commerce Street and was approaching the triple underpass. He had already heard on his police radio that there had been shooting at the motorcade and had seen the President's limousine travel at a high rate of speed from the underpass. In the area of the triple underpass, Tilson said he saw a man "slipping and sliding" down the embankment on the south side of Elm Street west of the underpass. Tilson said the man appeared to be conspicuous because he was the only one running away from the plaza immediately after the shots. Tilson said that because of his speed, the man rammed against the side of a dark car which was parked there. He then saw the man do something at the rear of the door portion of the car, like "throw something inside, then jump behind the wheel and take off very fast."[52]

Tilson gave chase, got the license number of the car, and gave it to homicide after abandoning the chase because his daughter was in the car with him. He never heard from homicide again about his report. Tilson said he knew Jack Ruby. He said the man looked enough like Jack Ruby to be his "twin." That impression was so strong in Tilson's mind that he noted Ruby showed a lot of "resourcefulness" in arranging to be identified in a newspaper office at the time of the assassination with a lot of influential witnesses.

So we know that Jack Ruby's involvement in the assassination was not limited to shooting Oswald to silence him. It appears he also had a part in the actual assassination. What was he doing running away from the assassination site as the President was struck down? The man who turned from Dealy Plaza and raced toward the railroad cars, who was seen "slipping and sliding" down the embankment may have been, in reality, a red herring. The police officers and citizens who saw the man running gave chase. What the running man did was divert attention from the actual killers of the President. For the true assassins, instead of running away from the scene, merely stood still and waited for the law enforcement officers to converge on them. As we shall see, the conspirators, when confronted by law enforcement officers, merely took out forged Secret Service identification.

Ruby pops up again between 1:00 p.m. and 1:30 p.m. This time, he is seen at Parkland Hospital. Malcolm Kilduff, the President's press secretary, was about to make the formal announcement of the President's death. The news media were assembling. They included Seth Kantor.

Kantor was a newsman based in Washington, D.C. when he was sent to Texas to cover the President's trip. Kantor had previously lived in Dallas from 1960 to 1962 and had known Jack Ruby. Ruby had provided him with half a dozen stories of various characters in town. Kantor relates the following:

> I was stopped momentarily by a tug on the back of my jacket. And I turned and saw Jack Ruby standing there. He had his hand extended. I very well remember my first thought. I thought, well, there is Jack Ruby. I had been away from Dallas 18 months but it seemed just perfectly normal to see Jack Ruby standing there, because he was a known goer to events. He called me by name. He said, "Isn't this a terrible thing?" I said, "Yes." But he asked me, "Should I close my places for the next three nights, do you think?"[53]

Another citizen, Wilma Tice, also saw Jack Ruby at Parkland Hospital. When challenged by a Warren Commission lawyer on the veracity of her statement, Tice replied, "If it wasn't him, then it's his twin brother."[54]

So Jack was at Parkland Hospital at the time the world was learning that JFK's laughter and wit and charm were no more. Some assassination researchers speculate that Ruby was at the hospital to place the "magic bullet" on the stretcher which would be used to incriminate Lee in the President's murder. I think not. It would have been much easier for the CIA to use one of their own agents to slip the bullet on to the stretcher. Besides, how would Ruby have known which stretcher to place the bullet on?

For the next 48 hours Jack seemed to be deteriorating mentally. It was as if he was having a nervous breakdown. Oswald was still alive, which was not according to plan. Now Jack's back up role in the assassination had to be activated. Someone had to go in and shut Lee up before he started talking, bringing down the entire assassination con-

spiracy which included Jack Ruby. Ruby knew his assignment and dreaded it. As we shall see, he even tried to prevent Lee's murder. But before we turn to Ruby's stalking Lee
and eventually getting into the Dallas Police Department's
basement to shoot him, let's find out if they knew each
other.

* * *

42

JACK AND LEE: A RELATIONSHIP HERE?

If Jack Ruby and Lee Oswald knew each other, then there was certainly a conspiracy. But did they? Henry Wade, the Dallas district attorney said before the Warren Commission that eight to ten people saw Ruby and Oswald together at various times and places. There was a waitress at the B & B Cafe, as well as four homosexuals. Wade told how the emcee at Ruby's club had seen Lee and Ruby together there. The emcee Billy De Mar, whose real name was William D. Crowe, spoke candidly to the Warren Commission. He was a ventriloquist and stand up comedian. On November 1, 1963, he was back at the Carousel, Ruby's club, performing. Crowe first announced that he had previously seen Oswald at the club on Sunday, after Jack had shot Oswald. He told a television interviewer about all the coincidences involved:

> I had been in Washington during the Inaugural of the President. And then being in Dallas during the assassination of the President, and then having what I had thought or recalled to have possibly seen Oswald in the club the week before and then working for the man who shot Oswald.[55]

Crowe's life had been threatened for his speaking out about having seen Lee Oswald with Jack Ruby at the club. He was, shortly thereafter, advised to hide or move out of Dallas because his life was in danger. Mr. Crowe continued, "I might say this. Bill Willis, the drummer in the band, said he seemed to remember Lee Harvey Oswald sitting in the front row on Thursday night, right in the corner of the stage and the runway."

Who else saw Ruby and Lee together at the club? For one, Larry Crafard, a handyman at Ruby's club, told the Warren Commission that Andy Armstrong (the bartender) had made the comment that Oswald had been at the Carousel at least on one occasion.[56]

Okay, so Lee may have dropped into the club a couple of times. But did anyone see Lee and Ruby together, conversing as if they knew each other? Robert Litchfield told a Warren Commission lawyer that during a poker game with Detective Green of the Dallas Police Department, he said, "I think I have seen that man with Jack up at the Carousel. I don't know but I'm pretty darn sure I have."[57] Lee had left an impression on Litchfield because of the sloppy way Lee was dressed. Litchfield thought at the time, "What is this individual doing up there?"

Leon D. Hubert, Jr., the Warren Commission lawyer, asked, "And you had the opportunity to observe him then as the man who got to see Jack before you did?" Litchfield replied, "Yes." Litchfield further said that Oswald was sitting in front of him at a table. Lee was with Jack, he said, for ten to 20 minutes before Oswald left, walking past Litchfield. "This fellow came out and then Jack came out and got me and I went back there with him."[58]

It appears, then, that Dallas District Attorney Wade was right. Eight to ten people did see Lee Harvey Oswald and Jack Ruby together and they appeared to have a relationship. The relationship must have had something to do with the

President's assassination. Along with eyewitness testimony, there is circumstantial evidence.

Bertha Cheek was interviewed by the Warren Commission. The first thing she wanted to know was if she was going to be prosecuted. Her question leads to a question of mine: What were you afraid of being prosecuted for, Bertha? What were you feeling so guilty about that you thought the Warren Commission might come after you? Bertha Cheek first met Jack Ruby in 1948. He approached her with the proposal that she buy into his club to the tune of $12,000. She turned him down, but the two kept in contact over the years. On November 18, four days before the assassination, Jack Ruby invited her to the Carousel. He told her he wanted to invest in another, more upscale, club and asked her if she would go in with him as a partner. She thought it over and declined.

What is relevant is that Bertha Cheek is the sister of Earlene Roberts. Earlene Roberts was the housekeeper at the A.C. Johnson residence, where Lee Oswald was a boarder. I think it is entirely possible that Lee had asked his friend Jack Ruby if Ruby knew of any inexpensive place where he could rent a room. Jack then called up his friend, Bertha Cheek, who owned several rental properties throughout Dallas, and asked if she knew where a friend of his could rent a room. Cheek checked with her sister Earlene Roberts, who told her there was a room to let where she worked. Hence, Lee Oswald ended up renting a room at 1026 Beckley, Dallas. This Earlene Roberts—Bertha Cheek—Jack Ruby connection is another bit of evidence that Ruby and Oswald knew each other. Coincidences can occur only so often before they can no longer be considered coincidences.

* * *

43

THE SHOOTING OF
LEE HARVEY OSWALD

Twenty-four hours had passed since the President's assassination and Lee Harvey Oswald was still alive. The problem with Lee being alive is that if he starts to figure out that he has been double-crossed by his own agency, he might begin to sing. Or if, while under constant interrogation by the Dallas Police, he might crack and if he does, the entire conspiracy would come falling down. It is imperative that Lee Oswald—be silenced which undoubtedly had been the plan all along. Lee's decision not to enter the police vehicle that had parked in front of his boarding room saved his life, at least temporarily. His arrest at the Texas Theater further delayed his death. Now with the capture of Oswald and his being taken into custody, the Central Intelligence Agency was forced to resort to Plan B. Someone had to penetrate the Dallas Police Department and kill Lee. Hence Jack Ruby was ordered to perform the hit.

Jack Ruby was an ideal choice for such an assignment. For over a decade, Jack had courted members of the Dallas

Police Department. Most of the officers knew him, many on a first name basis. Waitresses at his club and bartenders were on standing orders to offer cut rate prices on alcohol to any Dallas police officers who dropped in at his club. In return, the police department would grant him favors such as letting him carry his gun on his person and fixing any tickets he might get. Actually, with a little bit of luck, the world would never have heard of Jack Ruby. But with Oswald still alive after the President's assassination and, worse still, in police custody, Jack Ruby was about to become a part of history.

As soon as Oswald was brought in for the shooting of Officer Tippit, Jack seemed to be stalking him. On the evening of the President's assassination, Oswald was being interrogated on the third floor of police headquarters in the homicide office. Between 5:00 p.m. and 7:00 p.m., another visitor was wandering the third floor of police headquarters. While Chief of Homicide Will Fritz interrogated Lee Oswald, Jack Ruby tried to enter the door to Robbery-Homicide. Two officers pulled him back and prevented Ruby from entering the office.[59] I suggest if Ruby was carrying his pistol at this time, if he had actually been able to walk into Captain Fritz's office, he would have shot Lee then and there.

Ruby showed up again at a late night news conference with Lee Oswald as the star attraction. The conference room was filled with newsmen and police officers and our Jack was standing in the back of the room. While the newsmen were standing about waiting for Oswald to be brought down, Ruby took the opportunity to pass out cards advertising his club. When the district attorney briefed the media on the evidence that was pouring in pointing to Oswald as the President's assassin, Ruby corrected him at one point, stating that the organization that Lee belonged to was the "Fair Play for Cuba" committee. Interesting how Ruby would know that.

226 JFK VS. CIA

The following day once again finds Ruby making his phone calls. One of these calls was overheard. Garnett Hallmark, general manager of the Allright Auto Park, had known Ruby for four years. Mr. Hallmark saw Jack Ruby at the Nicols garage on November 23 at 3:00 p.m. Jack used the pay phone at the garage although his club was within walking distance. Hallmark said, "He was speaking to someone and told that person that his club would be closed, and the conversation, as you put it here, switched to some remarks concerning the transfer of Oswald." He heard Ruby say, "You know I'll be there."[60] Hallmark told the Commission that Ruby planned to be at the scene of the transfer.

But the intrigue continues. In the wee hours of the morning of Sunday, November 24th, the day of Oswald's transfer, the Dallas Police Department received a threat on Oswald's life. More important, the caller seemed to have inside information concerning the transfer. The FBI also had received a phone call that warned Oswald was going to be killed during his transfer to the county jail. Special Agent Milt Newson had received the call. In turn, Newson alerted the Dallas Police Department. Sgt McCoy of the Dallas Police tried to contact the chief of police but was unsuccessful. Chief Curry's telephone line was out of order. So McCoy called Sheriff Bill Decker. Sheriff Decker advised Sgt. McCoy to move Oswald immediately and to call back after he contacted his supervisors. Decker explained what happened next:

> He called me back shortly and stated that he had no success in contacting them. I asked him if he had any success to call me and that we would make arrangements to take care of the prisoner either way, and I meant by that, that we would transfer him or whatever was necessary to be done.[61]

Sgt. McCoy received another call later on in the early morning. The caller informed him that a group of one hundred men were going to kill Oswald while Oswald was in the process of being transferred. Sgt. McCoy said the caller was not excited but rather calm as he spoke. Captain W.B. Frazier was the officer in charge of the radio platoon during the graveyard shift. Captain Frazier told the Warren Commission that Sgt. McCoy had indeed received the phone calls and that Sheriff Decker wanted to talk to Curry, chief of police, but the chief's phone was out of order. Captain Frazier handed the problem to Captain Talbert, the officer who was in charge of the day shift, when he arrived.[62]

Captain Talbert told the Warren Commission that Captain Frazier had been unable to reach the chief of police because of a phone malfunction, so Captain Talbert called Chief of Homicide Will Fritz. Captain Fritz refused to authorize Oswald's immediate transfer, saying that only Chief Curry could authorize it. Next, Captain Talbert tried to call Chief Curry but to no avail, and finally ended up sending a patrol car to contact the chief and apprise him of the situation. The time was now close to 6:00 a.m.

But what about the chief of police's phone being out of order at a time when immediate contact with the chief of police was vital? The accused assassin of the President of the United States was in his jail and the world was aflame. Captain Talbert explained why they couldn't get through to the Chief: "I don't know sir but by all appearances, it was out of order. I think that latter item I was speaking of was around the entire neighborhood, almost."[63]

Once again, the parameters of the assassination identify the true assassins. What other organization than the CIA would have the power and ability to disconnect the Dallas chief of police's phone?

As far as the man who threatened Oswald's life with the phone call to the FBI then, later in the morning, to Sgt. McCoy of the Dallas Police Department, may I suggest the mysterious caller was none other than Jack Ruby. It makes perfectly good sense for Ruby to have made those calls. Jack Ruby was in the pickle of his life. On the one hand, if he were to succeed in killing Oswald, he could be rewarded with the electric chair. Dallas wasn't San Francisco and Texans frowned upon first-degree murder. On the other hand, if he didn't kill Oswald, he would certainly die a torturous death at the hands of the Mafia. But if he could attempt to shoot Oswald and be prevented from doing so by the Dallas Police, he would be off the hook with the mob and only serve a few years in prison. Ruby could explain to Sam Giancana that he did his part but the Dallas police were too quick; it wasn't his fault that Lee survived the murder attempt. It was a nice try and quite clever on Ruby's part.

When Jack awoke Sunday morning he was in quite a state. His cleaning lady called up prior to coming over, as was her regular practice, but Jack was largely incoherent. Her testimony was that he couldn't even remember who she was. When it finally did click in, Ruby canceled her appointment. Jack's good friend and recent roommate George Senator paints us an excellent picture of Jack's state of mind just hours before he went to the Dallas Police Department garage to shoot Oswald. Ruby had been crying repeatedly over the weekend concerning JFK's assassination and had a faraway look in his eye. It seems, in retrospect, Ruby's tears were more for his own predicament than for the fate of the fallen leader. However the Oswald murder turned out, Ruby was about to give up a large chunk of his own life. Describing that Sunday morning, Senator told the Warren Commission,

> And he still had this look which didn't look good. The way he talked, he was even mumbling, which I didn't understand. Then after he got dressed he was pacing the floor from the living room to the bedroom, from the bedroom to the living room and his lips were going. What he was jabbering, I don't know. But he was really pacing.[64]

The last thing Jack Ruby said as he was about to leave the apartment was, "George, I'm taking the dogs down to the Club."

A question that remains is how did Jack Ruby gain admittance into the Dallas Police Department basement? Prior to Oswald's being brought down, the entire basement was cleared of all persons—even the resident medical doctor whose task was to examine any suspects Dallas Police might bring in who had perhaps suffered a little street justice at their hands. After the basement was cleared, guards were placed at all its entrances. Then and only then were the news media allowed in. They were made to stand behind a barrier. Ruby's ability to penetrate the security of the basement shows us that Oswald was set up to be murdered, just as JFK had been set up. The setup begins with the announcement to the press by Chief Curry: "If you fellows are back here by ten in the morning, you won't miss anything."[65]

So the press was given an implied promise by Chief of Police Jesse Curry that it would be given an opportunity to view the transfer of Oswald to the custody of the Sheriff's department. Yet, the Dallas Police brass had more warnings about transferring Oswald in this manner. Forrest Sorrels of the Secret Service told Will Fritz, chief of homicide, "Captain, I wouldn't move that man at an announced time. I would take him out at three or four in the morning, when there is no one else around."[66]

Detective James Leaville suggested to Captain Fritz that he take Oswald to the first floor and out the door to avoid the newsmen. Captain Fritz explained he couldn't do that because Chief Curry had promised the reporters they would be able to witness the transfer. Indeed, with everyone from Sheriff Decker to the FBI, as well as the Secret Service and even his own detectives suggestions that Oswald be transferred in a more discreet manner, Chief Curry vetoed this good sense and ordered Oswald transferred in full view of the news media. Chief Curry was not a stupid man. Certainly he knew it was unwise to transfer Oswald in this manner. Especially in light of the death threats that came in informing the Police Department that Oswald would be killed precisely during the transfer. I doubt that Chief Curry had any willful role in the President's assassination or even in Oswald's murder, in light of his own phone's disconnection which cut off communication with his own department. But if Chief Curry wasn't involved in the conspiracy, why then did he insist on such an unsafe transfer?

Shortly after the assassination, the *Oak Cliff Tribune* ran an article that gives an indication of the forces surrounding Chief Curry: "Chief Curry taking the rap for 'higher ups' who had insisted that Oswald be transported to the county jail during daylight hours at the request of the press."[67]

Well, if it that were true, who were the higher-ups? One was Dallas Mayor Earle Cabell, the brother of Charles Cabell, formerly deputy director of the CIA, who was fired the year before by Kennedy for helping assassinate foreign leaders. The likelihood of General Cabell being involved in the President's assassination is quite high. Perhaps the general let his brother, the mayor of Dallas, in on the impending assassination. Yet Mayor Cabell received death threats for some months after the assassination, and someone was monitoring his entire family's movements which suggests that perhaps Mayor Cabell learned of the conspiracy after the fact. There is another more likely suspect—the only other person in Dallas above the Chief of Police—whom will be addressed below.

Who else felt the police chief was coerced into moving Oswald in such an uncautious manner? Lt. George Butler of the Dallas Police Department told the Warren Commission that Chief Curry was pressured and ordered to bring Oswald out and transfer him when the news media was there.[68] Ex-Sheriff Steve Guthrie voiced the same opinion. He told the Warren Commission that Mayor Cabell would not discharge Curry because Curry was acting on orders.[69] The only man above both Mayor Cabell and Chief Curry was the City Manager, Elgin Crull. Elgin Crull had the power to appoint or discharge, at will, all department heads and assistant department heads. It was Crull who appointed Jesse Curry chief of police and could likewise dismiss him at any time. Hubert of the Warren Commission asked the following question of Elgin Crull: "You have the authority to direct the chief to do or not to do any actions that you thought?" Crull answered, "That's right, any department head."

Crull in turn took orders from the Dallas Citizens' Council, the center of political power in Dallas. A Warren Commission lawyer asked the city manager if any pressure had been applied to Chief Curry as to when to move the prisoner. Crull answered that he had held discussions with Chief Curry and Assistant Chief Charles Batchelor concerning the President's assassination. It becomes quite clear that Elgin Crull pressured the chief of police to transfer Oswald in an unsafe manner. The reason? To facilitate Oswald's murder.

In this, once again we see an interplay between the CIA and the economic elite—in this case, they assist one another in removing a common thorn in their sides, John F. Kennedy. From the economic elite's demand for Kennedy's removal from political power to H. L. Hunt's involvement in the assassination, to Elgin Crull's part in the plot, it's clear that the economic elite were the real puppeteers of the Kennedy assassination. They found a willing accomplice to murder in the CIA; in this and other ways, the CIA was a conduit for the economic elite to achieve their purpose.

Still, how did Jack Ruby get into the basement of the Dallas Police Department and kill Oswald? The Warren Commission fiction has Jack Ruby going to the Western Union office a block away from police headquarters, sending off a money order to one of his strippers, then on the spur of the moment, descending into the basement of the garage via the main street ramp. He mingles with the press, who are waiting for Oswald's appearance. When Oswald is brought down, Jack takes a few steps toward Oswald and fires a bullet into his ribs.

But, it is more complicated than that. Patrolman Roy Vaughn was standing at the top of this ramp with orders not to let anyone enter the garage via this entrance. Supposedly, Ruby slipped by Officer Vaughn at the same time officer Vaughn was waving on Lt. Rio Pierce as he was exiting the ramp in his patrol vehicle. Pierce said he exited the ramp a few minutes before Oswald was brought down. However, he told the Warren Commission that Officer Vaughn merely stepped aside to allow the vehicle to depart the garage. Lt. Pierce had known Jack Ruby for 12 years. He did not see Ruby walk down the ramp nor did he see Ruby at the top of the ramp when he exited.[70]

During the investigation by the Dallas Police Department on how Jack Ruby had gained access to the basement, Captain Talbert told the Warren Commission that Lt. Rio Pierce was positive and vociferous that Ruby was lying—he could not have come in this main street side.[71] Captain Talbert also said the following, "The individual officer on Main Street (Vaughn) was one of, if not the best patrolman I have. He is the type [of] person you can depend on thoroughly, and quite sizable physically."[72]

Officer Billy Joe Maxey was in the police vehicle with Lt. Pierce as it ascended the ramp. He pointed out that there was only a 12-foot opening at the entrance and there wasn't enough room for a person to squeeze by the vehicle and the wall of the ramp.

Officer Vaughn finally appeared before the Warren Commission. He said that he knew Jack Ruby and no one, including Jack Ruby, went down that ramp. He had also passed a lie detector test on this subject. "The only time I ever moved out of my position there was when this car which was driven by Lt. Pierce exited by that ramp."[73] Officer Vaughn also told the Warren Commission that he did not go out into the middle of the street but stayed on the curb and merely waved them on—that he stood in the middle of the 12-foot opening. Just prior to the emergence of Lt.

Pierce's vehicle, he had been conversing with Napoleon Daniels, an ex-Dallas city police officer. After the murder of Oswald and Ruby's allegation that he entered the garage by walking down the Main Street ramp, Officer Vaughn phoned Daniels. He asked Daniels, "Well, did you see anybody go down that basement while the car was coming out?" Daniels said, "No, definitely not, there was nobody."[74]

Actually, the only person who claimed Ruby walked down that ramp was Ruby himself. Forrest Sorrels of the Secret Service interviewed Ruby soon after he shot Oswald. Agent Sorrels told Jack that he was friendly with several members of the Jewish community in Dallas, including Honest Joe, a local pawn broker. Ruby told Sorrels that was good enough for him and that he would answer Sorrel's questions. Months later, during the Warren Commission hearings, Sgt. Patrick Dean, who was present during Sorrel's interrogation of Ruby, said that Ruby had stated he had entered the basement by walking down the Main Street ramp. Agent Sorrels, being interviewed by the Warren Commission at the same time, said that Ruby never said anything of the sort.[75] FBI Agent C. Ray Hall also interrogated Ruby one hour after his shooting of Oswald. According to Hall, Ruby refused to answer how he got into the basement; nor would he say when he entered.[76]

The Warren Commission strongly suspected reserve Dallas Police Officer William Newman as the person who allowed Jack Ruby's entrance into the police station's basement. Officer Newman's falsehoods so infuriated Warren Commission lawyer Burt Griffin that at one point the lawyer exploded, "You're a damn liar."[77] The proceedings were recessed. When they resumed, another Warren Commission lawyer had taken over the questioning of Officer Newman. It was one of the rare times a Warren Commision lawyer ever lost his self-control. It appears Sgt. Dean was lying about being told by Ruby that Ruby entered through the Main Street ramp. Because Sgt. Dean had been placed in charge of security for the basement during the transfer of Oswald, Dean must be considered an accessory in the murder of Oswald.

Another key to understanding the conspiracy to kill the President and Oswald, besides how Jack Ruby gained admittance into the basement, is how he was able to stand in the middle of news reporters and police officers without being detected. Patrolman W.J. "Blackie" Harrison had known Jack Ruby for 12 years. On Sunday morning, shortly before 11:00 a.m., he had gone down to the basement for some cigars and was told to stand by for the transfer of Oswald. Harrison told the Warren Commission that he stood waiting for Oswald for 10 to 12 minutes before Lee was brought down: "I took up a position in the ramp area here and assisted with getting the newsmen on the east side of the ramp." [78]

He claims never to have seen Ruby at any time before Ruby leaped forward to shoot Oswald. Yet motion picture film shows Harrison standing next to Jack Ruby for minutes before Lee was brought down. How did Harrison, on duty in the basement, assigned specifically to protect Oswald from any harm during the transfer, fail to see Jack Ruby, who was standing right next to him? With a quick turn they could have kissed each other. Certainly Blackie Harrison knew Ruby was standing next to him. The question is, why didn't he ask Jack to leave or better yet, escort him out?

This omission goes beyond dereliction of duty and hovers near conspiracy. A police reservist, Officer William Newman, was standing next to Ruby as well.[79] So we have not one but two officers who knew Jack Ruby personally and allowed him to remain standing in the garage.

After Oswald was shot and rushed to Parkland Hospital, another reserve officer was removed from the basement security detail and transported to the hospital to stand guard. His name is Harold Holly. It is through Holly's testimony that we learn how Jack Ruby got into the basement and why two police officers, if not conspiring to murder Oswald, let his assailant roam at large in the basement. Holly told the Warren Commission that, while he was stationed at Parkland Hospital, another reserve officer told him how Ruby had entered the basement to shoot Oswald. Holly explained, "Yes, he was a reserve [officer]. And in the conversation he said that he either knew or he saw Ruby down in the City Hall, knew of him getting down in there. The conversation went like, well, how in the world could they ever let him in? Everybody knew him, which most reserves do know him [*sic*]. And he said he saw him down there—one of reserves had let him in, and he had a lapel pass on."[80]

During the Dallas Police Department's investigation into how Ruby had entered the basement, Captain James Solomon showed reserve Officer Holly photos of all of the Dallas Police reserve officers in order to help him identify the reserve officer who had told him he saw Ruby enter the basement. Holly picked out a photograph of Newman, the officer standing next to Ruby in the basement. Since Newman saw Ruby enter the basement and both he and Blackie Harrison did not attempt to remove him, there may be another reason for their inaction.

Detective L.C. Graves was among those escorting Lee into the basement. He told the Warren Commission of the rumor that had pervaded the Dallas Police Department after the tragic weekend. "I heard that Chief Batchelor and a couple of the detectives had walked down the ramp and Ruby walked in with them, and I heard that he probably had a pass, a press pass."[81]

Only four Dallas Police administrators knew precisely when Lee Oswald would be brought down to the basement. In order for the conspiracy to murder Oswald to work, timing was of the utmost importance. Without the conspirators' knowing the exact time that Oswald would be transferred, his murder could not be accomplished. If the gunman is a minute late Oswald will be in the police vehicle being whisked away. If the gunman is too early he may raise suspicions and be escorted out of the basement—especially someone so recognizable as Jack Ruby. Timing was everything in Oswald's murder. This means that at least one of the four Dallas Police administrators who were aware of the exact time of Oswald's appearance in the basement had to be in on the murder. Their information had to be passed on to Ruby. It cannot be left to chance. The four police executives with this knowledge were Jesse Curry, chief of police, Will Fritz, chief of homicide and Oswald's main interrogator, Deputy Chief M.W. Stevenson and last, but not least, Deputy Chief Batchelor.[82] One of these men had to be in on Oswald's murder. If one rules out Chief Curry and Will Fritz, that leaves either Deputy Chief Stevenson or Deputy Chief Batchelor, or both.

And if it was Chief Batchelor escorting Ruby into the basement, this explains why neither Officers Harrison nor Newman said a word to Ruby while he lay in wait for Oswald. You don't tell an assistant chief of police how to do his job. Not if you want to keep yours. That's, of course, if Blackie Harrison wasn't in on the conspiracy. Also, no reserve officer would question anyone escorted into the basement by Deputy Chief Batchelor. I suggest that Chief Batchelor, having received word while upstairs in the homicide office that Lee was about to be brought down, went to where Jack Ruby was waiting, perhaps on the main floor. Then, the two of them entered the garage through one of the doors that led to it from the main floor. When the reserve officer guarding the door looked up and saw it was Deputy Chief Batchelor, he allowed Batchelor and Ruby to enter the basement. Deputy Chief Batchelor then placed Ruby next to Harrison and returned to the third floor homicide office to give the word that the basement was secure. As Oswald's last interrogation was winding down, both Deputy Chiefs Batchelor and Stevenson made two trips down to the basement to check on security for the transfer. This by itself is perfectly innocent. What is not so innocent is that the newsmen lined up behind a barricade, who were ordered to remain behind the barricade or face ejection, were moved a second time just before Oswald was brought down. According to Captain Cecil Talbert, "Chief Batchelor did re-arrange the news media, I think on two different times. He was trying to arrange them in a better situation."[83]

Captain Will Fritz told the Warren Commission that the press was supposed to be behind the railing as he and the detectives and the prisoner were descending into the base-ment but that someone changed his orders down there.[84] When Captain Fritz and the detectives, along with Oswald, exited the elevator and began walking toward the waiting po-lice vehicle, the press surged forward. They practically sur-rounded Oswald. News reporter Ike Pappas was so close to Oswald he thrust a microphone toward Oswald's face while asking Lee a question. Just as he did, Ruby rushed past the crowd and shot Oswald. But the news media were already over the railing before the detectives and Oswald entered the garage. I believe that, when Deputy Chief Batchelor took his second trip down to the garage, supposedly to check the se-curity of the basement, along with picking up Ruby and walking him in, he changed Will Fritz's order and allowed the newsmen to come over the railing to wait for Oswald. Of course, in so doing, he allowed Jack Ruby access to Oswald as well. Ruby couldn't very well have been expected to shoot Oswald from across the railing. He might not have had a clear shot from there; Oswald would only be accessible for a minute while being ushered into the waiting patrol car.

As Lee and the detectives made their appearance in the basement, a hush fell over the crowd. The flood lights of the television cameras flashed on, all but blinding Oswald and his detective escort. With vision impaired, Ruby rushed forward and fired a fatal shot into Lee's side. The momentary stunned silence that followed the shooting was broken as a loud cheer went up among the spectators.

44

JACK RUBY'S CONFESSION

What is mostly unknown is that Jack Ruby confessed to Earl Warren, Chief Justice of the Supreme Court and head of the Warren Commission, to being part of a conspiracy to assassinate JFK. Jack Ruby was insistent on making an appearance before the Warren Commission. To placate Ruby, Earl Warren and Congressman Gerald Ford flew down to Dallas to interview him. The first thing Ruby did was plead for the Chief Justice to bring him to Washington, D.C.: "Gentlemen, unless you get me to Washington, you can't get a fair shake out of me. If you understand my way of talking, you have got to bring me to Washington."[85] Jack was scared to death about saying anything about the assassination while remaining in Dallas. "I may not live tomorrow to give any further testimony. The truth of everything and why my act was committed, but it can't be said here."[86]

What is interesting but devastating is that the great civil libertarian Chief Justice Earl Warren not only refused to bring Ruby to Washington, but tried to intimidate him into silence. Warren told Ruby that anything he said now would automatically be known to Dallas authorities. Again and again, the Chief Justice told Ruby he wasn't required to say anything and perhaps he should rethink his desire to talk about the assassination and the murder of Oswald. This was incredible. The very man assigned by President Johnson to find out the truth of President Kennedy's assassination was doing his utmost to shut up Jack Ruby. Finally, when it became clear that Ruby was going to tell his story in spite of the Chief Justice's opposition to his speaking, Warren let Ruby talk. And talk he did.

Throughout his confession, Ruby spoke in doublespeak. "At this moment, Lee Harvey Oswald isn't guilty of committing the crime of assassinating President Kennedy. Jack Ruby is. Unfortunately for me, for me giving the people the opportunity to get in power, because of the act I committed, has put a lot of people in jeopardy with their lives."[87] Of course, the Chief Justice didn't ask Ruby for clarification. Warren didn't want any facts of the conspiracy coming out. Ruby continues: "Consequently, right at this moment, I am being victimized as a part of a plot in the world's worst tragedy and crime at this moment."[88]

Ruby's statement was met with a wall of silence by Warren. One of the Warren Commission lawyers asked Ruby about an allegation that he had met with a Weissman, Officer Tippit, and a rich oil man shortly before the assassination. Ruby's response was, "Who was the rich oil man?

Notice Ruby doesn't deny the meeting. By asking who the rich oil man was, Ruby was directing the Warren Commission's attention to the conspirators. Certainly, we know who the rich oil man was. It was H. L. Hunt. Bernard Weissman actually attended this meeting. He was responsible for placing the Kennedy "wanted for treason" advertisement that greeted the President at breakfast when he opened a local Dallas newspaper the morning of his visit. Since H. L. Hunt, Bernard Weissman, Officer Tippit and Jack Ruby were all meeting at Ruby's club shortly before the assassination, this indicates a conspiracy. It also indicates that Officer

Tippit wasn't the angel the press made him out to be. After Ruby was arrested for shooting Oswald, Jack's car was searched. A great deal of H. L. Hunt's right-wing material was found in the trunk of the car. Ruby pressed on with his confession, using his trademark doublespeak. Commenting on his own murder of Oswald, Jack said, "If it were timed that way, then someone in the police department is guilty of giving the information as to when Lee Harvey Oswald was coming down."[89]

In response once again, SILENCE from Warren. Throughout Ruby's lengthy interview with the Chief Justice, Ruby continuously implied that he was part of a conspiracy that took President Kennedy's life. But to no avail. Earl Warren had put up a wall of silence. Ruby realized the cards were stacked against him. Now, in effect, even the federal government was standing on the side of the conspirators. Ruby ended his interview with this sad, lamented observation: "Consequently, a whole new form of government is going to take over our country, and I know I won't live to see you another time."[90] So right you were Jack, on both counts.

What was going on with Warren? The great civil libertarian and defender of criminal rights (including those of the child rapist, Miranda) was actively burying the truth of the JFK assassination. What gives? I would argue that he knew full well the truth and scope of the plot. How could he not? Before he was made a Supreme Court justice, he was governor of California. Before he was governor, he was district attorney of Alameda County in the San Francisco Bay area. As a district attorney, he had practiced criminal law. He had sent his share of bad guys to prison and was entirely at home with homicide and the rules of evidence.

He knew ballistics; the difference between entrance and exit wounds; the value of autopsies; and theories of motives. After all, the murder of the President was a homicide. Being such, it played to all of Warren's strengths and background.

Warren was the ideal man to head the investigation; yet he pressed for the lone assassin theory. To come to this conclusion, Warren disregarded crucial facts and evidence presented to the Warren Commission and suspended both his logic and training as a criminal trial attorney. Why?

At some point early on in the proceedings, the full truth was laid out before Earl Warren. I suggest that representatives of the CIA and the military met in private with the Chief Justice. It was explained to him that the CIA did in fact assassinate President Kennedy, with the full backing and participation of the military. It was explained that JFK was considered a national security threat. If the Chief Justice would sweep the assassination under the rug, the democracy would continue as it had done for the last century and a half. If, on the other hand, the conspiracy was revealed, the military was ready to suspend the constitution and stage a coup. Thus, Kennedy's prophecy—that if he had a third Bay of Pigs—the military would be obliged to try and seize power had been fulfilled. So Warren had a decision to make. Either come clean about the plot and risk a military coup or placate the forces of evil in order to salvage a democracy under threat. Earl Warren chose the latter. Ruby, disappointed with Warren but nevertheless undaunted, had one more trick up his sleeve. The man who was clever enough to warn the Dallas Police Department of the impending murder of Oswald demanded a lie detector test. With the lie detector test, Ruby would try to prove a negative. That is, Ruby would be asked incriminating questions, he would then lie by giving the expected answers which the polygraph machine would show were falsehoods, showing that the opposite of what he was saying must be true.

For instance, when he was asked if he was part of a conspiracy to kill JFK and Oswald, he would answer "No." This would register as a falsehood which would in turn mean the opposite must be true, i.e., he was part of a conspiracy. This would lead to a new trial and when the truth of the conspiracy came out Ruby, would escape the electric chair. Very clever, Jack.

Ruby got his lie detector test. It was administered by an FBI agent named Herndon. As Herndon began to go over the questions he was going to ask of Jack, Ruby tried to direct their content. Herndon: "Did you tell anyone that you were thinking of shooting Oswald before you did it?" Ruby's reply was, "Why don't you say this...that Sunday morning, specifically? Also, whether I received any phone calls from the time I went to bed and the time I woke up."[91] Ruby asked Herndon, "Aren't you going to ask me whether I knew anything as to whether or not he was going to come down, or anything like that?"[92] Ruby also pointed out something else that would hopefully lead to a conclusion of conspiracy. "Well, let me get this clear. I notice that the pictures brought out the facts that there are two sets of private boxes, close together in the post office. Did you gentlemen know this? Which is quite an insinuation."[93]

What Ruby was talking about is that Lee Harvey Oswald and Jack Ruby had rented P.O. boxes that were right next to one another. This is an old espionage trick designed to provide a cover for clandestine meetings. Go Jack Go! Ruby also wanted the polygraph examiner to inquire about the phone calls he had made all over the country just prior to the President's assassination: "There were a lot of phone calls as you recall, I'm sure you know about that and there should be a specific way to ask me, 'What was the purpose of all those calls?'"[94] Then Herndon asked Ruby, "Did you ever meet Oswald at your post office box?" Jack responded with, "No, pardon me—why don't you say, 'Did you ever meet him at the post office or at the club?' How many times did he come to the club, that's something else."[95]

Ruby, continuing to implicate himself in a conspiracy, wanted Herndon to ask him another question: "Also somebody said they saw Tippit, I myself, and Oswald at the club.

So go ahead, I don't want to throw you off." Ruby also requested to be asked, "Has any of the underworld ever contributed money to me for my clubs or was I put in here as a front for the underworld or things to that effect."[96]

Ruby, in setting up the questions for his own polygraph examination, had just given the Warren Commission a blueprint of his own role in the conspiracy to assassinate the President. More important, he had just given the Commission numerous leads that could lead to the center of the conspiracy. Ruby was hoping the Warren Commission would dig into these areas, find a conspiracy, arrest the men responsible for the President's assassination and hopefully get himself off the hook for his own participation in the assassination. He couldn't very well come straight out with the facts of the assassination—he could easily be killed in prison. Also, no doubt, his sister, Eva Grant and other family members were threatened as leverage to ensure his silence. But if the Commission on its own had tracked down the assassins, it would have been a different story. The ruse almost worked. Herndon asked the questions, Ruby answered them with lies, but Herndon recorded Ruby's lies as truths. Here are some examples.

Herndon: "Did you know Oswald before November 22, 1963?" Ruby: "No." Conclusion: No deception. Herndon: "Did you assist Oswald in the assassination?" Ruby: "No." Conclusion: No deception. Herndon: "Did you shoot Oswald in order to silence him?" Ruby: "No." Conclusion: No deception. Poor Ruby. They saw it coming and stayed one step ahead of him. The fix was in Jack. You had no more chance going up against these forces than JFK did. You get an A for trying.

Ruby made the following comment after his lie detector test:

> This is the ironic part of it, that wouldn't it be a tremendous hoax, that here is a fellow that didn't vote for the President, closes his club for three days, made a trip to Cuba, relayed a

244   *JFK VS. CIA*

message from Ray Brantley—looked at circumstantially, how guilty am I? If you want to put all of these things together. Then, I happen to be down there, at that particular second when the man comes out of whatever it was—an elevator or whatever it was—all these things—plus the fact of the post office box and other rumors that they saw us together at the club...[97]

Poor Jack Ruby. He wanted no more to be a part of the President's assassination than he wanted to go to the electric chair for killing Oswald. In 1967, Jack Ruby finally found a judge who would let him have a new trial. This time it was to be held outside the state of Texas. But the day after he was granted the new trial, Ruby was rushed to the hospital with a bad case of the flu. The following day he was diagnosed with terminal cancer. He was held incommunicado. Three months later, he was dead. Oswald's silencer was himself silenced. Yes, Jack, next time be careful who you choose for your friends.

* * *

45

RICHARD HELMS

It is not enough to understand that the Central Intelligence Agency assassinated President Kennedy. After all, the CIA is made up of men. Men came to the conclusion that the President had to be removed from office. Men developed the assassination concept and men carried it out. But who? Which men in the CIA were responsible for, and carried out, the assassination? The answer is not as difficult as it first appears.

If the CIA assassinated President Kennedy, the next question is, who was running the agency at the time of the assassination? By summer 1961, President Kennedy had accumulated evidence that the CIA was assassinating foreign leaders against his express orders. He received this information via the gangster Sam Giancana. So Kennedy began clearing the decks of those men he knew were behind the assassination concept. He appointed John McCone as DCI. Then, JFK searched for someone in the CIA to take Richard Bissell's place as deputy director of plans, the leader of covert action. Richard Helms was promoted. In February 1962, Helms took over. What kind of character can be attributed to Richard Helms? The year before Richard Helms took over, he played an integral part in the Trujillo assassination. On April 10, 1961, Helms signed an order approving a shipment of machine guns to its station in the Dominican Republic.[98] The machine guns were intended for Dominican dissidents, who were told to use them to assassinate Trujillo. Richard Helms was actually the fourth CIA executive who was instrumental in the formation of the assassination concept. But Kennedy was unaware of this. In February 1962 then, JFK had moved this silent killer into the second most powerful position in the CIA. As we shall see, Helms not only used his position to continue the CIA's own foreign policy, but he was actually running the agency.

Two months after being appointed DDP, Helms ordered William Harvey to reactivate the CIA-Mafia connection to assassinate Fidel Castro.[99] Harvey passed poison pills to the gangster Johnny Rosselli in April, 1962.[100] Equally incredible is the fact that John McCone, DCI, was never informed of the proceedings. In 1975, Harvey testified before the Senate Select Committee on Government Operations with respect to intelligence activities. He told the Committee that he received Helm's approval not to brief McCone about this resumption.[101] "We agreed it was not necessary or advisable to brief him at this time."[102]

John McCone also testified. He said that as DCI he had never been briefed by Dulles, Bissel, Helms or anyone else about assassination plots; and if he had been, he would have disapproved.[103] McCone also testified that he was never informed even of the CIA's "executive action" capability.[104] This capability included the CIA's own assassination teams. It was not until August, 1963, after reading an article in the *Chicago Sun Times* detailing a CIA-Mafia link to an assassination attempt on Castro, that the DCI learned what his agency was up to. After reading the article he ordered Richard Helms to brief him. Helms told him the agency had considered the attempt, but discarded the idea.

While Richard Helms was ordering William Harvey to reactivate the CIA-Mafia plots to kill Castro, Robert Kennedy, the Attorney General, had found out about the previous plot. On May 7, 1962, RFK met with Richard Helms. Later in the day, he was briefed by CIA personnel Sheffield Edwards and Lawrence Houston. The briefing was held at the Attorney General's request. It covered the topic of the CIA-Mafia relationship of the previous year.[105] Lawrence Houston, the CIA's chief counsel, told the Senate Select Committee the following: "If you have seen Mr. Kennedy's eyes get steely and his jaw set and his voice get low and precise, you get a definite feeling of unhappiness. There was not to be any more contact with the Mafia without prior consultation with him."[106] Houston added that Robert Kennedy had also said, "I trust that if you ever try to do business with organized crime again—with gangsters— you will let the Attorney General know."[107]

RFK met with J. Edgar Hoover, the Director of the FBI to discuss this matter. Mr. Hoover has left us with a memorandum of the discussion.

> The Attorney general told me he wanted to advise me of a situation in the Giancana case which had considerably disturbed him. He stated a few days ago he had been advised by CIA that in connection with Giancana, CIA had hired Maheu, a private detective in Washington D.C., to approach Giancana with a proposition of paying $150,000 to hire some gunmen to go into Cuba and to kill Castro.[108]

After the meeting in May 1962 between the CIA representatives and the Attorney General, Edwards prepared a memorandum on May 14, 1962, falsely stating that the operation involving Rosselli was being terminated.[109] In effect, not only did Richard Helms keep the DCI in the dark about covert operations, he also lied to the Attorney General in having Edwards write the false memorandum.

In fact, John McCone was no more running the CIA than he was running the Boy Scouts of America. Helms was running the agency. Helms continued with the assassination plots. In 1963, the CIA proceeded with its plans to assassinate Castro, this time without the Mafia.

CIA agent Desmond Fitzgerald met with a Cuban named Roland Cubela, code-named AM/LASH. Desmond Fitzgerald gave AM/LASH Robert Kennedy's personal assurance that the American government was behind Castro's assassination.[110] Fitzgerald's testimony is that Helms had told him, "Go ahead and say that from the standpoint of political support, the U.S. government will be behind you if you are successful."[111] Fitzgerald, falsely acting as the personal representative of RFK, met with AM/LASH on November 22, 1963, and offered him a poison pen to use against Castro.[112]

During President Johnson's administration, Helms sent a letter to Secretary of State Dean Rusk. The letter said, "The Agency was not involved with AM/LASH in a plot to assassinate Fidel Castro, nor did it ever encourage him to attempt such an act."[113] Clearly, Helms was running the CIA at the time of the Kennedy assassination. I suggest that Richard Helms was the intellectual author of the JFK assassination. Helms is the traitor par excellence of this saga.

Helms took over as deputy director of plans in February 1962. But before this time he had hardly been spending time in the mailroom. From 1953 until February 1962, Helms was the assistant deputy director of plans. He worked directly under Bissell. When Bissell decided to assassinate Patrice Lumumba of the Congo, Helms was there. When the CIA formed its own assassination squad, Helms was there. He was part of the ongoing attempts to assassinate Fidel Castro, and it was Richard Helms who signed off on the CIA's shipment of weapons to the dissidents who assassinated the Dominican dictator, Trujillo. In addition, while Helms was deputy director of plans, the CIA plotted to assassinate President Sukarno of Indonesia and "Papa Doc" Duvalier of Haiti. Weapons were shipped from the CIA to dissidents in both countries for the express purpose of assasinating these two leaders. Helm's bloody handprints aren't just on JFK's assassination. Helms was reveling in a blood bath. Even the President of South Vietnam was on Richard Helms's hit list. President Diem's demise was also courtesy of Helms.

On May 8, 1963, South Vietnamese soldiers fired on Buddhists celebrating Buddha's birthday. The Catholic President of South Vietnam had no love for Buddhists. The shooting triggered a nationwide Buddhist protest. On May 18, 1963, the U.S. Ambassador, Frederick Nollis, met with President Diem and expressed American outrage and disapproval. He wanted Diem to redress Buddhist grievances, admit responsibility for the incident, and compensate the victims. On June 8, 1963, Madame Nhu, the wife of the brother of the South Vietnamese President, while discussing the self-immolation of Quang Duc and other Buddhist monks, joked about furnishing mustard for the monk's barbecue. This brought a stern warning from President Kennedy that if Diem's government didn't solve the problem, it would cause a break in relations with the United States. President Diem's brother responded by launching a midnight raid, attacking pagodas throughout Vietnam, arresting monks and sacking the sacred buildings. Fourteen hundred people were arrested. By August 1963, JFK had had enough. The President cabled the American Embassy in Saigon and ordered it to tell Diem that the United States would find it impossible to support the South Vietnamese government militarily and economically unless the Nhus were removed from the scene. "We wish to give Diem reasonable opportunity to remove the Nhus."[114]

Shortly afterward, JFK gave his approval for the coup against Diem to take place. On August 29, 1963, Kennedy sent a cable to the embassy in Saigon allowing the coup to take place but specifically ordering that there be no U.S. involvement.[115] As a follow-up to his orders, the DCI sent a cable to the CIA station chief in Saigon stating, "We cannot be in a position of stimulating, approving, or supporting assassination." [116]

But as the time for the coup neared, President Kennedy started having second thoughts. In response to a query from the White House, the new ambassador to South Vietnam cabled back that he was unable to halt a coup. The President cabled back, "We cannot accept conclusion that we have no power to delay or discourage a coup."[117]

Certainly when these things are initiated, they gather a momentum and life of their own. So they're difficult to halt. Not surprisingly, the day after this cable was sent, the coup began. On November 1, 1963, rebels surrounded the Presidential Palace. President Diem refused to come out. Both he and his brother escaped through a tunnel, but were later captured and executed. Kennedy was highly disturbed when he received the report that the two brothers had been assassinated. That was not supposed to be part of the plan, or so Kennedy thought. But the CIA had had different ideas. To the CIA, by fomenting the coup and having Diem assassinated, victory over the communists in South Vietnam could be achieved. It didn't matter what Kennedy thought, for he was next. In effect, Richard Helms, during the month of November, 1963, performed a double hit.

* * *

46

RICHARD HELMS AND DEATH BY MURDER

Citizens started dropping dead in the aftermath of President Kennedy's assassination. Over two dozen citizens who were touched by the assassination were dead within 36 months. There was a special flurry of deaths of Warren Commission witnesses in 1966. This was the year Helms became DCI. Helms must have felt he was on top of the world. He had gotten away with assassinating foreign leaders the world over, including the President of the United States. But there was still some cleaning up to do. Witnesses had appeared in front of the Warren Commission. Their testimony exonerated Lee Oswald from having killed anyone. More important, their testimony pointed toward a conspiracy. Richard Helms rolled up his sleeves and went to work.

James Worrel. James Worrel testified before the Warren Commission of seeing a man "come busting" out the backdoor of the book depository within three minutes of the shooting. By early 1964, during the Warren Commission hearings, it had been established that Lee Harvey Oswald had

had a gun held on him by a police officer on the second floor lunchroom one minute after the cessation of shots. Lee Oswald was then seen walking out the *front* door of the building. It was no longer convenient to have testimony indicating Oswald had "come busting" out the back door of the building. In point of fact, James Worrel saw the gunman who fired at Kennedy from the book depository. On November 9, 1966 James Worrel died in a traffic accident.[118]

Lee Bowers. Lee Bowers's testimony pointed to two men standing behind a picket fence at the mouth of the overpass. The fence was atop the grassy knoll. He told the Warren Commission that when the shots were fired, he could only see the heavier man in the white shirt standing behind the fence—that the other man's clothes blended in with the bushes. The other man, whose clothes blended in with the bushes, was in fact firing from those bushes at the President. Lee Bowers gave other testimony that was most damaging to the conspirators. He died in a traffic accident on August 8, 1966. He smashed into a concrete abutment at 9:30 a.m. The doctor who attended Bowers said he did not have a heart attack and that he thought Bowers had been in some sort of "strange shock."[119]

William Whalley. Whalley was the cab driver who picked Oswald up after the assassination and drove him to his boarding home where Oswald rented a room. Whalley's testimony exonerates Oswald from having killed anybody. He told the Commission how Oswald sauntered up to the cab and asked most politely if it was occupied. When a little old lady stuck her head in the passenger side window and asked the cab driver to call her a cab, Oswald reached for the door handle and offered to let her have his cab. This kind of behavior is not indicative of flight. Whalley's testimony destroyed the Warren Commission's findings that Oswald was fleeing the scene of his crime. The picture Whalley paints exonerates Oswald from having shot anyone. Whalley died in a traffic accident on December 15, 1965.[120] He was the first Dallas cab driver to die in an accident while on duty since the 1930s. Either driving in Dallas suddenly became extremely perilous or somebody had put these citizens on a list to be murdered.

Al Bogard. Al Bogard was the salesman at Downtown Lincoln—Mercury who went with an Oswald impersonator on a demonstration ride shortly before the assassination. The CIA had an Oswald impostor go around Dallas in the weeks before the assassination with the express purpose of implicating Lee in the President's assassination. Bogard wrote Oswald's name on the back of one of his cards as a prospective buyer. Bogard recognized him as the President's assassin. Bogard testified extensively in front of the Warren Commission. Unfortunately for Bogard, the real Lee Oswald never learned to drive a car and was with his family in Irving, Texas, the weekend of the supposed demonstration ride. Al Bogard was found dead in his car in Hallsville, Louisiana on February 14, 1966. A hose had been connected to the exhaust with the other end put inside the sealed car.[121]

Within a little more than two years after the President's assassination, four star witnesses of the Warren Commission were dead. All expired within a 12-month period. One does not have to be a statistician to know how heavy the odds are against this happening.

James Worrel saw the gunman who fired from the book depository. He was now dead. Lee Bowers saw the gunman and his accomplice who were firing from the bushes of the grassy knoll. He was now dead. William Whalley's testimony exonerates Oswald from having shot anybody. He was now dead. Al Bogard had personal contact with the Oswald impostor and he died. If anyone at a later date wanted to build a case for conspiracy, the testimony of these four men would have been the heart of the case. What's more, dozens of other citizens whose lives were touched by the assassination

254 *JFK VS. CIA*

died during this same period, whether or not they'd testified before the Warren Commission.

Lt. William Pitzer. Lt. William Pitzer was the autopsy photographer of President Kennedy. He saw and photographed all of the President's wounds. Lt. Pitzer told friends that his debriefing after the autopsy was a "horrifying experience." He stated he was periodically visited by military personnel who reminded him never to reveal—for reasons of "national security"—what he had seen while taking those pictures. Lt. Pitzer died October 29, 1966 of a gunshot wound. A coworker at Bethesda Naval Hospital reported to the *Sun-News* of Waukegan, Illinois, on May 1, 1975, that Lt. Pitzer's death had been ruled "self inflicted." The coworker added, "He was shot with a .45 caliber pistol and was found with the gun in his right hand. But he was left handed.... I've always believed he was murdered. They said he was depressed but he was close to retirement and had just received an offer to work for a network television station at $45,000 a year."[122]

I suggest that in the aftermath of the JFK assassination, the CIA put dozens of citizens on a hit list. Those citizens whose testimony exonerated Oswald and pointed specifically to a conspiracy were killed in case, at some point, their testimony and what they saw could be used against the CIA. Anyone who had firsthand knowledge was eliminated. Employees of Jack Ruby. Police officers and reporters. Congressmen and innocent bystanders who were in the wrong place at the wrong time were put on the hit list.

I suggest Richard Helms was covering his tracks by systematically eliminating witnesses whose testimony could lead to the undoing of the conspiracy and thus the end of the Central Intelligence Agency. The CIA wave of terror seems to have lasted from 1964 to 1967. In any case, Helms's mass murder campaign to cover up the assassination paid off in dividends. In 1978, the House Select Committee on Assassinations was formed. The call went out to all those citizens who testified before the Warren Commission. Many of those citizens had died in the intervening 12 years. Others could not be found. Perhaps they were not located because they, too, were six feet underground in coffins. The Butcher of Langley had done his job well.

* * *

47

RICHARD HELMS, THE MANCHURIAN CANDIDATE AND RFK

RFK was assassinated in June of 1968. He had just won the California primary. It looked like Senator Kennedy would become the next President of the United States. The question is, did the CIA assassinate Robert Kennedy as it did JFK? The CIA didn't hesitate to assassinate a President of the United States. Why would it hesitate to murder a mere Senator? Did the Agency have any motive to assassinate Senator Kennedy? I argue that the Agency had overwhelming and compelling reasons to assassinate Senator Kennedy.

Certainly by 1968, Robert Kennedy knew that Lee Harvey Oswald had not killed his brother. Mark Lane's book *Rush to Judgment* had been published in 1966. His book once and for all proved that President Kennedy had been caught in a crossfire. Sylvia Meaghers's *Accessories After the Fact* was published the following year. Her analysis of the 26 volumes of exhibits and testimony that the Warren Commission had based its conclusions on effectively destroyed those conclusions. Several other assassination critics had their works published in the 1960s (those works have held up most admirably). Doing the work the government should have been doing were Josiah Thompson, Harold Weissberg and Penn Jones, just to name a few of the original Warren Commission critics. Year after year, honest citizens were chipping away at the findings of the Warren Commission, using the Commission's own documents. Certainly by 1968, RFK knew that his brother had died as a result of a conspiracy. He also knew that only the power of the Presidency could unlock the secret.

President Johnson was also aware that CIA had assassinated his predecessor. In April 1967, President Johnson told Marvin Watson, special assistant to the President, that he was now convinced the CIA had assassinated President Kennedy.[123] Marvin Watson then contacted Cartha Deloach of the FBI. He informed him of President Johnson's statement. Deloach then wrote up the memo and sent it to his boss at the FBI, Clyde Tolson, (who died, not surprisingly, in 1975) as these hearings were underway. We know this because Senator Schweiker was grilling Deloach during the Senate Select Committee hearings investigating the FBI. Schweiker had in front of him the document that Deloach had written to Tolson back in 1967.

One wonders if the realization on the part of President Johnson that the CIA had assassinated President Kennedy was the real reason he did not run for office in 1968. He thought he could be next. In any event, RFK knew a conspiracy had taken his brother's life. I suggest that one of the reasons he was running for the Presidency was to be able to hunt down his brother's assassins. Removing Hoover from the FBI and Richard Helms from the CIA would be a start in the right direction. The overwhelming and compelling reason for the CIA to assassinate Bobby was that if RFK became President, Richard Helms and others would go to prison. Richard Helms knew full well that, as President, RFK would

258   JFK VS. CIA

circumvent the FBI and use the other branches of the Department of Justice to reach his brother's killers. He might also have those men in the military who were loyal to the democracy search out and hand over those men in the Armed Forces who had assisted the CIA in the assassination.

If RFK became President, it would simply have been the end of the CIA. Richard Helms was not a fool, nor into suicide. It was either him or Bobby, and Helms was going to make sure Bobby would die. Just like he did five years before with JFK, Helms now plotted RFK's assassination. This time no Wild West ambush. You can only pull that one once. A much more diabolical and sophisticated method would be used for Senator Kennedy's death. If I am right that Helms, as DCI, ordered Bobby Kennedy's assassination in order to get away with John's, how did he do it? In order to pull off this type of assassination, Sirhan Sirhan would have to be brainwashed. The CIA would have to develop a "Manchurian Candidate"-type brainwashing program. Did CIA have this capability in 1968?

Project MKULTRA. By the mid-1970s, rumors abounded into the halls of Congress that the CIA had the capability to turn citizens into assassins via a brainwashing program. Supposedly, experiments had been conducted on unsuspecting citizens as the program developed. The Senate Subcommittee on Health explained what they were up against.

> The records of all these activities were destroyed in January of 1973, at the instructions of then CIA director Richard Helms. In spite of persistent inquiries by both the Health Subcommittee and the Intelligence Committee, no additional records or information were forthcoming. And no one—no single individual—could be found who remembered the details, not the Director of the CIA, who ordered the documents destroyed, not the official responsible for the program, nor any of his associates.[124]

Fortunately for Congress and the American people, some of the Project MKULTRA materials had been misplaced and thus were not destroyed when Richard Helms tried to hide from Congress what the CIA had been up to. In 1976, with the election of a new President, Jimmy Carter, and a new appointed DCI, Stansfield Turner, the Senate Subcommittee on Health, finally learned the truth about Project MKULTRA.

The CIA had indeed conducted experiments on humans. Over 30 universities and institutions were involved in an extensive testing and experimentation program which included covert drug testing on unwitting citizens.[125] A 1963 CIA Inspector General's report revealed that "present practice is to maintain no records of the planning and approval of test programs."[126] The technical services division of the CIA had initiated 144 subprojects related to the control of human behavior between 1953 and 1963. Forty-four colleges and universities, 15 research foundations, 12 hospitals, and three penal institutions were used for this ten-year project.[127] Among the many subprojects initiated were the following:

1) Research on hypnosis, including eight subprojects, two involving hypnosis and drugs combination.

2) Nine projects on studies of human behavior, sleep research, and behavioral change during psychotherapy.

3) Seminars and international conferences on behavioral modification.

4) Six subprojects on drugs, toxins, and biologicals in human tissue, provision of exotic pathogens, and the capability to incorporate them in effective delivery systems.

5) Three subprojects on activities whose nature cannot be determined.[128]

Who originally proposed this program? We learn it was none other than *Richard Helms*. His goal was for the agency to develop "capability in the use of biological and chemical agents and materials."[129] He described his project as follows:

> We intend to investigate the development of a chemical material which causes a reversible, nontoxic aberrant mental state, the specific nature of which can be reasonably well-predicted for each individual. This material could potentially aid in discrediting individuals, eliciting information, and implanting suggestions and other forms of mental control."[130] (ADDP to DCI 4/3/53)

The last clause of Helm's proposed project back in 1953 is of paramount importance: "...and implanting suggestions and other forms of mental control." On December 17, 1963, shortly after having successfully assassinated the President of the United States, Helms wrote the CIA's deputy director a memo pertaining to his pet project: "For over a decade the Clandestine Services has had the mission of maintaining a capability for influencing human behavior." Helms argued that the individual must be "unwitting" as this is: "the only realistic method of maintaining the capability, considering the intended operational use of materials to influence human behavior as the operational targets will certainly be unwitting."[131] Helms continued: "The present investigation is concerned with chemical agents which are effective in modifying the behavior and function of the central nervous system."[132]

We learn the bottom line for this project in Helms' last three points.

1) Materials which will render the induction of hypnosis easier or otherwise enhance its usefulness.

2) Materials and physical methods which will produce amnesia for events preceding and during their use.

3) Substances which alter personality structures in such a way that the tendency of the recipient to become dependent upon another person is enhanced.[133]

It turns out that the man who told the Senate Subcommittee on Health that he had no recollection of this project was in reality the father of the project. Let us be candid. The real reason for the CIA's extensive 10-year human experimentation program was to assist in assassination. The agency, in particular, Helms, wanted a way to program assassins. Helms wanted to set the assassins on their targets and either be killed in the return fire or, if captured, not remember a damn thing about how they got into the situation. In this way, the target is killed, someone is captured and takes the fall, and the CIA is never suspected.

Those last three capabilities that Richard Helms wanted realized for the project give away the RFK assassination. We learn a great deal about the RFK assassination from the three volumes of summary reports of the Los Angeles Police Department's investigation into it.

A beautiful blonde girl came into Sirhan Sirhan's life in the few months before he shot at Robert Kennedy. She was seen everywhere with him and apparently was the first (and last) girlfriend he had. This beautiful girl was seen with him on campus at Pasadena Junior College and at a firing range the day before Robert Kennedy's murder where Sirhan practiced with his pistol. She was seen with him at the Ambassador Hotel the night RFK was shot, but mysteriously disappeared the next day. Point three of Helms's edict covered "substances which alter personality structures in such a way that the tendency of the recipient to become dependent upon another person is enhanced." The blonde girl was the bait. Eyewitnesses to the shooting said that Sirhan seemed to be in a trance when he shot at Senator Kennedy and while being wrestled to the floor. When Helms first pitched his project, the last phrase in his proposal was "implanting suggestions and other forms of mental control." To this day, Sirhan cannot remember how he got to the Ambassador Hotel or anything about shooting RFK. How can a person's memory register a complete blank when it comes to shooting a Senator? Perhaps we should ask Helms, for his second disideratum was: "Materials and physical methods which will produce amnesia for events preceding and during their use." In other words, brainwashing.

RFK was also assassinated by the CIA in order to cover up the first assassination. Fortunately for Helms, by 1968 the CIA had Project MKULTRA—the behavior modification program—and proceeded to use it on Sirhan Sirhan. The Butcher of Langley had struck again.

* * *

48

RICHARD HELMS
AND LATIN AMERICA

With John Kennedy out of the way, a reign of terror began that stretched southward from Dallas to Argentina. Kennedy's support for democracy in Latin America and his strong opposition to dictatorships were well-known. With JFK's murder, forces of darkness unleashed vengeful legions of death.

In the early 1960s, the leftist governments of Latin America behaved exactly as J.C. King, head of Western Hemisphere operations for the CIA, had said they would. In 1959, he predicted that Latin American governments would start to seize American businesses in a nationalist frenzy. American and European corporations lost billions of dollars as their businesses were confiscated. The Latins were playing by their own rules and violating international law in the process. The only way the Americans were going to get back their businesses, and the billions of dollars invested in those businesses, was by force. Hence we have an alliance between the American business community and the CIA with a common goal of overthrowing elected governments in Latin America and replacing them with right-wing military dictatorships. One by one, like dominoes, each Latin American country fell to CIA-engineered coups. And leading the CIA all the way was Helms. In 1970, it was the South American country of Chile that was about to fall to the ax of the Butcher of Langley.

The Senate Select Committee on Governmental Operations with Respect to Intelligence Activities in 1975 studied the CIA's role in engineering coups in Latin America throughout the previous decade. Their scope, the reasons why, and their effectiveness has been revealed in government documents. The purpose of this chapter is to show the evil genius of the man who killed Kennedy and further illuminate his predilection for doing so.

Multinational corporations operating in Chile feared that Salvador Allende, a Marxist, would be elected president of Chile. Allende's public statements indicated his intention, if elected, to nationalize basic industries and to bring Chilean ownership to service industries such as telecommunications.[134] As Allende took office, American business had $1.1 billion invested in Chile and other foreign corporations had $1.6 billion invested there.

Throughout the 1960s the CIA had been able to keep Allende from power through a massive infusion of funds to his opponents and anti Allende propaganda. Still, in 1970, Allende was elected president. The American business community knew full well what was in store. Another Castro, minus the guns, was about to stick it to them. In response, American business and the CIA struck a premptive first blow. After Allende was elected but before he could take office, U.S. Ambassador Korry informed the Chilean armed forces that should Allende ascend to the presidency, there would be no more military aid from the U.S. At the same time, the CIA contacted 21 key military and police officials and assured them of strong U.S. support for a coup.[135]

Ambassador Korry next met with the sitting president, Eduardo Frei, who, with only six weeks before Allende took over, was told by Ambassador Korry, "Not a nut or bolt would be allowed to reach Chile under Allende."[136]

Three weeks after the election, the CIA had coopted journalists from ten different countries to act as its agents in Chile. The CIA also had agents in place in managerial capacities in the broadcast and print media. In the six weeks before Allende took office, 726 articles, broadcasts, and editorials were produced as a direct result of agency action.[137] With this scare campaign, the CIA was hoping to create a financial crisis that would in turn goad President Frei or the military into taking steps to stop Allende from actually taking power. But the campaign failed.

So Helms decided to initiate "Track II." This plan was to employ direct military action and assassination to topple Allende's government. In the meantime, Allende struck back at the Americans. He nationalized both the telephone company and the copper mines. In a matter of months the foreign companies operating in Chile saw $2 billion in investments expropriated. The Americans and Europeans countered by cutting off Chile's credit. Now, Chile couldn't borrow from their banks. This created even more financial tumult and instability. Parts for American machinery were withheld from Chile. Critical sectors of the Chilean economy, such as copper, steel, electricity, and petroleum production (and transportation) were especially hit hard.

U.S. bilateral aid to Chile dropped from $35 million in 1967 to $1.5 million in 1971. U.S. import bank credits dropped from $234 million in 1967 to $0 in 1971. Loans from multinational interAmerican development banks dropped from $46 million in 1970, when Allende took office, to $2 million in 1972. If Allende wanted to practice Marxist politics and economics, the Americans were happy to show him the fruits of his ideology.

266 JFK VS. CIA

While the financial squeeze was being put on Chile by the business world, Helms ordered the CIA station chief in Santiago to prepare operational intelligence that would be instrumental in the event of a coup. Arrest lists were made, key civilian installations charted, and personnel who might need protection were located. But a major barrier to a military coup remained in the form of General Rene Schneider, commander-in-chief of the Chilean armed forces. While not a supporter of Allende, he did support democracy in his homeland. When approached to lead the coup, he refused. General Schneider insisted that the constitutional process be followed. So, naturally, Helms ordered his assassination.[138] The Chilean conspirators, out of respect for the General, decided to kidnap him to get him out of the way. The CIA station chief in Santiago, Chile wired headquarters in Langley, Virginia the following message on the day of the attempted kidnapping: "Military will not admit involvement in Schneider's abduction which is to be blamed on leftist."[139]

Just to be on the safe side, the CIA sent, through a diplomatic pouch, machine guns intended for the conspirators. The kidnapping failed and the general was assassinated the next day. Helms had struck again. This time he had slaughtered one of the rarest breeds on the planet, a Latin American general who was honest, brave, patriotic and, most of all, pro-democracy.

Eventually the Chilean military succeeded in its coup, costing Allende his life. General August Pinochet took over the reigns of government. Political parties were banned, Congress was put in indefinite recess, censorship was instituted, supporters of Allende were jailed, and elections were postponed indefinitely.[140] The CIA helped the new government organize and implement the new policies, gave the generals an economic plan to follow, and renewed its liaison with the Chilean government's security and intelligence forces.[141]

It seems like an awfully hard fate to punish a people for making the wrong choice for President. Especially if you were a Chilean who ended up in one of 11 torture centers operating in Santiago and throughout the country. Especially, if you were a mother who never saw your son again after he was kidnapped off the street by security forces going down the list provided them by the CIA. The Chilean episode well characterized the nature of the management running the CIA throughout this period. In effect, Helms signed General Schneider's death warrant. Richard Helms playing God, destroying so many lives across the planet in a single decade.

Do the ghosts of the Kennedy brothers ever haunt Richard Helms in his dreams? Does Bobby ever come to him with those piercing eyes and ask, "Why ?" Do the ghosts of Salvador Allende and of the dozens of Americans and thousands of Latins sent to early graves, in service to his homicidal passion, pass by him in bewilderment? Surely if there is a God, He has reserved a special place for him in hell. A traitor not just to America, but to mankind.

* * *

PART VI—PRELUDE TO THE ASSASSINATION

49

FOURTEEN MONTHS
AND COUNTING

It is with the testimony of Jose Aleman during the House Select Committee's investigation into the assassination of President Kennedy that we learn the date on which the decision was made to assassinate the President.

Aleman testified that in the middle of September, 1962, Santos Trafficante asked to have lunch with him in Miami. Aleman had been a good friend of Castro's and had fought with him against Batista. After the revolution, Castro started leaning toward Communism and Aleman became disenchanted and left the island. Trafficante was hoping that he could use Aleman in his attempt to assassinate Castro.

At the luncheon, Trafficante rambled on about many things and then the conversation turned to Kennedy. Aleman pointed out to Trafficante that Kennedy would probably be reelected. Trafficante disagreed and finally remarked, "No Jose, you don't understand. He is going to be hit."[1] Aleman confirmed that Trafficante personally told him that President Kennedy was going to be hit and that Trafficante made it clear to him that he had not been speculating about the killing.[2] The questions raised are, how did Trafficante, in September of 1962, know that President Kennedy was going to be assassinated? Also, why would he have been privy to this information?

To find out the answers to these questions we must go back two years. As previously mentioned, in August of 1960, the CIA made contact with Johnny Rosselli, a West Coast gangster, to see if the Mafia could be used to dispose of Castro. The CIA was hoping the Mafia could use its contacts on the island to effect Castro's murder. For the Mafia's part, elimination of Castro would mean they would be able to resume the gambling and other underworld pursuits Castro had shut down when he took control of Cuba.

By February of 1961, Rosselli had brought Sam Giancana, the Mafia boss of Chicago, into the conspiracy. A meeting was held at the Fountainbleu Hotel in Miami between a CIA representative, Rosselli, Trafficante, Robert Makeu, a private detective who worked for Howard Hughes and a Cuban national who had access to Castro. The CIA agent passed poison pills to Rosselli, who passed them to the Cuban national. The Cuban worked in a restaurant Castro frequented and was to drop the poison pills in liquid that Castro would subsequently drink. The only reason the plan did not materialize was because the Cuban got cold feet.[3]

The project was handed to William Harvey in April of 1962 by Helms. Harvey was ordered to make contact with Rosselli and reactivate the assassination mechanism of using the Mafia. Harvey went over the latest plans to assassinate Castro with Rosselli in Miami on September 7 and 11. These meetings between Harvey and Rosselli are crucial in understanding why Trafficante knew by the middle of September that Kennedy was going to be hit. Trafficante knew by this date either because he was at the meeting with Harvey and Rosselli and Harvey let it slip out or Harvey, in a moment of macho bluster, told Rosselli that Kennedy wasn't going to be around much longer—the implication being that the CIA would assassinate him. William Harvey was in an ideal situation to know about the impending assassination. Not only was he, in effect, the CIA's field commander for the Castro assassination, he was in charge of the execution squad known as the "International Team" that had been set up the year before under Allen Dulles.

Also, since the meeting was held in Miami and Trafficante was the city's Mafia boss, he became privy to Mafia business. His close friendship with Rosselli, as well as his own previous association with CIA-Mafia plots against Castro, were helpful. Aleman testified that the conversation took place in the middle of September. On September 7 and 11, the meetings between Harvey and Rosselli took place.[4] This means that by September of 1962, at the height of the economic elite's hysteria over Kennedy's turning the country into another socialist state, the Central Intelligence Agency was going forward with its plans to assassinate the President.

* * *

50

NINE MONTHS
AND COUNTING

On February 22, 1963, at a party, the Oswalds were introduced to several members of the Russian emigre community living in Dallas. Everitt Glover, who organized the party, also invited a woman named Ruth Paine. Paine knew Glover from a singing group they belonged to. The group would socialize and sing madrigals. Glover thought it would be beneficial to both Marina as well as Paine if they could meet and be friends. Marina, with her limited English skills, would have someone to converse with, and Ruth Paine, an American living in the Dallas suburbs, would be able to sharpen her Russian skills.

This probably was not the real reason for the party. I suggest the real reason was to introduce Ruth Paine to Marina Oswald. This introduction was tied to the assassination. I suggest that Ruth Paine was working for the CIA. Her assignment was to make sure Marina was living with her in Irving, Texas, a suburb of Dallas, by the fall of 1963.

Ruth Paine told the Warren Commission about this first meeting with the Oswalds. "I did ask for her address and I asked if I could write her. I wanted to go visit her at her home"[5]

Wherever Marina and her daughter June were living, that is where Oswald would also be. It was imperative that Oswald be in Dallas by the fall of 1963—that was when the CIA was going to strike at the President. Marina and her daughter were living with Paine outside Dallas at the time of the assassination. This means that as early as February 1963, a tentative place, as well as a patsy, had been picked for the President's assassination.

The fall guy chosen by this early date was Lee Harvey Oswald. He was an excellent choice, since Oswald was an undercover CIA operative. It was much easier for the agency to control one of its own. Dallas was also the perfect city in which to assassinate the President. The Mayor of Dallas was the brother of General Cabell. General Cabell was the assistant director of the CIA when Kennedy fired him for assassinating foreign leaders. Indeed, one has to wonder if he wasn't one of the military brass working on the President's assassination. Dallas was also virulent right-wing anti-Kennedy territory. Now, with a tentative patsy and place set for the President's assassination, the CIA had to get both President Kennedy and Lee Harvey Oswald in the same city and at the same time.

* * *

51

EIGHT MONTHS
AND COUNTING

On March 13, 1963, a Chicago sporting goods company named Kleins received an order for a rifle. This rifle was sent on March 20, 1963 to an A.J. Hidell at P.O. Box 2915, Dallas, Texas.[6] Across the country we have a similar occurrence. George Rose & Co. of Los Angeles prepared an invoice for a handgun order on March 20, to A.J. Hidell at P.O. Box 2915, Dallas, Texas.[7]

Lee Harvey Oswald was renting this P.O. Box and A.J. Hidell was an alias that Oswald used. The orders for both weapons were in Oswald's handwriting. The problem we confront is that at this point in his life, Oswald did not have the funds to purchase even one of these weapons, let alone both. Oswald put it most succinctly when being questioned about the order of the rifle by Captain Fritz, chief of homicide: "How could I afford to order a rifle on my salary of a dollar and a quarter an hour?"[8] Also, why purchase such weapons through the mail? Why not just walk into any sporting goods store in Dallas and buy a rifle on the spot? If

Oswald was contemplating assassinating the President in March, why leave such a paper trail leading straight to himself?

In March 1963, a paper trail was being laid, but the source was not Lee Harvey Oswald. It was the CIA. The agency was laying a paper trail that was going to be used to tie Oswald to the assassination in the fall. It was through this paper trail that the rifle that was "found" on the sixth floor of the book depository was traced to Oswald's ownership. The CIA was framing Oswald even at this early stage of the assassination.

* * *

52

SECRET SERVICE WARNING

The Secret Service received a warning of the President's impending assassination in March. A postcard was sent to the Secret Service warning them that the President was going to be assassinated while in a motorcade.[9] Someone was letting the cat out of the bag quite prematurely. Someone with intimate knowledge of the planning of the assassination was doing their patriotic duty in warning the Secret Service. This postcard also tells us that with eight months to go, the assassination plan was already well-advanced. The method picked for the President's death would be gunfire while riding into an ambush during a motorcade. But before he can be shot in a motorcade the President must be directed into one.

* * *

53

FIVE MONTHS
AND COUNTING

President Kennedy spoke at the Air Force Academy on June 5, 1963. Later in the day at the Cortez Hotel in El Paso, Texas, the President and Vice-President met with Governor Connally. This was when the original conversation of a special Presidential trip to Texas was discussed. The President's commitments prevented him from coming to Texas any sooner than November 21, 1963, the date finally set for his visit.[10]

Thus, as early as June 5, 1963, the President's itinerary was to include a visit to Texas on November 21, 1963. The CIA now had the date of the President's visit to Texas to work with and five months to prepare the final scene. Now the agency sought to make sure Oswald would be in Dallas on this date, too.

When we turn back to the Oswalds during this period, we see that Ruth Paine was busy at work. Ever since their meeting in February, Ruth Paine had been steadily ingratiating herself with the Oswalds. She visited Oswald's residence in March. In April she sent a letter to Marina asking her to come live with her for economic reasons (Oswald was not doing very well supporting his family and Marina was pregnant). Ruth Paine was separated from her husband and was living with her small children in Irving, Texas.

On April 24, Paine persisted: "I had discussed with her the possibility of her coming at the time the baby was expected." The baby was expected in the fall, the same time as the assassination.

* * *

54

FOUR MONTHS
AND COUNTING

It is now July and Ruth Paine is getting desperate for Marina to live with her in Irving, Texas. The Oswalds were then in New Orleans. Lee Oswald cannot be set up to take the fall for the President's assassination if he is in New Orleans while the President is shot in Dallas. Lee Harvey Oswald must be in Dallas at the time of the assassination. The CIA realized that wherever Marina and his children were, that's where Oswald would be.

So Paine wrote once again to Marina in New Orleans on July 17: "Marina, come to my home the last part of September without fail. Either for two months or two years. And don't be worried about money."[11] The CIA had told Paine that it was imperative to have Marina there by late September. She need only put up Marina and family for two months. Two months, because the President was going to be assassinated on November 22.

I do not believe Ruth Paine understood, at that time, the ulterior purpose behind the CIA's request to have Marina living with her by the end of September. Indeed, Paine probably had no idea of the impending assassination. Yet, she was a tool for the agency in its assassination of the President. The agency may have told her that Oswald was a Communist, a subversive whom they wanted to keep an eye on. In any event, she was instrumental in the planning of the President's death. It was Ruth Paine who brought Marina, and thus Oswald, to Dallas. It was Paine who got him the job at the book depository—on the route the President would eventually take. It was Paine who led police officers to the blanket in the garage in which, supposedly, the gun lay wrapped. And it was Paine who, in her testimony, harangued Lee Harvey Oswald throughout the Warren Commission hearings. On July 12, another letter from Ruth Paine to Marina: "Come here the end of September. We could give you $100.00 a month and pay for the doctor and hospital. I love you Marina and want to live with you. I hope that you and Lee will agree. If it is easier for you, I can come for you and June in September."[12]

Now bribery was being used. A hundred dollars a month and having her maternity bills paid was too good to turn down. The Oswalds were living in an impoverished state because of Oswald's minimum wage jobs. Paine also offered to drive from Irving, Texas to New Orleans to pick them up and bring them back to Texas. What a devout friend Paine was being to a person she barely knew and had just met. The reality is that Ruth Paine had instructions to make sure the Oswald family was near Dallas by the end of September. These instructions she fulfilled.

* * *

55

TWO MONTHS
AND COUNTING

In the summer of 1963, with the military coming to the conclusion that JFK was a national security threat, the assassination plot was speeding toward its climax. Marina moved in with Ruth Paine on September 24; Oswald would follow soon.

* * *

56

FIVE WEEKS
AND COUNTING

Oswald arrived at the Paine residence on October 4th.[13] While visiting at a neighbor's house down the street, Ruth Paine was informed of a possible job opening for Oswald. At the nearby Randall home, Linnie Mae Randall told Ruth Paine that her brother Wesley Frazier thought they needed another person at the book depository. Ruth Paine called the book depository and talked to Roy Truly, the Superintendent, securing Oswald an interview. Oswald started work on October 15, 1963.[14]

The book depository lay on the route the President's motorcade would eventually be following. Seemingly, five weeks before the assassination no one had yet routed the motorcade. No one, that is except the Central Intelligence Agency. Oswald was offered the job at the book depository in order to place him at the known site of the assassination. The site for the shooting had been chosen well in advance. The Presidential motorcade would travel onto Elm Street, pass in front of the School Book Depository, and encounter a classic military ambush. Men firing in front of the President, from the bushes on the grassy knoll, as well as assassins firing from behind him in the book depository building, would catch him in a deadly crossfire. And now, with Oswald where they wanted him, the fall guy was in place.

* * *

57

TWO OSWALDS

Starting in November, the same month in which the assassination took place, a "twin" Oswald started appearing in public. The CIA sent an Oswald impostor to various locations in the Dallas area. The purpose was to have him act in such a way as to later incriminate Oswald—in effect, to frame him for the President's murder.

Several citizens testified to the Warren Commission as to having done business with "Oswald" in the weeks before the assassination. As we shall see, dates and other information rule out the possibility that this man was the Oswald married to Marina and who was arrested for the President's assassination. The second Oswald running around Dallas impersonating and implicating Marina's Oswald makes it clear that the CIA went to the extreme of having plastic surgery performed on the impostor. This was nothing new to the CIA. Three years before, WI/ROGUE, the CIA's contract assassin, had had plastic surgery and donned a toupee so that fellow Europeans would not recognize him.[15] This was done in conjunction with the Patrice Lumumba assassination.

The Furniture Store. Edith Whitworth was the owner of a furniture store in Irving, the suburb of Dallas where Marina was now staying with Ruth Paine. Whitworth told the Warren Commission that on November 1, 1963, a family drove up in front of her store. The man who was driving got out of the car and inquired about a gunsmith who had been renting space in her furniture store. She told him that the gunsmith had gone out of business. She then directed the customer to the Irving Sports Shop.[16] The customer then said "You have furniture in here? I'm going to need some in a couple of weeks or so."[17] The customer's wife followed the man along with a baby and a little girl. The man told Whitworth that the young baby was born on October 20.[18] This was the date Rachel was born to the Oswalds. Whitworth remembered joking with the customer about swapping babies with him. Whitworth told the Warren Commission that the customer was Lee Harvey Oswald.

Gertrude Hunter was with Whitworth at the time the customer showed up in front of the store. She was sitting in front of the store. She told the Warren Commission the man drove up in a two-toned blue Ford. She remembered Edith Whitworth's joke about switching babies. She told the Commission that Whitworth said to the customer, "Let me trade you a boy for this girl and we will both have a boy and a girl." Hunter told the commission that the man first inquired about a gunsmith. She told the commission the man was driving and was accompanied by a woman and two children.[19] Hunter also told the commission that the man was Oswald and the incident occurred on a Wednesday or a Thursday.

The testimony of these two women gave the Warren Commission cause for concern. Previous testimony had pointed to Oswald's inability to drive a car. Previous testimony had also placed Oswald at work during the week at the book depository. It had Oswald coming home to Irving only on weekends. But here was testimony that had not just

Oswald but Oswald's entire family including his two-week-old daughter visiting a furniture store.

To repeat, according to Whitworth, while at the store Oswald pointedly referred to the fact that he would be needing furniture in a couple of weeks. Of course, in a couple of weeks the President would be assassinated. The implication of this statement was that, in two weeks Oswald, having been paid to kill, would have sufficient money to buy furniture.

To resolve this dilemma, the Warren Commission brought in Marina as well as Hunter and Whitworth, to try to sort things out. Marina, when confronted with Whitworth and Hunter's testimony, told the Warren Commission, "I have never seen Lee drive the car in my lifetime. Lee never drove a car with me or the children in it.[20] Marina continued: "The only possible person who could have driven the car when we were in the store could have been Mrs. Ruth Paine. She knows all the stores where we went because we never went there without her."[21]

Marina also told the Warren Commission, "I never wore any ribbons or bows in the hair. Maybe it was somebody just like me." Whitworth piped up, "I saw him get out of the car and come to the west door absolutely."[22] Marina then pointed out that Lee never was in Irving on a Wednesday or Thursday and only came to Irving on weekends.[23] Marina did confirm that her daughter Rachel was born on October 20, 1963, the date the customer assumed to be Oswald told Edith Whitworth his daughter was born.

Clearly, an Oswald imposter was going around the Dallas area leaving clues that would later implicate Marina's Lee as the President's assassin. Clearly, the imposter had had plastic surgery to look very similar to Oswald. Once again the parameters of the assassination identify the assassins. Only the CIA had the scope and apparatus to arrange plastic surgery for an agent in order to frame Oswald for the

President's murder. In the next few weeks, the imposter would show up in several more places.

The Rifle Range. The Oswald imposter appeared at the Sports Drome Rifle Range on September 28 and again on November 9, 10 and 17. Malcolm Price told the Warren Commission that on September 28, at dusk, a car pulled up to the Sports Drome. The man wanted to have his telescope sighted in on his rifle. Malcolm Price helped him sight-in his telescope. Price told the commission: "...he fired three shots and he scored bull's-eyes with all three—a very tight pattern, and he said, 'Well, I'm completely satisfied.'"[24] Price continued: "When I saw him on television, when they were transferring him from the Dallas jail, I called the FBI the next day."[25] Price last saw the man assumed to be Oswald at the Sports Drome on November 17.

Unfortunately for the CIA, the real Oswald didn't show up in Irving, Texas until October 4. Thus, an imposter was having the gun sighted-in on September 28. Let's not forget Nelson Delgado's testimony: Oswald consistently shot "Maggie Drawers" in the Marines. That is, the real Oswald had trouble just hitting the target, let alone hitting three bull's eyes. Floyd Davis, also an employee of the Sports Drome, saw "Oswald" on November 9, 10, and 17. Davis told the Warren Commission, "The only other thing I would like to say is that several other people mentioned that they saw Oswald on November 17, but they said they didn't want to get involved."[26] Garland Slack also testified. He told the Commission that he saw Oswald at the Sports Drome on November 10 and 17. "And I went to the rifle range and these four or five people knew he had been there, but they were afraid to say anything about it."[27] Slack continued: "He didn't have a very good likeness of him, like the paper pictures. That was him as I saw him at the rifle range, and as I saw him one second before, no, one tenth of a second before he was shot."[28]

Dr. Homer Wood and his son Sterling also saw "Oswald" at the rifle range. This was the week before the assassination. "Oswald" was shooting at his son's right, in the next lane over. His son Sterling spoke to "Oswald". Sterling told the Commission that "Oswald" shot almost always in the bull's eye. He went up to "Oswald" and said, "Sir, is that a 6.5 Italian carbine?" "And he said 'Yes, sir.'"[29]

Dr. Wood told the commission, "I saw him flashed on the television screen at home several times. They would interrogate him and bring him down the hall and bring him back to his cell. This particular time I mentioned to my wife, I said to her, "Honey, that looks exactly like the fellow that was sitting next to Sterling at the rifle range."[30] Dr. Wood said his son also reacted when he saw Oswald on the television screen. "Well, I would say within thirty minutes or an hour he was flashed on the screen and he said to me, 'Daddy, that is the fellow that was sitting next to me out on the rifle range.'"[31]

The imposter was seen by several people on November 9 and 10 at the rifle range. The man looked identical to Oswald. Yet it wasn't Oswald because on these dates, Lee was sitting at home in Irving, Texas with his wife and children. Along with Marina's testimony that Lee was home with her on this weekend is Ruth Paine's corroborating testimony. "There was no long period of time that I was away from the home when he was there."[32] Also, as we've seen, Lee could not drive an auto. But this man was seen driving. Lee's lack of driving ability, by the way, also blew the cover on another impersonation.

The Car Dealership. Two weeks before the assassination, the Oswald imposter visited the Downtown Lincoln Mercury dealership in Dallas. The purpose of the visit was once again to implicate Oswald in the President's murder. He posed as a customer dropping hints that he would soon be coming into a lot of money. He made an obnoxious bore of himself in order to be remembered. This was the final impersonation of Oswald in the frame-up plan for the assassination.

Frank Pizzo. Frank Pizzo was the dealership's assistant manager. His salesman, Albert G. Bogard, waited on Oswald. Pizzo remembered Bogard coming to him and telling him, "He ['Oswald'] doesn't have the down payment, but he will have $200-$300 in a couple of weeks."[33] Pizzo remembered that the demonstration model "Oswald" drove was a red Comet Caliente. Pizzo told the Warren Commission that between 4:00 p.m. and 5:00 p.m. on the day of the assassination someone made the remark that "Al Bogard lost his prospect."[34] In discussing "Oswald" after the assassination, Bogard told Pizzo the following: "Well, you should remember because when I took that man for a ride he drove like a wild man, and besides we had Gene Wilson's car and Gene got mad at me because we used up all his gas." He said, "He drove so fast, he scared the daylights out of me. Don't you remember me coming back and saying how mad I was."[35]

Albert Guy Bogard. Bogard told the commission that "Oswald" came into the dealership on Saturday, November 9, in the afternoon. Bogard told the commission that "Oswald" took him for a ride on the Stemmons Expressway and that "Oswald" drove the demonstration model. Bogard said that "Oswald" drove 60-70 miles per hour. When they came back to the showroom, "Oswald" told Bogard he wasn't ready to buy, that he would be back in a couple or three weeks, and that he had some money coming in.[36]

Bogard informed the commission: "And when he finally started to leave I got his name and wrote it on the back of one of my business cards and never heard from the man anymore. And the day the President was shot, when I heard the name, that he shot a policeman over in Oak Cliff, I pulled out some business cards that I had wrote his name on the back and said, "He won't be a prospect anymore because he is going to jail," and ripped the card up.[37] A commission lawyer wanted to be certain that "Oswald" drove during the demonstration ride, that he did drive 60-70 miles per hour and whether it appeared that "Oswald" knew how to handle a car. Bogard answered affirmative to all three questions. Bogard said he recognized "Oswald" as the man who assassinated President Kennedy and commented that his boss, Frank Pizzo, had also recognized him.[38] He finished his testimony by telling the Warren Commission the following: "We were all standing around listening to the radio and the name came on the radio, and I pulled out this business card with 'Lee Oswald' wrote across it."[39]

Summary of the Impersonation. Once again we have a man who looked almost exactly like Marina's Lee but who was in reality an impersonator. On the day of this impersonation, the real Oswald was actually home with his family in Irving, Texas. Lee also cannot drive. Marina and John Pic, one of Oswald's brothers, and several other people who knew Oswald testified that Lee did not know how to drive a car. Ruth Paine told the commission that Lee had told her he never learned to drive. [40] It was Paine who tried to teach him how to drive and who insisted, not surprisingly, that Oswald at least take the written portion of the state driving test.[41]

I suggest that the reason Paine was so insistent upon Lee's learning to drive was (unbeknownst to her) so that the imposture and framing of Oswald could be complete. As it turned out, Lee never did learn how to drive. So the massive evidence of an "Oswald" driving to a furniture store with his family, and an "Oswald" driving to a rifle range as well as an "Oswald" taking a demonstration ride at a car dealership was quietly dropped from use to incriminate Oswald in the assassination.

First, we have "Oswald" inquiring about a gunsmith at Edith Whitworth's furniture shop. Looking for a gunsmith was meant to show that "Oswald" was putting a telescope on the rifle in anticipation of commiting the President's assassination. While at the furniture store "Oswald" dropped hints about coming into some money shortly, so that

"Oswald" would be seen retrospectively as expecting financial gain, presumably for participating in the assassination. This in turn indicates that others additionally (probably Castro) would be blamed for the President's assassination. To make sure that "Oswald" would be remembered, the CIA had a whole family accompany the imposter. To make sure it was Lee Harvey Oswald who would be identified as the person having visited the furniture shop, the Agency had "Oswald" mention the birthdate of the baby that was accompanying his "family." "Oswald" told Edith Whitworth that his baby had been born on October 20, which was indeed the real Oswald baby's birthdate.

The impersonation of Oswald at the rifle range was intended to implicate him in the assassination as well. Here he could be remembered as an expert marksman thus, fully competent to assassinate the President.

The impersonation of Oswald at the car dealership also was made to implicate him as well. He did make an impression, since several salesmen remembered him. Once again, because Marina's Lee never learned to drive nor obtained a driver's license, all the pre-framing of Oswald with the Oswald imposter was wasted. Not only could the framing not be used but it now could be used against the agency. Once again, it is the parameters of the assassination that identify the assassins.

The continual mentioning by the Oswald imposter of expected financial gain clearly means that the CIA was originally going to involve someone else in the assassination. For Oswald to receive money for killing JFK, someone would have to pay that money. The question is, on whom did the agency plan to pin the assassination besides Oswald. I suggest that with the President's assassination, the CIA was going to kill two birds with one stone. In late September, just before showing up in Irving at Paine's house, Oswald tried three times to obtain a Cuban passport. While visiting the Cuban consulate in Mexico City, Oswald was quite adamant

294 JFK VS. CIA

about receiving a passport. The Cuban Embassy was equally adamant about not letting him have one. This, in spite of his defection to the Soviet Union and his avowed Marxism. As previously mentioned, Oswald was also a member of the Fair Play for Cuba Committee and had been arrested in New Orleans for disturbing the peace while handing out pro-Castro literature. Apparently Cuban intelligence was on to Oswald

I suggest the CIA's original plan was to shoot the President, blame Oswald through circumstantial evidence, and then tie Oswald to Fidel Castro, in order to make Oswald out to be a paid assassin for Cuba. Thus, the CIA could have killed JFK via the assassination team and then, by tying Oswald and Castro together, could have used this as an excuse for the U.S. military to invade Cuba and get rid of Castro, too. With this plan going awry as soon as the shots died down, the CIA decided to be content with what it considered the death of America's number one enemy—John Fitzgerald Kennedy.

* * *

58

THREE WEEKS
AND COUNTING

Actually at this point the assassination plot began to fall apart. The Secret Service learned that an individual named Thomas Arthur Vallee, a Chicago resident who was an outspoken critic of President Kennedy's foreign policy, was in possession of several weapons. Vallee's landlady had reported that he had requested time off from his job on November 2, 1963. On November 2, the President was scheduled to go to Chicago. Vallee was arrested by the Chicago police who found an M-1 rifle, a handgun, and three thousand rounds of ammunition in his automobile. He was a Marine Corps veteran with a history of mental illness while on active duty. He was also a member of the John Birch Society and an extreme critic of the Kennedy administration.[42] Some questions that should have been asked of Thomas Vallee were, how did he get his hands on a U.S. military rifle? Where did he get the money to purchase 3,000 rounds of ammunition? Where was the ammunition purchased? But these questions weren't asked. The President's trip to Chicago on November 2, 1963 was canceled. The Select Committee on Assassinations, which reinvestigated JFK's assassination in 1978, could not determine why the trip was canceled.

The Committee on Assassinations also obtained the testimony of Abraham Bolden, who had been assigned to the Chicago office of the Secret Service during this time period. Bolden alleged that shortly before November 1, the Secret Service received a teletype message in its Chicago office from the FBI. The message stated that an attempt to assassinate the President would be made on November 2. The message elaborated: A four-man team using high-powered rifles would be used and that at least one member of the team had a Hispanic surname. Bolden claimed that while he did not personally participate in the surveillance of the subjects, he learned about it by monitoring Secret Service radio channels in his automobile and by observing one of the subjects detained in the Chicago office.[43]

I suggest the reason President Kennedy's trip to Chicago was canceled was because of the assassination plan. The Secret Service forced the cancellation of the Chicago trip on the President. The President would have demanded the details of why the Secret Service was canceling his trip. I suggest the Secret Service informed him of the assassination conspiracy they had just busted up and that the information had been furnished to them by the FBI.

That there was an assassination attempt set for Chicago in early November meant that Dallas and Oswald were one set of perhaps several sites and "patsies" picked for the President's assassination. That seems only logical. The CIA in early 1963 could only be sure that, at some point in the year, the President would be leaving the confines of the White House to travel across the country. Though it knew that in June the President's trip to Texas had been set for November 21-22, that date could not be counted upon. Presidents change their plans. The trip to Texas could be canceled at anytime. Hence, the CIA had to develop alternate plans, cities, and fall guys.

The record suggests that if Chicago had been picked as a possible assassination site, and if the President had been assassinated in Chicago, Thomas Vallee would have been the fall guy, as Lee Oswald was in Dallas. Bolden had listened to the arrest of the gunmen sent to assassinate the President. He also witnessed the interrogation of one of them. I suggest that, after their arrest, the CIA secured the assassination team's release and the team regrouped two weeks later in Dallas to prepare for the President's visit. I also suggest that the canceling of his trip to Chicago on November 2 made the President stubbornly insistent as to not being a captive in the White House and ironically ensured his making the trip to Dallas on November 22. On the evening of November 19, the President summoned Richard Helms to the White House. If the President inquired as to the validity of the assassination threats, Helms was in a perfect position to play down or deny the existence of a plot, all the while knowing the President was slated for execution within three days.[44]

* * *

59

TWO WEEKS
AND COUNTING

The FBI was investigating one Joseph Milteer for the bombing of a black church. Milteer was a prime candidate, since he belonged to the Ku Klux Klan as well as to several right-wing organizations. The FBI convinced a lifelong friend of Milteer's to become an informant. The informant, William Somerset, tape recorded a conversation. After speaking at length on the church bombing, the conversation turned to Kennedy. Milteer said that a plan to assassinate the President was "in the works." He pointed out several steps that would become the case against Oswald during this taped conversation. Some of the steps were the following:

(1)   That the President could be assassinated using a high-powered rifle fired from an office building.

(2)   That the rifle could be broken down, carried into the building, reassembled then used to fire with.

(3)   That a patsy would be picked up by the police very soon after to throw the police off and satisfy the public.[45]

Furthermore, on the day of the assassination, Milteer, in Dallas, made a long distance call from Dallas to Somerset, saying, "You won't see your friend Kennedy in Miami again." [46] There is also a photograph taken along the motorcade route which shows Joseph Milteer standing on the sidewalk among the crowd.[47] Following the assassination, Somerset again met with Milteer. Milteer commented that things had gone as predicted. Somerset asked if Milteer actually had known in advance of the assassination or had just been guessing. Milteer asserted that he had been certain beforehand.[48]

William Somerset brought the taped recording of his conversation with Milteer to the Miami Police on November 9, 1963. He was an informant for them as well. Both the Miami Police and the Miami Office of the Secret Service were concerned about the threat since the President was coming to Miami on November 18. The Secret Service had Somerset call Milteer at his home in Valdosta, Georgia on November 18 to verify that he was not in Miami.[49]

Between the November 2 assassination attempt on the President in Chicago and the Milteer taped conversation on an impending assassination attempt one week later, certainly both the Secret Service as well as the FBI knew that some organization was intent on assassinating the President. The question for the FBI and the Secret Service was—which organization? There were several right-wing organizations that would be logical suspects. The John Birch Society, the Minutemen Organization, the Ku Klux Klan, even the Mafia could all be suspects. The one organization that was not suspect was actually the one responsible for the assassination, and was about to give itself away.

* * *

60

FIVE DAYS
AND COUNTING

I suggest that after the assassination attempt in Chicago, the FBI launched an all-out offensive against the men conspiring to assassinate the President. With the November 9 taped conversation of Milteer's warning of an impending assassination, the FBI pressured every one of its informants, be they in the Ku Klux Klan, the Minutemen, or the Mafia, to come up with information on the planned assassination. FBI agents who were working undercover in these organizations were told to be alert and pressure informants in order to discover anything relating to an assassination attempt. This all-out effort on the part of the FBI climaxed November 17, 1963.

William S. Walter, in a deposition to the House Select Committee on Assassinations in 1978, stated that on November 17, 1963, while he was on night duty in New Orleans as an FBI security clerk, he received a teletype from FBI headquarters warning of a possible assassination attempt against President Kennedy. The attempt was to take place on

November 22 or 23. Walter recalled that the teletype was addressed to all special agents in charge of FBI field offices; it instructed them to contact criminal, racial, and hate group informants in order to determine whether there was any basis for the threat. Walter contends that this teletype was removed from the New Orleans FBI office files soon after the assassination.[50] Walter also stated that after the assassination he found a single file pertaining to Oswald in special agent in charge, Harry Maynor's locked file cabinet. The name of special agent Warren D. Dubreys appeared on the file jacket.[51]

This second allegation fits neatly with another allegation of one Orest Pena, who claimed that Oswald was an FBI informant who reported to Dubreys. Pena, a bar owner in New Orleans, testified that during the early 1960s he himself was an FBI informant who reported to Dubreys. He told the committee that on several occasions he saw Oswald in the company of Dubreys and other government agents in a restaurant and that he believed Oswald and Dubreys knew each other well.[52] Pena also alleged that Dubreys was "transferred" to Dallas at the same time Oswald was "transferred" there. He added that he was "very, very, very, sure," that Dubreys went to Dallas before the assassination of President Kennedy.[53] Pena also maintained that a few days before he went to testify before the Warren Commission, Dubreys threatened him physically and warned him not to make any accusations against him.[54]

Adrian Alba, an employee and part owner of the Crescent City Garage in New Orleans, also testified before the Assassination Committee. He said he observed an FBI agent in a government vehicle hand Oswald a white envelope. Oswald turned and walked away with it. He'd become acquainted with Oswald, who worked next door at the Reily Coffee Company, in the summer of 1963. He related that one day an FBI agent entered his garage and requested to use one of the Secret Service cars garaged there.

The FBI agent showed his credentials, and Alba allowed him to take a Secret Service car, a dark green Studebaker. Later that day or the next day, Alba observed the FBI agent in the car handing a white envelope to Oswald in front of the Reily Coffee Company. There was seemingly no exchange of words. Oswald, in a bent position, turned away from the car window and held the envelope close to his chest. Alba believed that he observed a similar transaction a day or so later as he was returning from lunch. But on this occasion he was farther away and failed to see what was handed to Oswald.[55]

Henry Wade, the district attorney of Dallas County, told the Warren Commission back in 1964 of a conversation he had with a newspaperman named Hudkins. Hudkins told him, "Now, I have got all kinds of evidence that he is working for the FBI."[56] Wade told the Warren Commission that some of the press had mentioned that Oswald had two voucher numbers in his little black book and this indicated he was working for the FBI and CIA.[57] One of the voucher numbers was #209.[58]

The testimony of Alba and Pena to the House Select Committee on Assassinations, as well as Wade's testimony to the Warren Commission, give credence to Oswald's having been an FBI informant. This, in turn, gives credence to William S. Walter's testimony of having seen an FBI informant's jacket on Oswald, and discovering that his handler was Warren Dubreys. Since certainly Walter was speaking the truth about seeing this file on Oswald, the veracity of his other allegation that the FBI had what amounts to a five-day warning of the impending assassination should not be doubted.

Another bit of evidence that lends credibility to Walter's testimony is the following. Oswald's routine had been to stay at a rooming house in Dallas during the week and come home to the Paine residence on weekends to stay with his wife and children. He did this every weekend without fail—

except once. Oswald did not return to the Paine residence the weekend of November 16 and 17. I suggest that the men who were going to be responsible for the President's assassination met over this weekend in Dallas and went over final plans and details. I also suggest that the reason the FBI found out about the impending assassination, even getting its time and location, was the result of the stepped up investigation of Joseph Milteer and pressure on informants as well as agents in place. Perhaps it was even Lee who tipped off the FBI the evening of November 17, after this last meeting of the conspirators.

May I suggest that Oswald was both an FBI informant as well as CIA agent. The extra money as an FBI informant would have come in handy as the CIA had put him on hold. Whatever Oswald's mission to the Soviet Union was as a CIA agent, it was over. Whether he had succeeded in his mission or blundered cannot be determined. After returning Oswald to the States, the Agency now had someone with impeccable left-wing credentials to infiltrate left-wing organizations. But with the decision to assassinate the President made in late 1962, Oswald was to have a more important role. That role was to take the fall.

So with five days and counting, the CIA had assembled an assassination team in Dallas and finalized plans for the President's assassination. Oswald attended those meetings. By midnight of the 17th, the FBI had learned the planned time and place for the attempt. The only question that remained was whether they could prevent the President's death.

* * *

61

ONE DAY AND COUNTING

Margie Barnes worked in the communications center of the Dallas Police Department. The day before the assassination, she received an engraved invitation to attend the President's luncheon at the Trade Mart. Margie Barnes had no idea how it came about that she was picked to attend the luncheon. She was not political and had not sought the invitation. The following day she was at the Trade Mart waiting for the President's arrival.[59] I suggest Margie Barnes was moved out of the Dallas Police Communications Center specifically because the officers in the dispatch office the day of the assassination were involved in the assassination. As we shall see, the department's communications went down not once but twice that day.

* * *

62

MORNING OF THE

ASSASSINATION

Julia Ann Mercer gave a description of the gunman who fired from in front of the President, giving him a fatal head wound. The shots came from the bushes atop the grassy knoll, to the right and front of the President. Her deposition states that on November 22, 1963, she was traveling down Elm Street and had come to a halt because a truck had stopped in the middle of traffic. One man remained in the driver's seat while the second man got out and reached into the back of the truck, taking out a gun case. The driver, she said, was a man in his '40s, heavy-set. Mercer continued: "The man who took this out of the truck, then proceeded to walk away from the truck and, as he did, the small end of the case caught in the grass or sidewalk and he reached down to free it. He then proceeded to walk across the grass and up the grassy hill which forms part of the overpass."[60]

Mercer described the man with the gun case walking up the hill of the grassy knoll as wearing brown pants and a plaid shirt. Julia Ann Mercer's affidavit is supported by the

Dallas Police Department's radio log of Channel 1 the morning of the assassination:

11:07 a.m.   Could you send a city wrecker to the triple underpass on Elm Street to clear a stalled truck from the route of the escort?

11:16 a.m.   Disregard the wrecker at the triple underpass. We got a truck to pull him out of there.[61]

The assassins were positioning themselves for the President's arrival.

* * *

63

ONE HOUR AND COUNTING

It appears that police officers working in the Dallas Police Department's communications center were in on the assassination. One hour before the President's assassination, and 40 minutes before Air Force One landed in Dallas, Police Channel 1 went silent. From 11:29 a.m. to 11:38 a.m., a full nine minutes, channel 1 was inoperable.[62] This would happen once again later in the day. At exactly the moment the President of the United States was being struck down and for five minutes afterward, Dallas Police Channel 1 was down. I suggest that this first shutdown of police communications was a trial run for the assassination. The CIA, by blanking out police communications at crucial times, helped the true perpetrators to escape.

* * *

64

TWENTY MINUTES
AND COUNTING

Lee Bowers, in his testimony to the Warren Commission in 1964, inadvertently identified the gunmen who were shooting at the President from the bushes located in front and slightly to the right of the President as he approached the underpass. In position as the tower man for Union Terminal, he operated the switches and signals controlling the movements of the trains. From his vantage in the control tower, he had a perfect view of the assassination site. The tower that he worked from was 14 feet above ground. Between his tower and Elm Street was a parking lot, and the grassy knoll. Bowers testified in detail about the two men he saw standing behind a fence atop the grassy knoll:

> Directly in line, toward the mouth of the underpass, there were two men. One man middle aged, or slightly older, fairly heavy set, in a white shirt, and fairly dark trousers. Another younger man, about mid-twenties in either a plaid shirt or plaid coat or jacket.[63]

Lee Bowers description of the two men is extremely similar to Julia Ann Mercer's description of the two men she encountered earlier that morning while driving down Elm Street. Her description of the driver of the truck blocking her way was of a man in his forties and heavy set. Her description of the man who got out of the truck and pulled the gun case from the back of the truck then proceeded up the hill was of a man in his twenties in a plaid shirt.

Lee Bowers continued: "They were facing and looking up toward Main and Houston, and following the caravan as it came down." Bowers said the two men were directly in his line of vision toward the mouth of the overpass. Bowers said he saw the man in the white shirt standing there at the time of the shots, but that he could not see the younger man in the plaid clothing because of the trees, which made him hard to distinguish.[64]

I suggest that Lee Bowers identified the two men who were responsible for the shots that were fired from the bushes of the grassy knoll. The heavy-set man in his 40s in the white shirt was serving as a lookout for the younger man in the plaid shirt who was shooting at the President. It is this younger man in the plaid shirt firing from the bushes who shot the President in his right temple and knocked the President backward. This man is the real assassin.

* * *

65

TWENTY MINUTES AND COUNTING: WEST COAST

Another interesting incident happened at 12:10 P.M. A phone company supervisor overheard a lady saying over and over again, "They're going to shoot the President, they're going to shoot the President." The incident was reported to the authorities.[65] The call had come from Oxnard, California. To me this signifies how widespread the conspiracy was and how much support it had. It is very possible that one of the wives of the economic elite had just been told what was about to take place and became hysterical.

* * *

66

THREE MINUTES
AND COUNTING

Police channel 1 went down again at 12:27 p.m. The outage lasted until 12:34 p.m.[66] Thus, no communication on the main Dallas Police Channel was possible for seven minutes. The President of the United States was gunned down at 12:29 p.m. I suggest this was no accident. A trial run had knocked out Channel 1 an hour earlier. That outage had lasted nine minutes. I suggest that Channel 1 was made inoperable in order to abet the President's assassination. CIA agents worked with certain members of the Dallas Police to knock out communications at a critical time. It would be in those very few minutes before the President's vehicle made the turn onto Elm Street that the gunmen would have been most exposed. The gunman behind the fence would be going into the bushes at this time to take his position. Also, the gunman in the window of the book depository would have to come out of the shadows and position himself to shoot the President. This means that the rifle would have been seen sticking out of the window as he aligned his sight on the

312 JFK VS. CIA

street below. Channel 1 came back on four minutes after the President was shot. Four minutes was sufficient time for the perpetrators to vacate the area. Even more important, with police communications hijacked, Parkland Hospital may not have been notified as hospital staff were caught unaware as the presidential vehicle came to a stop in front of the emergency room. Secret Service agents rushed into the emergency room to retrieve stretchers to place the President and Governor Connally on.

* * *

67

SECRET SERVICE
INVOLVEMENT

The Select Committee on Assassinations found the following:

1) The postcard from March which warned the Secret Service that the President would be shot while being driven in a motorcade was not forwarded to the Dallas office of the Secret Service. Nor was Roy Kellerman, head of the White House detail accompanying the President on his trip to Dallas, made aware of the threat.[67]

2) Neither the documented arrest of Thomas Vallee on November 1st nor the allegations of Secret Service agent Bolden, forwarded to the Dallas office of the Secret Service; nor was Roy Kellerman notified of the arrest.[68]

3) The November 9th taped recording of the Milteer threat warning that the President was going to be assassinated and that it was "in the works" was not sent to the Dallas office of the Secret Service nor was Kellerman notified of its existence. This threat also said the President would be shot from an office building, that a rifle would be used, and that a patsy would be picked up by the police to

throw them off and to satisfy the public. This tape recording was made only 13 days before the President's motorcade through Dallas. The Miami office of the Secret Service was so concerned about the threat that extra precautions were taken, including the phone calls placed to Milteer's hometown of Valdosta, Georgia just to verify that he was not in Miami.[69]

This information should have been routinely routed to the Dallas office of the Secret Service by the Protective Research Section of the Secret Service. It is that section's responsibility to evaluate all information that could be construed as a security threat in any of the cities that a President will visit. That the President was scheduled to visit Dallas on November 22; to travel in a motorcade down streets surrounded by office buildings; and that he would be riding in an open convertible; these should have struck Protective Research as conditions ominously similar to those suggested in the Milteer recording. Especially since Milteer said that it was "in the works." Also, Dallas should have been considered hostile territory because of its virulent right-wing atmosphere, as well as the presence of various right-wing groups there.

Yet this information was never sent to the Dallas field office or made available to the White House detail leaving with the President for Dallas. Existing procedures should have insured that the threats of November, as well as the postcard from the month of March, reached the Dallas office of the Secret Service in time. That the Dallas office was ill-informed means only one thing: There was a conscious effort somewhere to prevent its being sufficiently transmitted. Who was responsible? The head of Protective Research, Robert Houck, or his boss, James Rowley, Chief of the Secret Service, were in an excellent position to stop the information from being transmitted. One of them was the CIA's inside man. In any case, there could have been only one purpose in obstructing the information—to facilitate the assassination of the President. Therefore, at least one member of the Secret Service was a traitor to his President.

But was there a third Secret Service Agent involved in committing treason? A point man as it were, who would guide the President to his death—someone like a treacherous Indian scout leading an army into an incipient ambush, who, just before the attack, slips away to let his confederates complete the butchering.

Winston Lawson of the Secret Service had been sent to Dallas to help the Dallas Police prepare for the President's motorcade. He had been notified November 4 that he would be responsible for arranging the Presidential trip. Lawson, however, had an ominous background. Prior to becoming a Secret Service agent in 1959, Lawson was a counterintelligence agent for the army. He apparently didn't have to serve many years in the boonies before being promoted to the White House detail of the Secret Service. In order for the President to have been ambushed, he would have had to be directed into the ambush. Gunmen were waiting for the President both from the rear, in the book depository, and from the front, in the bushes of the grassy knoll. They wouldn't have been waiting for the President unless they had been certain that he was going to appear in their sights. Kennedy's motorcade was placed deliberately on Elm Street. Whoever was responsible for putting the President on Elm Street was clearly one of the conspirators. Lawson and Forrest Sorrels, who was in charge of the Dallas office of the Secret Service, first rode the proposed motorcade route on November 14, one week before the assassination.[70] The original motorcade route never included a turn off of Main Street and passing in front of the book depository. The President's motorcade was to go from the airport at Love Field to Cedar Springs, Mockingbird Lane, Lemma Avenue, Turtle Creek, Cedar Springs, Harwood and finally to Main Street.[71] The Presidential motorcade would continue on Main Street until Main Street flowed into the Stemmons Freeway.

Warren Commission lawyers repeatedly asked police officers why the Presidential motorcade was routed off of Main Street since there was no logical reason for these movements. Officer Joe Marshall Smith was the traffic officer standing in front of the book depository and whose job was to stop traffic coming from Houston and Elm Streets while the Presidential motorcade passed. He was asked the following question by a Warren Commission lawyer: "What would have prevented the motorcade from going directly down Main Street under the triple underpass, remembering now that the motorcade wanted to go onto Stemmons Freeway?" Smith answered, "I don't know, sir." The Warren Commission lawyer, taken aback by the officer's answer, asked it again: "So far as you know, there was no reason why the motorcade could have gone straight down Main Street and gotten onto Stemmons Freeway down here?"

Officer Smith replied, "Yes, sir." Officer Smith told the lawyer that Main Street flowed into the Stemmons freeway.[72] Thus, what one sees on a map of Dealey Plaza, that Main Street flowed directly into the Stemmons Freeway, was confirmed by traffic Officer Smith.

Dallas Police Department officials told the Warren Commission that the Secret Service was in charge of the motorcade route and made the decision to make the turn off of Main Street to Houston and then to Elm Street. Dallas Chief of Police, Jesse Curry, told the Warren Commission that, "The Secret Service suggested the turn onto Houston Street two days before the arrival."[73]

Other Dallas Police brass confirm that the decision to change the motorcade route to include a turn off of Main onto Houston and then pass in front of the book depository, was made on November 21, at 3:00 p.m., which is the day before the assassination.[74] The decision was made by the Secret Service. Whether the decision to change the route was made the day before the President's arrival, or two days before, isn't as important as the fact that the change was made and that it was made by the Secret Service. And when you are talking about the Secret Service in regard to the motorcade, you are talking about Winston Lawson. What did Lawson have to say about this change in plans? The Warren Commission brought in Winston Lawson, the only Secret Service agent to appear with his own attorney, and questioned him about this decision: "Mr. Lawson, can you tell us why you didn't plan the motorcade so that it went straight down Main Street to turn right onto the entrance to the freeway instead of taking this dogleg on Houston and Elm?"[75] Lawson replied that he was told there wasn't any entrance that way.

This was clearly a fabrication on the part of Winston Lawson. Lawson had already driven over the original route not once but twice prior to the President's arrival. The first time was on November 14, when the route was set which had the President's motorcade staying on Main Street as it flowed into the Stemmons Freeway.

The second time he drove the original route he was in the company of Forrest Sorrels, Chief Batchelor and another command officer of the Dallas Police Department. This was on November 17, five days before the President's visit. Lawson knew full well that Main Street flowed directly into the Stemmons freeway, since he had driven it twice. Yet it was Lawson who made the decision to have the motorcade turn off of Main Street and which led straight to the President's ambush. Could Army Intelligence have been so prescient to place one of their own in the Secret Service in preparation for the Presidential election of 1960? I think it is entirely possible. Thus, Winston Lawson is also a prime suspect in the President's assassination.

* * *

68

FBI NOTIFICATION OF IMPENDING ASSASSINATION

Yet when we look back at the assassination and realize that the FBI had five days' notice of the impending assassination, how is it that the assassination took place and President Kennedy is dead? When William S. Walter received the teletype from FBI headquarters warning of the upcoming assassination attempt, he wasn't the only one being warned. The attempted assassination of an American President is a national security emergency. As such, the CIA and the military and the Secret Service would have been notified as well. The problem was that Helms, at the CIA, and James Rowley, head of the Secret Service, along with the head of Army Intelligence, were the very men conspiring to kill Kennedy.

That is, Hoover's teletyped warning of a possible assassination attempt on President Kennedy had reached the desks of all three department heads the next morning. First thing Monday morning then, November 18, these three individuals had a decision to make. Security for the Dallas operation had been blown—although the FBI had not, as yet, figured out specifically who would be participating in the assassination attempt, it had the time and place of the attempt.

Richard Helms, the mastermind behind the assassination, was now at a turning point. The attempt in Chicago had been thwarted with the arrest of the "executive action" squad members, including Thomas Vallee. If there had been a second plan, for Miami, in anticipation of the President's visit on November 18th, it had been aborted because of the taped conversation of Joseph Milteer. This left Texas and Lee Harvey Oswald. Of course, Helms could cancel the assassination, but that might mean that another chance to kill the President would not present itself for perhaps several months. With the FBI breathing down the necks of the conspirators, it was just a matter of time until it broke up the assassination conspiracy for good. On the other hand, Helms could go with the alternate plan that had been so meticulously set for Dallas. This would mean that J. Edgar Hoover and the FBI would have to be brought into the assassination. This, then, was the decision. So after November 17th but before the 22nd, J. Edgar Hoover was brought into the conspiracy. Once it was explained to Hoover that the CIA and the military were trying to assassinate the President, and that the plan had the full backing of the economic elite as well, Hoover jumped at the chance to help bring down his nemesis. The teletype was ordered destroyed. Henceforth, the FBI's main role would be to find evidence to incriminate Oswald as the President's lone assassin.

* * *

PART VII—THE ASSASINATION OF A PRESIDENT

69

PRELIMINARY
INFORMATION
NECESSARY FOR SUCCESS

There is certain preliminary information that the gunmen needed to enhance their probability of success. I suggest that a traitor in the motorcade was transmitting information to the gunmen waiting for the President in Dealey Plaza. I suggest the traitor was the Army Intelligence Colonel who was riding in the pilot vehicle of the motorcade. The CIA assassination team was monitoring the motorcade's progress via its own frequency. The location of the President's vehicle in the motorcade as well as the seating position of the President was relayed to the assassins. As soon as the President's vehicle entered Elm Street, there would be only a few seconds to shoot at him. So this preliminary information had to be transmited to the gunmen before the President entered Elm Street. The gunmen fired upon an audible signal and I believe this audible signal may have been a starter pistol. This "firecracker" noise caused the President such alarm after his limousine started down Elm. The President is seen looking to his right with a look of consternation and then rapidly turns to his left as if trying to discover the source of the shot.

As the President starts to look forward again, his hands rise up to his throat. The President at this point has been hit with one of the shots. The wound is not fatal. William Greer, the driver of the limousine, stepped on the brakes, slowing the vehicle from 12 miles per hour to 0. At this point, a citizen standing to the President's right began to rapidly and repeatedly unfurl an oversize umbrella. But why was he the only one (of the 200,000 Dallas citizens who had turned out to see the President) carrying an umbrella? It was 70 degrees outside. The Warren Commission never bothered to identify this man. The House Select Committee on Assassinations in 1978 found this citizen. The story he told the Select Committee was highly unbelievable from beginning to end. His rapid unfurling of the umbrella at President Kennedy was a protest intended for Joseph Kennedy, JFK's father, formerly Ambassador to the Court of St. James (in President Franklin D. Roosevelt's administration). I think it is highly doubtful that the man testifying before the Select Committee was the "Umbrella Man" standing alongside Kennedy when the President received the fatal shot. His explanation of why he was carrying an oversize umbrella is also unbelievable.

I believe the "Umbrella Man" was signaling for more shots. The first rounds didn't do the job. Potentially more important to the mechanics of the assassination was the man standing next to the "Umbrella Man." As citizens in the area dive for cover, these two men calmly watch as the President's vehicle takes off under the overpass. Next, they sit down on the curb and talk to each other. Between the time the shots poured into the President and the time they sat down next to each other, the second man looked back toward the bushes of the grassy knoll. He appears to be speaking into a radio as citizens and police officers are rushing up the hill to the fence behind the bushes. I suggest that this second man was in radio communication with his fellow CIA agents and was, in fact, warning them of the crowd that was rushing upon them.

70

THE ESCAPE

James Worrell was a citizen who was standing in front of the book depository at the time the shots were fired. With shots being fired from windows straight above him, Worrell wanted to get out of the line of fire. So he ran alongside the book depository building to Houston Street. He then crossed the street and paused to catch his breath. Worrell told the Warren Commission that while catching his breath he saw a man "come busting" out of the back exit of the book depository.[1] Worrell estimates that this occurred within three minutes of the cessation of the shots. He originally told the FBI that the man he saw "come busting" out the back was Oswald.[2] Yet Oswald has been documented as being in the second floor lunchroom with an officer's gun pointed at his stomach within a minute of the assassination. Oswald was then seen calmly walking out the front door of the depository with a Coke in his hand.[3]

Deputy Sheriff Roger Craig picked up sight of this running man on the other side of the building. Craig testified to the Warren Commission that he was standing on Elm Street when he heard a shrill whistle. He looked up to see a man running from the southwest corner of the building down the grassy knoll where the knoll curved under the overpass. Sheriff Craig said that a light-colored Rambler station wagon was moving "real slow" on Elm Street and the driver was leaning to his right, looking up the hill at the running man. Craig testified that the man was about 5'8" and was wearing blue trousers.[4] Craig said the man was Lee Harvey Oswald.

Oswald was confronted in the second floor lunchroom. He then walked out the front door of the book depository; he caught a taxi cab; who then was the man James Worrell saw "come busting" out the back exit door of the building? As this man ran around the corner of the building thus cutting off sight from James Worrell, Sheriff Craig picked him up. Both men identified the man as Oswald. Why was this man running out the back exit of the school book building? Why did he look identical to Lee Harvey Oswald? What was he doing in the building?

The man James Worrell saw "come busting" out the back door of the book depository was a party to the assassination, but he wasn't Oswald. He was the gunman firing from the sixth floor of the schoolbook building. Since he bore such a close resemblance to Lee Harvey Oswald, he was certainly the Oswald imposter who was running around Dallas in the three weeks prior to the assassination. Since the Oswald imposter looked exactly like the real Oswald, the imposter would not have raised any eyebrows upon entering the building. This CIA agent entered the building at the lunchhour through the backdoor. He then proceeded up the backstairs to the sixth floor. Then he, and perhaps a compatriot, built a sniper's nest and waited for the President. After firing at the President, he ran across the floor of the northwest corner by the stairway, hid the rifle, built a semicircle of cartons around it, ran down the backstairs and out the back door. He then rounded the corner of the back of the building and waited until he saw his escape vehicle slowly moving down Elm Street.

Once he saw the light-colored Rambler he ran down the hill toward the overpass and hopped into the car. This was when Sheriff Craig heard a shrill whistle and turned around to see "Oswald." This was the work of a genius. Even if Lee Harvey Oswald had not shown up for work that day, the Oswald imposter could have walked into the building at noon and, going almost unnoticed, proceed to the sixth floor to shoot the President.

* * *

71

IDENTITY OF THE ACCOMPLICES

Officer Joe Marshall Smith testified to the Warren Commission that he had had his back to the book depository at the time of the shooting. A woman came running up to him in hysterics screaming "They are shooting the President from the bushes."[5] Although Smith was standing directly in front of the book depository, Smith told the Warren Commission that he thought the shots had come from the bushes down near the overpass.[6]

Joe Marshall Smith related how he sprinted down Elm Street and ran up the grassy knoll, hopped the fence atop the knoll and confronted a man on the other side. He pulled his gun on the man and, as he did, the man behind the fence took out Secret Service identification.[7] In an interview in 1978, Smith said that the man behind the fence displayed "regular identification" of the Secret Service.[8]

At the other end of the street where the book depository was located, a similar encounter with fake Secret Service agents occurred. Officer D.V. Harkness rode his motorcycle around to the back of the book depository. As he was about to enter the building through the back entrance, he noticed a group of men who were standing there. His testimony to the commission was the following: "There were some Secret Service agents there. I didn't get them identified. They told me they were with Secret Service."[9]

So there were men identifying themselves as Secret Service agents present in the exact two locations whence the shots came. Within a minute of the shooting, a Secret Service agent is standing behind the stockade fence directly behind the bushes where one set of shots was fired. There are also men identifying themselves as Secret Service agents standing at the back exit to the book depository.

The reality is that there were no Secret Service agents on foot in Dealey Plaza at anytime during the motorcade. Sorrells, head of the Dallas office of the Secret Service, had testified as much. He pointed out that the Secret Service had only a limited number of agents, most of whom were waiting at the cavernous Trade Mart, the destination of the President's motorcade. One agent remained with the plane; the rest were in the motorcade guarding the President and Vice-President. He also stated that he was the first agent back to Dealey Plaza after the President was dropped off at the hospital and, even so, it took him 20 minutes because of the traffic jam caused by the shooting.[10]

Who were these men really, and why were they identifying themselves as Secret Service agents? How did they get their hands on false Secret Service identification? Why weren't the men that Officer Harkness encountered at the back exit to the book depository rushing into the building as Harkness, proceeded to do? The timing was such that the man who Worrel saw "come busting" out of the back door would have run straight into their arms. And why didn't the Secret Service agent standing behind the stockade fence capture the gunman firing from the bushes? Were there any other witnesses who saw "Secret Service" men in Dealey

Plaza immediately after the assassination? A citizen named James Romack told the commission the following:

> I saw a policeman running north toward me. He was running to look to see if somebody was running out of the back of this building. There was two other gentlemen which I never said anything about that taken over. They were FBI or something standing right here at the very entrance, and just stood there.[11]

To clarify things, the commission lawyer said, "You are pointing again to the back stairway that leads up from the street to the dock on the north side of the building."[12] This occurred within four minutes. At the same time, down by the overpass, atop the grassy knoll similar meetings between "Secret Service" agents and citizens were occurring.

Jean Hill, an elementary school teacher who pursued the running man who fled toward the railroad tracks told the Warren Commission that after she hopped the fence she was stopped from pursuing the man by a "tall and slender" man in a suit who "flipped out" identification, claiming he was a Secret Service agent. This appears to be the same man that Officer Joe Marshall Smith pulled a gun on after he hopped the same fence. It was after she was stopped by the "Secret Service" agent that Jean Hill heard several people yelling, "Did he get away, did he get away?"[13]

Officer Seymour Weitzman, who later in the day would find the German Mauser found on the sixth floor of the Book Depository, also encountered "Secret Service" agents. Standing a block over from Elm Street, Weitzman heard the shots fired at the President. He told the commission he heard three distinct shots. "First one, then the second two seemed to be simultaneous." Weitzman continued: "Somebody said the shots or firecrackers (whatever it was at that time—we still didn't know the President was shot) came from the wall. I immediately scaled that wall.[14] Weitzman continued:

> Yes sir, other officers, *Secret Service* as well,... there was something red in the street and I went back over the wall and

somebody brought me a piece of what he thought to be a firecracker and it turned out to be, I believe, I wouldn't quote this—but I turned it over to one of the Secret Service men and I told them it should go to the lab because it looked to me like human bone. I later found out it was supposedly a portion of the President's skull."[15]

Implicit in Weitzman's testimony is that there were at least two Secret Service agents over the wall and fence area.

Another citizen's testimony gives us more information. S.M. Holland testified to the Warren Commission about the shot originating from the bushes atop the grassy knoll. From his position on the overpass, he could witness the entire assassination scene. After the shots were fired, Holland ran off the overpass and went straight for the bushes and stockade fence area, where he said the shot came from. He witnessed a hundred footprints in one little spot behind the stockade fence.[16] He noticed mud on a car bumper that had backed up against the fence. Holland also saw something else; "...a number of your federal agents went out there then and SECRET SERVICE men."[17] The "Secret Service" agents started searching for bullet shells behind the fence.

Howard Brennan was another citizen who had extensive contact with the men identifying themselves as "Secret Service" agents. While sitting on a retaining wall in a park across the street from the book depository, Brennan looked up and saw a man with a rifle sitting in the sixth floor window of the book depository. The man was sitting sidewise on the windowsill.[18] He saw the man shoot at the President and afterward pause after the shot watching to see if he'd hit his mark.[19]

After the shots were fired, Brennan immediately told a police officer that he had seen a man firing from the window. The police officer took Brennan to a parked vehicle located in front of the book depository.[20] The car was parked on Houston Street and was filled with "Secret Service" agents. Brennan told the "Secret Service" agents what he saw. Brennan also told the Warren Commission that it was less than five minutes from the time of his diving from the retaining wall as the shots were fired, to the time he crossed the street and spoke with the policeman and was taken to the parked car.[21] Clearly, if it was near five minutes from the time of the shots to the interview with the "Secret Service" agents in the parked vehicle, the agents were not bona fide Secret Service agents.

Remember that Secret Service agent Sorrell's testimony that there were never any Secret Service agents on foot in Dealey Plaza at anytime during the motorcade and that all agents in the area left with the motorcade as it raced to Parkland Hospital. Agent Sorrell also told the Warren Commission that he was the first agent to reach Dealey Plaza after the assassination and that it took him twenty minutes to do so because of the traffic jam. So the question is raised once again, who were these men sitting in a parked vehicle in front of the book depository as the President was being gunned down on Elm Street? Who were these men? What were they doing in Dealey Plaza at the very moment the President was shot? Why didn't they capture the gunmen who were doing the firing?

* * *

72

MILITARY INTELLIGENCE

The Warren Commission never pursued an investigation of these men though their existence was known to the Commission. This is *guilt by omission*. Fortunately, the House Select Committee on Assassinations in 1978 did manage to identify these fake Secret Service agents. In so doing, the Select Committee made the mechanics of the President's assassination even clearer. First, let us consider the Final Report on the Assassination: The Committee did obtain evidence that military intelligence personnel may have identified themselves as Secret Service agents or that they might have misidentified themselves as such. Robert E. Jones, a retired Army Lieutenant Colonel who in 1963 was commanding officer of the military intelligence region encompassing Texas, told the Committee that from eight to twelve military intelligence personnel in plainclothes were assigned to Dallas to provide supplemental security for the President's visit. He indicated that these agents had identification credentials and, if questioned, they would most likely have stated that they were on detail to the Secret Service.

The Committee sought to identify these agents so that they could be questioned. The Department of Defense, however, reported that a search of its files showed "no records," indicating any Department of Defense protective services in Dallas. The Committee was unable to resolve the contradiction.[22] Jones also testified that the eight to twelve military intelligence agents who performed liaison functions with the Secret Service in Dallas on the day of the assassination wrote "after action" reports and these reports were maintained in the Oswald file.[23]

To Jones' knowledge, neither the FBI nor any law enforcement agency ever requested a copy of the Military Intelligence file on Oswald. To his surprise, neither the FBI, Secret Service, CIA or the Warren Commission ever interviewed him.[24] Access to Oswald's military intelligence file, which the Department of Defense never gave to the Warren Commission, was not possible because the Department of Defense had destroyed the file as part of a general program aimed at elimination of all of its files pertaining to nonmilitary personnel.[25]

The House Select Committee on Assassinations in 1978 revealed a photograph taken of the sniper's nest shortly after the shots had been fired at the President. The photograph was snapped by an army intelligence officer named Powell. Powell was standing diagonally across the corner of Elm and Houston. From whom did Officer Powell receive orders to be in Dealy Plaza? What are the names of his fellow army intelligence officers working with him during the President's trip to Dallas? What was their assignment? Why have we never heard from this Army Intelligence team? Finally, the report tells us that Colonel Jones was the one responsible for letting the FBI know that the name A.J. Hidell was an alias of Oswald's.[26]

* * *

73

ANALYSIS OF THE TESTIMONY OF LT. COLONEL JONES

Again, Lt. Col. Jones testified that he had eight to twelve Army intelligence agents acting in liaison with the Secret Service during the President's trip to Dallas on the day of the assassination. Yet, Department of Defense records show that no Defense Department protective service personnel were in Dallas.

Also, Lt. Col. Jones testified that his military intelligence agents wrote "After Action" reports of the assassination and he was the one who contacted the FBI and gave them information about Oswald having an alias of A.J. Hidell. He stated that neither the Warren Commission, the FBI, nor the CIA inquired about any of the information military intelligence had on Oswald.

Why was this information absent from the otherwise comprehensive 26 volumes of Warren Commission evidence, consisting of police reports, Secret Service reports, FBI reports, extensive background checks of both Oswald and Jack Ruby, the testimony of citizens who were in Dealey Plaza at the time of the shooting, expert medical opinions, requests to the Soviet Union about Oswald's time there, etc.? In fact, every detail about the assassination that the Warren Commission could uncover was included.

Millions of dollars were spent on the investigation, yet Lt. Col. Jones would have us believe that the Warren Commission and the FBI did not have the least interest in the "After Action" reports of a group of military intelligence officers acting in liaison with the Secret Service at the time of the assassination. Not to mention wanting to know how it was that military intelligence knew about Oswald using the alias of A.J. Hidell. Or that Lt. Col. Jones would not have volunteered the information that military intelligence had if the FBI or the Warren Commission lawyers had not requested it. Especially since he so readily volunteered information that Oswald had an alias, an alias that could tie him to the murder weapon.

Should we also believe that the Department of Defense would destroy its intelligence file on Oswald as a matter of routine? Why can't it be determined who gave the order to destroy the file or which person actually destroyed it?

A military intelligence team was sent to Dallas to "run interference" for the gunmen who were shooting at the President. When the decision was made by the U.S. military to sanction the CIA's plan for the assassination, the military then took an active interest in its outcome. Hence, Lt. Col. Jones and his military intelligence team were sent to Dallas to assist in the assassination. The men posing as Secret Service agents were members of the military intelligence team that Jones referred to. Supposedly they were acting in liaison with the Secret Service during the President's visit. The "Secret Service" agents behind the book depository identified themselves as Jones testified they were supposed to do if confronted. Only their complicity explains why these "Secret Service" agents were not rushing into the building through the back entrance, to capture whoever was firing from the building. These men also did not capture the man, seen by James Worrell, who fled out the back exit of the building, of course. The shots fired at President Kennedy from the front came from the bushes of the overpass which were directly in front of the stockade fence where another "Secret Service" agent was standing. Why didn't this "Secret Service" agent capture the man who fired at the President? Indeed, why didn't he capture the man before the assassin fired the shot? We also know for certain that an army intelligence colonel rode in the pilot vehicle of the motorcade. We also know that an army intelligence officer by the name of Powell was on Elm Street at the time of the assassination.

Why was the military intelligence unit centered in Dealey Plaza where the President was assassinated? Why not have stationed them at the Trade Mart or at the airport or anywhere else along the motorcade route? The answer, of course, is that the military intelligence team was assisting in the President's assassination.

* * *

74

THE PRE-AUTOPSY

There are certain things the CIA could plan for in regard to the assassination and there were going to be things happening that could not be foreseen. So the agency would have to rely on its improvisational skills. Those improvisational skills proved to be as well executed as its planning genius. Take the CIA's handling of the discovery of the 7.6 caliber German Mauser by Dallas Police. This should have been absolutely devastating to the agency. But someone with a cool head thought it out and decided to combine the discovery of the German Mauser with the 6.5 caliber Italian Mannlicher Carcano which was to be used to frame Oswald—to make them one and the same. Thus, the Agency was able to turn a minus into a plus.

The Abraham Zapruder film of the assassination could also have been extremely devastating to the conspiracy. Certainly, the agency was prepared to pounce on any citizens taking moving pictures of the assassination, and probably seized their share of film taken by citizens. Unfortunately for the agency, in regard to the Zapruder film, Sorrels reached Abraham Zapruder before the CIA. He then immediately made copies of the film. Once again the agency relied on its improvisational skills. A news organization bought the film rights from Abraham Zapruder and locked the film away from the public for ten years. That was the next best thing to not having the film in the first place. Certainly, the CIA was behind the purchase of the film.

One aspect of the assassination that could be planned for and would be expected was that an autopsy would be performed on the President. The CIA knew than an autopsy could also bring down the conspiracy. Several bullets had flown in the direction of the President from different directions, front and back. For example, a ballistics test could prove that a recovered bullet *was not* fired from Oswald's Italian Mannlicher Carcano. This would lead to a conclusion that more than one weapon was used to shoot at the President, which would mean a second assassin, which in turn would point to a conspiracy.

The only way to make sure no evidence of a conspiracy was discovered at the autopsy was by arranging for a pre-autopsy to remove any evidence from the body that would give away the conspiracy. A pre-autopsy could also be used to disguise any wounds made from shots he took in front, making it look like all the shots were taken from behind—hence, that they all came from the book depository. How did the CIA get away with it?

The official version is that the President's casket was wheeled out of Parkland Hospital and flown aboard Air Force One to the Bethesda Naval Hospital. The official autopsy would be conducted and all would be well and proper. Diane Hamilton Bowron was a nurse at Parkland Hospital. What does she say happened with the President's body after he was pronounced dead.

"After he died, she [Mrs. Kennedy] kissed his hand, then took off her wedding ring and slipped it on his wedding finger. It came just up to the knuckle. We all wept with Mrs. Kennedy."[27] Nurse Bowron then helped lift the President's body into the bronze casket which had been brought to the hospital. In an affidavit written shortly after the assassination, Bowron gives more detail:

> Miss Hinchcliff and myself prepared the body by removing the remaining clothes, we then washed the blood from the President's face and body, and covered him with a sheet. We placed the President's body on a plastic sheet in the casket.[28]

During her testimony, Diane Bowron also told the Warren Commission: "We wrapped some extra sheets around his head so it wouldn't look so bad."[29] These extra sheets will actually give away the conspiracy and prove that a pre-autopsy was performed on the President. Doris Nelson also helped in preparing the President's body.

> Mr. O'Neill of O'Neill Ambulance Company arrived with a bronze casket. Miss Hinchcliff came out and asked for some plastic to put inside the casket. I sent Mrs. Hutton to the second floor to obtain a plastic mattress cover. I asked David Sander to assist the nurses in preparing the President's body before placing it in the casket.[30]

The fact that a bronze casket was delivered to the hospital and the President was placed in this casket will also point to a pre-autopsy being performed on the President. Doris Nelson continued:

> The President was having extensive bleeding from the head and they had wrapped four sheets around it but it was still oozing through, so I sent her to the second floor to obtain a mattress cover to put in the casket prior to putting his body in the casket.[31]

Pat Hutton was the nurse sent to fetch the plastic mattress cover. She and David Sanders lined the inside of the coffin with the plastic.[32] This all took place in the hour after the President was pronounced dead but before he was taken out of the hospital by the Secret Service. If everything is legitimate, the following would have happened: The President would have arrived at Bethesda Naval Hospital in an expensive bronze casket, he would have been lying on a plastic mattress, he would have had four sheets wrapped around his head and a sheet would have been covering his body. But this is hardly how the body arrived at Bethesda. David Lifton, the author of *Best Evidence*, interviewed Paul O'Connor, the medical assistant who opened the casket when it arrived at Bethesda. He describes the casket as a grey shipping casket. The President was in a "body bag." A towel was wrapped around the President's head. So between Dallas and Bethesda, an expensive bronze casket transformed into a grey shipping casket. A plastic mattress cover became a body bag. Four bloody sheets metamorphosed to one towel wrapped around his head. Clearly, someone effectively intercepted the President's body. The reason for intercepting the body was clearly to remove evidence that multiple gunmen had fired at the President. All bullets and bullet fragments had been removed from the body.

But how did the CIA hijack the body? Our first clue is given to us by Jane Carolyn Wester, who worked at Parkland Hospital and was on duty when she received a phone call.

> At noon, around noon—noontime—I'm not sure as to the exact time it was. I was relieving the secretary for lunch and the phone rang. Someone in the pathology department asked if the President was in the operating room and I answered them, 'No'; and they said that a Secret Service agent was down there and as soon as the President did arrive in the operating room, would I please call them.[33]

A short time later she received a second phone call.

> I received a phone call from the emergency room asking us to set up for a craniotomy. That's an exploration of the head. Immediately following that, I received a call to set up for a thoracotomy, which is an exploration of the chest. Shortly thereafter, Governor Connally arrived in the operating room by stretcher."[34]

Looking at her statement, the first thing we are confronted with is that she received the first phone call before the President arrived at Parkland Hospital. The President wasn't shot until 12:30 p.m. More important, there were never any Secret Service agents in the pathology department and certainly not at the time when the President was being brought into the hospital. Yet here is Wester receiving a phone call from pathology. She is told that a Secret Service agent is standing by. We know from the record that there was a group of men all over Dealey Plaza identifying themselves as "Secret Service" and that these men were in reality Army Intelligence and played a role in the President's assassination. I suggest the "Secret Service" agent standing by in pathology was just such an agent. Army intelligence was standing by to recover the President's body at Parkland Hospital.

The order of the phone calls is important. If the calls were legitimate, Wester should have first received the call to set up the operating room for the craniotomy and the thoracotomy. Then later, at least until after the President was pronounced dead at 1 p.m., she should have received the call from pathology. But the order is reversed. First comes the call from pathology even before JFK arrived at the hospital or certainly before the Parkland doctors started working on him. I believe army intelligence was waiting at Parkland Hospital before the President was shot. It was ready to receive the President's body and transport it to the pre autopsy which was likewise set up and staffed with military surgeons who were to eliminate physical evidence pointing to a conspiracy. The question is, how did they do it?

Dr. Earl Rose, the Dallas County medical examiner, insisted that the President's body remain at Parkland Hospital in Dallas. The Secret Service agents, beside themselves with grief for having lost not just a President but a friend, were equally insistent that the President's body go back to Washington. Things got very ugly and finally the Secret Service pushed pass Dr. Rose and brought JFK's body to Air Force One. Many people think that what Dr. Rose did was very noble and correct in trying to keep the President's body in Dallas. I wonder though. If you are going to assassinate the President in Dallas and have the pre-autopsy in Dallas, the last thing you would want is to have the President's body be removed from Parkland Hospital, at least by the Secret Service.

Perhaps Dr. Rose is innocent and was just doing his duty. Then again, perhaps he was adamant because the pre-autopsy was set up to be done in Dallas and his part was to make sure the conspirators had some time with the body before the official autopsy began. If the pre-autopsy was to be done in Dallas, how would the conspirators gain access to the body?

Frank Price was the administrator of Parkland Hospital. He tells us of an incident simultaneous with the scuffle for the body and cleaning of the President's body. A Secret Service agent approached him and asked if there wasn't another way the President (Johnson) and Mrs. Kennedy could be taken out of the building: "I told him there was another exit and if he would come with me I would walk it off for him. We walked down to inspect the tunnel, then returned to the surgery area of the hospital."[35]

The administrator and the Secret Service agent had taken the emergency Room elevator down to the basement, where a winding tunnel led to an exit. When they returned topside, President Johnson and the Kennedy entourage had departed the hospital.

I suggest the following happened. After the President's body was placed in the casket but before the Secret Service whisked the coffin away, FBI agents or intelligence personnel closed off the trauma room that contained the President's body. They lifted the President's body from the casket and placed it on a gurney. They may have placed some leaded weights in the casket. With the President's body secure on the gurney with a sheet covering him and surrounded by FBI agents, the weight-laden casket was handed to the Secret

Service. As soon as the Secret Service left with the reporters and politicians, the FBI and/or intelligence personnel sequestered the President's body, took it to the emergency room elevator, directed it through the tunnel in the basement and out of Parkland to a waiting vehicle. The vehicle then took the body to another location in Dallas and the pre-autopsy began. Because the surgeons were already set up to do the pre-autopsy and because high-speed military aircraft were used, the conspirators were able to beat Air Force One back to Bethesda, Maryland.

Until personnel at Parkland Hospital, an administrator, a nurse or security person, comes forward with information that Kennedy's body did not leave Parkland when everyone thinks it did, the only thing we can be sure of is that there was a pre-autopsy, which completed the perfect murder.

* * *

PART VIII—CONCLUSION

75

1975

From the time the Warren Report was published in 1964 until the early 1970s, the American public was satisfied that Oswald had acted alone in assassinating President Kennedy. However, as the years went by, the Warren Report was reduced to questionable findings by the first generation assassination researchers. At the same time, political assassinations continued. RFK was assassinated along with Martin Luther King in 1968. George Wallace was cut down during his Presidential bid in 1972. With American leaders being struck down left and right, first the public and then Congress became aware of the game being played upon them.

By 1974, Congress was deeply suspicious that the CIA may very well have assassinated John F. Kennedy. In 1975 the Senate Select Committee on Governmental Operations with respect to Intelligence Activities was formed. The CIA was about to be raked over the coals. The revelations of the Church Committee (as it was commonly known) brought about serious consideration on the part of Congress that the CIA was involved. A movement to renew the investigation of the Kennedy assassination was snowballing. The Senate came very close to reopening the matter but it was eventually left to the House of Representatives to conduct the second major investigation into the assassination. This investigation occurred over 1977-1978.

In 1975, the CIA was panicking. The Senate was breathing down its neck. Each revelation of CIA wrongdoing and treason was a hammer blow to the agency's credibility. It became clear that the one thing that could destroy the agency and bring about its permanent demise would be for Congress to discover that it had, in fact, assassinated President Kennedy. To prevent this, starting in 1975, the CIA began the slaughter anew.

Sam Giancana. Sam Giancana was murdered in 1975, shortly before he was to testify before the Senate Select Committee on Governmental Operations with respect to Intelligence Activities. The common assumption is that Giancana was murdered by the Mafia. Yet, what Sam Giancana could have told the Church Committee was far more damaging to the CIA than to the Mafia.

If Giancana would have told the Church Committee that John Kennedy had used him to spy on the CIA, if Giancana would have added that JFK fired the top three men at the Agency after discovering they were going behind his back in trying to assassinate Fidel Castro, the Select Committee and Congress could then have perceived that the CIA had a motive to assassinate Kennedy. And remember, Giancana was a direct player in the assassination himself. At the very least he assisted the CIA by ordering Jack Ruby to kill Oswald. Giancana could have swapped immunity for confessing his and the CIA's role in the assassination.

It was the CIA that had everything to lose, not the Mafia, if Giancana appeared before the Select Committee. I suggest that Giancana was murdered by the CIA in order to protect its existence as a function within government.

Johnny Rosselli. Johnny Rosselli, of course, knew everything that Giancana knew about the CIA. Once again, Rosselli wouldn't tell the Select Committee anything that could hurt the Mafia in regard to CIA Mafia plots against Castro. What worried the CIA was not Rosselli's squawking about CIA-Mafia plots, although they were certainly bad enough, but that he'd spill the beans about the Kennedy assassination. Certainly Rosselli was aware the CIA had assassinated JFK. Rosselli was told about the impending assassination in September 1962 by William Harvey. With all the information that Johnny Rosselli had, he was a walking time bomb. In all likelihood the CIA was behind Rosselli's murder. Rosselli was killed in 1976.

Roger Craig. Roger Craig was the Deputy Sheriff who saw a man who looked identical to Oswald run from the book depository down the hill and hop into a slow-moving vehicle that was traveling down Elm Street. His testimony brought great trials and tribulations to the Deputy in the years afterward. In May of 1975, Roger Craig wrote an answer to a question put to him by Congressman Thomas Downing of Virginia. Congressman Downing was calling for a reopening of the JFK assassination. Roger Craig informed Congressman Downing that three shells found in the snipers lair of the book depository were lined up next to each other. That same month Roger Craig died—on May 15, he was found dead from a gunshot wound. The death was ruled a suicide. Roger Craig was one of the few witnesses remaining from the Warren era who had not died during the CIA's subsequent reign of terror. I think it entirely possible that the CIA, planning ahead, wanted to eliminate this man as a witness, should he be called to testify, should another investigation be reopened. The legacy of terror paid off in dividends. When the House Select Committee on Assassinations conducted their hearings throughout 1977 and 1978, hardly a witness from 1964 could be found. What is of interest is that the CIA did not just go after private citizens and top Mafia leaders in its continuing effort to block the discovery of its role in assassinating President Kennedy. The CIA as it turns out, eats its own.

CIA Eats Its Own. Sheffield Edwards testified to the Senate Select Committee about his role in setting up the CIA-Mafia partnership to eliminate Castro. After testifying in 1975, the Select Committee wanted to call him back for additional testimony. Unfortunately, Edwards died in the interim. Desmond Fitzgerald was another CIA agent taking orders from Richard Helms. Fitzgerald died a few years after the assassination as well.

William Harvey testified at length in 1975. He told the Select Committee about the execution squad he commanded and of the CIA-Mafia alliance against Castro. He placed the responsibility for all that he had undertaken squarely on the shoulders of Richard Helms, from whom he took orders. Harvey's testimony was quite an eye opener for the Committee. William Harvey became deceased in 1976.

It must have appeared to the Senate Select Committee on Governmental Operations with respect to Intelligence Activities that appearing before the committee, or just being called to appear was a death sentence. I suggest that the murders of Sam Giancana and Johnny Rosselli, as well as the sudden deaths of CIA personnel, stimulated the House of Representatives to reopen the Kennedy assassination and try to get to the bottom of the matter. Hence, we have the formation of the House Select Committee on Assassinations in 1977.

It was after the Church Committee held its hearings and before the House opened up its investigation of JFK's assassination, that the U.S. government finally struck back at CIA. In 1976, Jimmy Carter became President. He appointed Stansfield Turner as DCI. Director Turner fired 200 top CIA agents. Why were these 200 agents fired in a single move? I suggest that Congress was aware that the CIA had assassinated JFK. Among the men who made Turner's hit list were those CIA agents who had taken part. I suggest these 200 men had spent their careers committing treason. In order to gain control of the agency, yet not leave the country defenseless, the decision was made to leave the CIA intact but to purge it of its more extreme elements.

It was all for naught though. A fantasy. In 1977 while the House Select Committee was deep in its investigation of the President's assassination, six FBI agents involved in the original investigation were scheduled to testify. All six died within six months of one another and before testifying. The evil autonomy had been institutionalized. The CIA was back.

* * *

76

CONCLUSION

A question in the minds of many Americans is how did the CIA get away with it? With the CIA combining with the military to assassinate JFK, as well as the FBI being used to cover up the murder, there are too many cooks standing over the fire and certainly someone, somewhere, sometime, would have leaked word. How, then, could the conspirators have gotten away with it? The answer, of course, is that they didn't. Starting in the mid-1960s, assassination researchers pouring over the 26 volumes of Hearings and Exhibits produced for the Warren Commission, learned that Oswald didn't shoot anyone. They also were able to determine that the President was led into an ambush and caught in a crossfire. The first generation of assassination researchers also learned there had been a coverup by the government. By 1967, even the next President of the United States, Lyndon Baines Johnson, was convinced that the CIA had assassinated JFK. In the early 1970s, Congress was coming to the same conclusion. In 1979, the conclusion of the House Committee on Assassinations was that JFK had died as a result of a conspiracy. The matter was then handed over to the Department of Justice, where it has since been laid to rest.

So, the CIA didn't get away with it. By 1979, both Houses of Congress, as well as every President after Kennedy, as well as the first generation of assassination researchers, all knew of the CIA's role. The only ones walking around in the dark on the entire planet are the American people. Oliver Stone, with his motion picture "JFK," finally brought the truth to the last ones to find out, the citizenry. So the answer to the question of how did they get away with it is they didn't. But a more relevant question is, why have they gone unpunished?

The conspirators have gone unpunished based on practicality. Once Congress, and especially the Senate, understood the CIA's role, it had two alternatives. On the one hand, it could dismantle the agency. If they did this though, what organization would there be to protect America from terrorists and foreign enemies? Having an organization that can act in extra-legal ways is invaluable in combating such foreign enemies—as long as America is successful, she will always have her enemies. For Congress to dismantle the CIA for killing Kennedy would have left the nation defenseless from present and future enemies. On the other hand, if Congress brought the agency under political control and weakened it, as well as reformed it by eliminating those CIA personnel bent on autonomy, then the agency could still be used to thwart present-day enemies. I believe Congress chose the lesser of two evils. The decision was made to allow the CIA to remain in existence but eliminate its autonomy and bring it under political control. To confront the American people with the horror of the Central Intelligence Agency having assassinated President Kennedy would bring about a demand from the citizens to dismantle it. Our Senators didn't think that would be the wisest choice.

Still, why did it take over a decade for Congress to figure things out? In organizing the President's murder, the CIA used three tactics to its distinct advantage in both perpetrating the murder and covering it up. The first was the element of surprise. Hardly any American citizens knew what the CIA was, let alone imagined that this agency might be behind the President's assassination.

It was only after the James Bond movies of the mid-1960s that the American people learned that there were such things as secret agents with a license to kill. Even so, these movies could be dismissed as fiction. A more important obstacle was the innocence and inborn patriotism of the American people. It was incomprehensible that an American institution would assassinate an American President. It was so unAmerican. It was only after the scandal of Watergate in the early 1970s that the American people began to realize that government may not be all that clean. The wholesomeness of what we learned in eighth grade civics class might, in fact, be tainted with immorality. Over a decade had to pass before Americans could look back retrospectively to the Kennedy assassination to make a fresh and hitherto unthinkable analysis of his murder. Only after the Senate investigated the CIA in 1975 did the pieces start to fall into place. Only then did the CIA's advantage in the element of surprise come to an end.

The second tactic the agency used was the concept of compartmentalization. To understand the usefulness of compartmentalization in the President's assassination, let us take a look at the men who were firing at the President. These men were professional gunmen in the CIA's employ. The first assassination team had been formed in 1961. Perhaps the original assassination team were the ones firing at the President. Perhaps though, this assassination team was formed in 1963 for this particular project. The bottom line, though, is that they were professional gunmen, hardly any different then the gunmen who were hired by cattle barons to kill homesteaders on America's open plains a century before. These men had a job to do and they did it well. Even if they had been caught in the act of firing at the President their knowledge of the assassination would have been severely limited. Of course, they know it is a CIA-sanctioned hit. And they know that William Harvey, their team leader, is CIA. But they certainly don't know any more than this. All they know is that the target will be riding into their gunsights down Elm Street and that they will have only several seconds to kill the target. All these men cared about was doing a professional job, getting paid, and leaving town. The gunmen only knew what they needed to know in order to do their job and nothing more. This is compartmentalization.

When we look at the army intelligence unit that was in Dealey Plaza acting as backups for the gunmen, certainly they know their own organization backed the assassination. Lt. Col. Robert E. Jones, their commander, was head of Army Intelligence, Southern Command. Certainly they know that he had to have received his orders from higher up.

No one in the military does anything without orders. But they may very well not have known anyone else in the military high command who sanctioned this hit. These men did not do the actual shooting at the President nor are they part of the framing of Oswald. Nor did they have anything to do with the shooting of Oswald in the basement of the Dallas Police Department. The role of this army intelligence team is to provide the logistical support for the assassination. Certainly James Rowley, the Chief of the Secret Service, was in on the assassination since he was actively blocking information from reaching the Dallas office of the Secret Service that indicated an assassination attempt would be made in Dallas on the Presidential trip. Winston Lawson is highly suspect for having placed the President's vehicle on Elm Street, but this is their limited role in the President's assassination. The CIA will do the rest. FBI agents picked by J. Edgar Hoover would be responsible for covering up the assassination but the FBI took no part in the actual assassination beyond allowing it to transpire.

Even Charles Batchelor and Patrick Dean of the Dallas Police Department, who are most likely involved in Ruby's killing of Oswald, needn't have been involved in the President's murder. Thus, the entire assassination from top to bottom is compartmentalized and effectively insulates the CIA from being detected as the organization responsible for the President's assassination.

But it is in the third tactic of the composition of the assassination that proved to be the most useful tool to the conspirators in their act of treason. The third tactic is murder. Murder was the single most effective tool the CIA had at its disposal in keeping the lid on the Kennedy assassination. In case any leaks occurred, in case any FBI or CIA or military personnel with firsthand knowledge started to let the secret slip, the CIA was there with the ultimate tool of censorship. We see a wholesale slaughter of American citizens occurring in the first years after the President's assassination. James Worrel, who saw the assassin who fired from the book depository rushing out the back exit of the building, was dead within two years of his testimony to the Warren Commission. Lee Bowers, who saw the two assassins at the mouth of the overpass in the bushes atop the grassy knoll, was also dead within two years of his testimony.

William Whalley, the cab driver who picked up Oswald, as well as Albert Guy Bogard, the car salesman who gave a demonstration ride with the Oswald impersonator, also were dead within two years of their testimony. One can only guess at how many dozens of other citizens were murdered by the CIA for something they saw or something they said or something they knew. We have another wholesale slaughter taking place from 1975 to 1978, as the CIA tried desperately to avoid the Senate's censorship and perhaps its legislating it out of business. CIA agents died after testifying in front of the Senate Select Committee on Intelligence. A half dozen FBI executives during the Kennedy Administration who were called to testify never made it, dying during the same year. Even the mob could find no cover from CIA attack. Mob figures who had been involved in the President's assassination were murdered. Sam Giancana, the mob boss of Chicago who ordered Jack Ruby to kill Oswald, died just before he was scheduled to appear before the Intelligence Committee. Johnny Rosselli, the West Coast gangster who had been up to his neck in plotting assassinations with the CIA in the precious decade, was killed shortly after he testified in front of the Intelligence Committee. Even Robert Kennedy's old nemesis, Jimmy Hoffa, died in 1975. By 1978, the Florida mob boss, Santos Trafficante, was so afraid of being murdered he would not venture outside his front doors.

Throughout the decade and a half after the President's assassination, when any chink in the conspirators' armor appeared, the CIA rushed in with their professional assassins. By using the tactics of surprise, compartmentalization and murder, what is surprising is that any information has escaped about the truth of the assassination, let alone bringing the traitors to justice. But can there be no justice for JFK and the American people? The traitors who murdered JFK are like Nazi war criminals who escaped to South America before the fall of Berlin. Like aging Nazi dinosaurs, these men walk free, enjoying their government pensions, which have served only to reward them for committing treason and murder and evil.

The assassination conspiracy is like a long chainlink fence but this fence has many weak links. It can also serve as a blueprint for justice. Enough pressure at any number of weak points can break the chain and the whole fence will come crashing down. One weak link is that there were 12 Army intelligence officers in Dealey Plaza when President Kennedy was struck down. The Army claims not to have a record of these men, since everything connected to the Kennedy assassination was supposedly destroyed, but this, of course, is a fabrication. The Army did not want the House Select Committee on Assassinations to find these men because they were involved in assassinating the President.

Arrest these men, isolate them, and hand them over to Special Forces for interrogation and the truth of the Kennedy assassination will be known in less than 24 hours. There were FBI agents at Parkland Hospital and who were working out of the Dallas office of the FBI during the Kennedy assassination. Arrest all of these agents and interrogate them the way you would a suspected member of the Viet Cong during the Vietnam War. There was a group of Bureau of Alcohol, Tobacco and Firearms (ATF) agents who rushed into the book depository after the shootings. These men in my opinion were really CIA agents with fake Treasury identification. First, go into the Bureau and determine that the Bureau never had any men assisting in the President's visit to Dallas. Then use this information to go after those CIA personnel who participated in the assassination. Ex-CIA agent Howard Hunt looks practically identical to a photograph of one of the tramps taken from the railroad cars beyond Dealey Plaza. Start with his arrest and interrogation. There are only so many CIA agents who were in the covert section of the CIA working under the Directorate of Plans in 1963. Make a list of these agents and, one by one, arrest and interrogate them. Richard Helms could not have assassinated the President by himself. He would have needed other CIA personnel at the management level to assist him. Start with whomever was the assistant to the Deputy Director of Plans. This position was vital to carrying out the President's assassination. From this position, go down the CIA's pecking order of management in the Directorate of Plans and arrest everyone who is still alive. Arrest and interrogate the Chief of Western Hemisphere in 1963 for the original plan was to include Castro in the Kennedy assassination. Certainly there are other CIA personnel involved in ZR Rifle, the CIA's assassination capability other than William Harvey. Find out which CIA agents recruited foreign assassins, for one of these CIA agents recruited the gunmen who were waiting for the President in Dealey Plaza.

A list of top military brass in 1963 should be drawn up. Lt. Col. Jones didn't take it upon himself to assist in the assassination of the President of The United States. Someone gave him his order. Who was Lt. Col. Jones's superior? Certainly he receives his orders from the head of army intelligence. Who did the commander of army intelligence report to? Those men who were 40 years old in 1963 are only in their 70s today. These witnesses to treason are for the most part still alive. Arrest the behavioral scientists and CIA agents involved in Project MKULTRA, the CIA's Manchurian candidate program for assassination. Solving Robert Kennedy's assassination would lead to the solving of the President's murder. But to break the backs of the conspirators and have them fleeing in terror from truth and justice and to solve the crime of the century, merely arrest one man: *Richard Helms*. Arrest Richard Helms for treason and murder and end the doubt plaguing our national conscience.

Yes, they took him from us, and probably many others, too. First John, then Bobby. For all we know, Martin. We cannot bring JFK back from the grave. But we can capture his spirit and listen to his wisdom, and feel his bravery.

And we can understand one more thing. When the CIA opened fire on JFK in Dealey Plaza, the Agency declared war on America. Isn't it time for America to declare war on the CIA?

Michael Calder

* * *

NOTES

PART I—THE WARREN COMMISSION

1. *Report of the Warren Commission on the Assassination of President Kennedy.* Bantam Books, 1964, p. 112.

2. *Hearings Before the President's Commission Investigating the Assassination of President John F. Kennedy.* (Government Printing Office, 1964) vol. VII, p. 338

3. ibid., p. 345

4. ibid., p. 346

5. *Hearings*, op. cit., vol. II, p. 74.

6. ibid., p. 78

7. ibid., p. 76

8. ibid., p. 78

9. ibid., vol. VI, p. 243.

10. ibid., p. 244

11. ibid.

12. ibid., p. 230.

13. ibid., vol. XIX, p. 490

14. ibid., vol. VII, p. 571

15. ibid., p. 572

16. ibid., vol. VI, p. 209

17. ibid., vol. VII., p. 532

18. ibid., p. 535

19. ibid., p. 535

20. ibid., vol. XVIII, p. 755

21. *Report*, op. cit., p. 139

22.   *Saturday Evening Post,* December 14, 1963, p. 24.

23.   ibid., p. 26.

24.   ibid., vol. XXII, p. 673

25.   ibid., p. 675.

26.   ibid., p. 647

27.   ibid., vol. II, p. 242

28.   ibid.

29.   ibid., vol. XXII, p. 663

30.   ibid., p. 794

31.   *Report,* op. cit., p. 141

32.   *Hearings,* vol. III, p. 252

33.   ibid.

34.   ibid., p. 293

35.   ibid.

36.   ibid., p. 275

37.   ibid., p. 274

38.   ibid., p. 279

39.   ibid., vol. II, p. 253

40.   ibid., p. 261

41.   ibid., p. 255

42.   ibid., p. 256

43.   ibid.

44.   *Report,* p. 86

45.   *Hearings,* vol. VII, p. 107

46. ibid., p. 108

47. ibid.

48. ibid., p. 106

49. ibid., p. 109

50. ibid.

51. ibid., vol. XXIV, p. 228

52. ibid., vol. III, p. 294

53. ibid., vol. II, p. 239

54. ibid., vol. II, p. 243

55. ibid., p. 249

56. ibid., vol. IV, p. 68

57. ibid., p. 88

58. ibid., vol. VI, p. 316

59. ibid., vol. XVII, p. 461

60. ibid.

61. ibid., p. 368

62. ibid., vol. VI, p. 321

63. ibid., p. 323

64. *Report*, op. cit., p. 183

65. *Albany Metropolitan* (newspaper), November 24, 1963

66. *Hearings*, op. cit., vol. VIII, p. 233

67. ibid.

68. ibid.

69. ibid., p. 239

70. ibid.

71.   ibid.

72.   *Report*, p. 182

73.   *Hearings*, vol. VIII, p. 403

74.   ibid., p. 405

75.   ibid.

76.   ibid., p. 409

77.   ibid., p. 395

78.   ibid., p. 396

79.   ibid., p. 443

80.   ibid.

81.   ibid., p. 444

82.   ibid., p. 444

83.   *Report*, p. 84

84.   *Hearings*,vol. III, p. 402

85.   *Hearings*, vol. VII, p. 101

86.   ibid., p. 102

87.   ibid.

88.   ibid., p. 101

89.   ibid., vol. VII, p. 403

90.   ibid., vol. III, p. 286

91.   *Report*, p. 85

92.   ibid., p. 98

93.   ibid., p. 88

94.   ibid., p. 90

95.   ibid., p. 91

96.   *Hearings*, vol. II, p. 374

97.   ibid., p. 375

98.   ibid., p. 375

99.   ibid., vol. V, p. 68

100. ibid., vol. IV, p. 113

101. ibid., p. 114

102. ibid., vol. V, p. 80

103. ibid., p. 82

104. *Report*, p. 516

105. ibid., p. 88

106. ibid., p. 90

107. ibid., p. 91

108. *Knickerbocker News,* Albany, NY, November 23, 1963

109. *Hearings,* vol. XX, p. 353

110. ibid., vol. VI, p. 81

111. ibid., p. 81

112. ibid., vol. XIX, p. 490

113. ibid., vol. II, p. 81

114. ibid., p. 93

115. ibid., p. 94

116. ibid., vol. II, p. 141

117. ibid., vol. XVIII, p. 744

118. ibid., p. 760

119. *Report*, p. 516

120. *Hearings,*vol. IV, p. 23

121. ibid., p. 24

122. ibid., vol. IV, p. 260

123. *Report*, p. 130

124. *Hearings*, vol. IV, p. 268

125. ibid., p. 269

126. ibid., p. 94

127. ibid., p. 94

128. ibid., p. 96

129. ibid., p. 97

130. ibid., p. 37

131. ibid., p. 269

132. ibid., p. 38

133. ibid., p. 39

134. ibid., p. 55

135. ibid., p. 55

136. *Report*, p. 120

137. *Hearings*, vol. VII, p. 189

138. ibid., p. 191

139. ibid., p. 548

140. ibid.

141. ibid.

142. ibid., p. 549

143. ibid.

144. ibid., p. 209

145. ibid., 194

146. ibid., vol. IV, p. 226

147. ibid., p. 289

148. ibid., p. 281

149. ibid., p. 281

150. ibid., p. 288

PART II—JFK VS. BUSINESS

1. C. Wright Mills, *The Power Elite,* Oxford University Press: 1956, pp. 168-169

2. Ralph G. Martin, *A Hero for Our Time,* Fawcett-Crest: 1983, pp. 387

3. Mills, op. cit., p. 168

4. "Address in Atlantic City at the Convention of the United Auto Workers," *Public Papers of the President,* vol. II, May 8, 1962.

5. Mills, p. 169

6. "Press Conference," *Public Papers of the President,* vol. II, April 11, 1962.

7. Milton Friedman, *Capitalism and Freedom,* University of Chicago Press: 1962, p. 2

8. "Inaugural Address," *Public Papers of the President,* vol. 1, Jan. 20, 1961.

9. Jefferson, *Autobiography, Notes on the State of Virginia Public and Private Paper, addresses, letters;* Literary Classics of the United States, 1964, p. 666

10. ibid., p. 677

11. ibid., p. 679

12. ibid., p. 682

13. ibid., p. 684

14. ibid., p. 685

15. ibid., p. 673

16.   ibid., p. 699, 700

17.   ibid., p. 1305

18.   "Special Message to Congress Protecting the Consumer's Interest," *Public Papers of the President*, March 15, 1962.

19.   ibid.

20.   "Remarks on the Consumer's Advisory Council," *Public Papers of the President*, vol. II, July 19, 1962

21.   "Special Message to Congress on Taxation, " *Public Papers of the President*, vol. II, April 20, 1961.

22.   "Message to Congress Presenting the President's first Economic Report," *Public Papers of the President*, vol. II, January 22, 1962.

23.   Mills, p. 121

24.   "Special Message to Congress on the Regulatory Agencies," *Public Papers of the President*, vol. 1, April 13, 1961.

25.   "Letter to Representative Harris on Pending Legislation Relating to the Federal Trade Commission," *Public Papers of the President*, vol. 1, August 31, 1961

26.   "Businessmen's Concern Over Attitude of Government Toward Business," *U.S. News and World Report*, July 10, 1961.

27.   "Bobby Kennedy's Address Before the Economic Club of New York," *U.S. News and World Report*, November 27, 1961

28.   "Letter to the Chairman, Senate Special Committee on Aging, Concerning Health Insurance Legislation, " *Public Papers of the President*, vol. 1, September 1, 1961.

29.   ibid.

30.   "Statement by the President Upon Signing the Community Health Services & Facilities Act," *Public Papers of the President*, vol. 1, Oct. 5, 1961.

31.   "Annual Message to Congress on the State of the Union," *Public Papers of the President*, vol. II, January 4, 1962.

32.   "New York Rally in Support of the President's Program for Medical Aid for the Aged," *Public Papers of the President*, vol. II, May 20, 1962.

33. "Statement of the President on Establishing the Presidential Commission on Campaign Costs," vol. I, *Public Papers of the President,* October 4, 1961

34. Mills, p. 167

35. "Special Message to Congress on Education, " *Public Papers of the President,* vol. II, February 6, 1962.

36. "Federal Water Pollution Control Act, Amendment," *Public Papers of the President,* vol. 1, July 20, 1961

37. "Special Message to Congress on Gold and the Balance of Payments Deficit," *Public Papers of the President,* vol. III, January 30, 1961

38. "Donald Hardenbrook Speech" *NAM News,* December 15, 1961

39. *U.S. News and World Report,* December 25, 1961, p. 54

40. "Executive Officers of NAM," *NAM News,* December 15, 1961

41. "Press Conference," *Public Papers of the President,* vol. VI, April 11, 1962

42. "Top Officials Lash Out at JFK for Forcing a Rollback in Steel Prices," *U.S. News and World Report,* May 7, 1962

43. "Editorial," *American Banker,* April 17, 1962

44. "Why are Profits Unpopular?" *U.S. News and World Report,* March 27, 1961, p. 118.

45. *Journal of Commerce,* May 1, 1962, p. 5

46. "Business Reacts," *Journal of Commerce,* May 25, 1962, pp. 1, 20

47. ibid., pp. 1, 6

48. ibid.

49. *Business Week,* April 21, 1962, p. 29

50. ibid.

51. "Planned Economy," *U.S. News and World Report,* April 30, 1962

52. "Address at Atlantic City Convention of the United Auto Workers," *Public Papers of the President,* vol. II, May 8, 1962

53. "Press Conference," *Public Papers of the President,* vol. II, May 9, 1962

54.   "Press Conference," *Public Papers of the President,* vol. II, May 17, 1962

55.   "New York Rally in Support of the President's Program for the Medical Aid for the Aged," *Public Papers of the President,* vol. II, May 20, 1962.

56.   "Letter to the President of the Senate—Bill to Carry Out Recommendations of the Commission on Campaign Costs," *Public Papers of the President,* vol. II, May 29, 1962.

57.   "Commencement Address at Yale University," *Public Papers of the President,* vol. II, June 11, 1962.

58.   "Radio TV Report to the American People on the State of the National Economy," *Public Papers of the President,* vol. II, August 13, 1962

59.   "Remarks Upon Arrival at Cincinnati Airport," *Public Papers of the President,* vol. II, October 5, 1962

60.   "Remarks at the University of Pittsburgh," *Public Papers of the President,* vol. II, October 5, 1962

61.   "Remarks at City Hall, McKeesport Pennsylvania, " *Public Papers of the President,* vol. II, October 13, 1962.

62.   "Remarks at Indianapolis Airport," *Public Papers of the President,* vol. II, October

63.   "Remarks at Vanderbilt University," *Public Papers of the President,* vol. III, May 18, 1963.

PART III—JFK VS. THE MILITARY

1.   C. Wright Mills, *The Power Elite,* Oxford University Press: 1956, p. 211.

2.   "American University Address," *Public Papers of the President,* vol. III, June 10, 1963.

3.   "Statement by the President Upon Signing Bill Modifying the Anti-Communist Oath Requirement for Student Loans," *Public Papers of the President,* vol. II, October 17, 1962.

4.   "Press Conference," *Public Papers of the President,* vol. II, January 24, 1962

5.   "Annual State of the Union Message to Congress, " *Public Papers of the President,* vol. II, January 11, 1962.

6.   "Inaugural Address," *Public Papers of the President,* vol. I, January 20, 1961

7. "Radio and Television Report to the American People on Returning from Europe," *Public Papers of the President*, vol. I, June 6, 1961

8. "Radio and Television Report to the American People on the Berlin Crisis," *Public Papers of the President*, vol. 1, July 25, 1961

9. "Press Conference," *Public Papers of the President*, vol. II, June 7, 1962

10. "Khrushchev Doctrine," *U.S. News and World Report*, October 15, 1962, p. 18

11. "Press Conference," *Public Papers of the President*, vol. II February 14, 1962

12. "Goldwater Platform," *U.S. News and World Report*, January 23, 1961

13. "General Lemnitzer's Testimony before Congress," *U.S. News and World Report*, July 17, 1961, p. 6

14. "Mutual of Omaha Insurance Company Award: J. Edgar Hoover," *U.S. News and World Report*, Dec. 18, 1961, p. 6

15. "Address at the University of Washington," *Public Papers of the President*, November 16, 1961

16. "Military Muzzling," *U.S. News and World Report*, September 18, 1961.

17. "Furor over Muzzling of the Military," *U.S. News and World Report*, August 14, 1961

18. ibid.

19. ibid.

20. "Press Conference," *Public Papers of the President*, vol. II, February 7, 1962

21. ibid., February 14, 1962

22. ibid., "Special Message to Congress on the Defense Budget," March 28, 1961

23. ibid., "Remarks at West Point to the Graduating Class of the U.S. Military Academy," June 6, 1962

24. ibid., "Press Conference," vol. III, February 14, 1963

25. ibid.

26. Paul Fay, Jr., *The Pleasure of His Company*, Dell Publishing: 1966, p. 162

27. "New Staff System," *U.S. News and World Report*, August 7, 1961, p. 35

28. ibid.

29. ibid.

30. "New Agency in Charge of Purchasing," *U.S. News and World Report*, September 4, 1961.

31. "Military Men No Longer Call The Tune," *U.S. News and World Report*, April 23, 1962.

32. "Fundamental Changes Taking Place in Defense," *U.S. News and World Report*, April 10, 1963, p. 3

33. "Dispute between Military Men and Civilians in the Pentagon," *U.S News and World Report*, April 22, 1963, p. 51.

34. United States Senate Select Committee to Study Goverment Operations with Respect to Intelligence Activities; vol. III, Alleged Assassination Plots Involving Foreign Leaders, 1975, p. 74

35. "Press Conference," *Public Papers of the President*, vol. I, April 12, 1961.

36. Theodore Sorensen, *Kennedy*, Harper and Row/Bantam edition: 1965, p. 339.

37. ibid., p. 338

38. "Press Conference," *Public Papers of the President*, vol. III, January 24, 1963.

39. "Press Conference," *Public Papers of the President*, vol. II, August 29, 1962.

40. "Invasion Force," *U.S News and World Report*, January 14, 1963, p. 13.

41. "Special Message to Congress on World Defense and Assistance," *Public Papers of the President*, vol. III, April 2, 1963.

42. "Communism in the Americas," *U S News and World Report*, February 25, 1963, p. 6.

43. "Press Conference," *Public Papers of the President*, vol. III, April 3, 1963.

44. "First Faint Feelers," *U.S. News and World Report*, July 8, 1963.

45. Jean Daniels, "Unofficial Envoy: An Historical Report from Two Capitals," *New Republic*, December 14, 1963

46. Khrushchev, *Kruschev Remembers*, Little, Brown & Co.: 1970, p. 497-498.

47. "Statement by the President Concerning the Conference on the Discontinuance of Nuclear Weapons Testing," *Public Papers of the President,* vol. I, March 14, 1961.

48. "Proposing the Establishment of a United States Disarmament Agency," *Public Papers of the President,* June 29, 1961

49. "Address in NYC to the General Assembly of the United Nations," *Public Papers of the President,* vol. I, September 25, 1961.

50. ibid.

51. "Brazil," *U.S. News and World Report,* June 18, 1962.

52. "Press Conference," *Public Papers of the President,* vol. III, November 14, 1963

53. "American University Address," *Public Papers of the President,* vol. III, June 10, 1963

54. "High Officers in the Armed Forces Concerned Over U.S. Defense Policy 'Disarm by Example,'" *U.S. News and World Report,* July 15, 1963.

55. Unanimous Opposition of Chiefs, *U.S. News and World Report,* August 5, 1963, p. 36.

56. United States Senate: *Nuclear 'Test Ban Treaty-Hearing Before the Committee on Foreign Relations,* 85th Congress, 1st Session, Government Printing Office, 1963, p. 54.

57. ibid., p. 164.

58. ibid., p. 345, 372.

59. "Address to the American People on the Nuclear Test Ban Treaty," *Public Papers of the President,* vol. III, July 26, 1963.

60. ibid., p. 603

61. ibid., p. 605

62. "Address in NYC to the General Assembly of the United Nations," *Public Papers of the President,* vol. I, September 25, 1961.

63. "Unanimous Opposition of the Chiefs," *U.S. News and World Report,* August 5, 1963

64. Allan Nevins, ed. *The Strategy of Peace,* Popular Library: 1961, pp. 89-90

65. *Vietnam and Southeast Asia: Report to the Committee on Foreign Relations,* Government Printing Office: 1963, pp. 7-8.

66. "Press Conference," vol. III, *Public Papers of the President,* Vol III, May 22, 1963.

67. "Televised Interview with Walter Cronkite Inaugurating a CBS Television News Program," vol. III, *Public Papers of the President,* September 2, 1963.

68. "Press Conference," *Public Papers of the President,* September 2, 1963

69. Paul Fay, Jr.,*The Pleasure of His Company,* Harper and Row: 1966, p. 190

PART IV—JFK VS. CIA

1.   United States Select Committee to Study Government Operations with Respect to Intelligence Activities, vol. III, *Alleged Assassination Plots Involving Foreign Leaders,* Government Printing Office: 1975, p. 92

2.   ibid., p. 92

3.   ibid., p. 19

4.   ibid.

5.   ibid., p. 29

6.   ibid., p. 51

7.   ibid., p. 181

8.   ibid., p. 182

9.   ibid.

10. ibid., p. 46

11. ibid., p. 123-124

12. ibid., p. 138

13. ibid., p. 139

14. "Address in Seattle at the University of Washington's 100th Anniversary Program," *Public Papers of the President,* vol. I, November 16, 1961.

15. United States Select Committee to Study Governmental Operations With Respect to Intelligence Activities, vol. III, *Alleged Assassination Plots Involving Foreign Leaders*, Government Printing Office: 1975, p.76.

16. ibid., p. 191

17. ibid., p. 212

18. ibid., p. 213

19. ibid., p. 129

20. Judith Exner, "The Dark Side of Camelot," *People*, February 19, 1988, p. 111.

21. ibid., p.113

22. United States Select Committee to Study Governmental Operations With Respect to Intelligence Activities, vol. III, *Alleged Assassination Plots Involving Foreign Leaders*, Government Printing Office: 1975, p.84

PART V—THE PLAYERS

1. *Hearings Before the President's Commission Investigating the Assassination of President John F. Kennedy*, vol. XXII, p. 826

2. *Hearings*, vol. XI, p. 456

3. *Hearings*, vol. XIX, p. 622

4. *Hearings*, vol. XVI, p. 719

5. *Hearings*, vol. V, p. 265

6. ibid.

7. *Hearings*, vol. XXII, p. 17

8. *Hearings*, vol. V, p. 333

9. *Hearings*, vol. XXII, p. 102

10. ibid., p. 118

11. *Hearings*, vol. VIII, p. 341

12. *Hearings*, vol. X, p. 202

13. *Hearings*, vol. X, p. 77

14. *Hearings,* vol. X, p. 36

15. *Hearings,* vol. X, p. 38

16. *Hearings,* vol. X, p. 61

17. *Hearings,* vol. XX, p. 636

18. ibid., vol. VII, p. 41

19. ibid., p. 58

20. ibid., p. 59

21. *Hearings,* vol. IV, p. 214

22. *Hearings,* vol. VII, p. 267

23. *Hearings,* vol. IV, p. 213

24. *Hearings,* vol. VII, p. 135

25. ibid.

26. ibid., p. 267

27. ibid.

28. ibid., p. 279

29. ibid.

30. ibid, vol. XV, p. 748

31. ibid., vol. VI, p. 443

32. ibid, vol. VII, p. 77

33. ibid., p. 81

34. ibid., p. 47

35. ibid., vol. XVII, p. 416

36. ibid., vol. VIII, p. 255

37. ibid., vol. VI, p. 449

38. ibid., p. 448

39. ibid., vol. VII, p. 80

40. ibid., vol. III, p. 475

41. ibid., p. 476

42. ibid., vol. XX, p. 444

43. ibid., vol. XXII, p. 898

44. ibid., p. 923

45. ibid., vol. XXIII, p. 334

46. ibid., p. 205

47. ibid., vol. XXII, p. 361

48. *Hearings,* vol. XXIII, p. 205

49. *Hearings,* vol. XXIII, p. 631

50. *Hearings,* vol. VI, p. 210-211

51. *Hearings,* vol. XIX, p. 492

52. House of Representatives: Select Committee on Assassinations, *Subcommittee—JFK Assassination,* 95th Congress, 2nd session, vol. III, p. 15, Government Printing Office, 1979

53. *Hearings,* vol. XV, p. 80

54. ibid., p. 391

55. ibid., p. 105

56. ibid., p. 46

57. ibid., p. 102

58. ibid., p. 106

59. ibid., vol. XXI, p. 309

60. ibid., vol. XV, p. 491

61. ibid., vol. XII, p. 49

62. ibid., p. 54

63. ibid., p. 110

64. ibid., vol. XIV, p. 236

65. ibid., vol. XII, p. 2

66. ibid., vol. VII, p. 358

67. ibid., vol. XIX, p. 395

68. ibid., vol. XX, p. 370

69. ibid., vol. XXII, p. 360

70. ibid., vol. XII, p. 340

71. ibid., vol. XV, p. 189

72. ibid.

73. ibid., vol. XII, p. 360

74. ibid., p. 369

75. ibid., vol. XIII, p. 80

76. ibid., vol. XV, p. 68

77. ibid., vol. XXII, p. 329

78. ibid., vol. XII, p. 246

79. ibid., p. 153

80. ibid., p. 262

81. ibid., vol. XIII, p. 11

82. ibid., vol. XV, p. 125

83. ibid., p. 187

84. ibid., p. 150

85. ibid., vol. V, p. 191

86.   ibid., p. 196

87.   ibid., p. 198

88.   ibid., p. 198

89.   ibid., p. 206

90.   ibid., p. 210

91.   ibid., vol. XIV, p. 527

92.   ibid., p. 540

93.   ibid., p.542

94.   ibid., p. 548

95.   ibid., p. 557

96.   ibid., p. 566

97.   ibid., p. 567

98.   United States Senate Select Committee to Study Governmental Operations with Respect to Intelligence Activities, vol. III, *Alleged Assassination Plots Involving Foreign Leaders,* p. 202

99.   ibid., p. 83

100. ibid., p. 84

101. ibid., p. 92

102. ibid., p. 102

103. ibid., p. 99

104. ibid., p. 187

105. ibid., p. 131

106. ibid., p. 133

107. ibid.

108. ibid., p. 132

109. ibid.

110.   ibid., p. 87

111.   ibid.

112.   ibid.

113.   ibid., p. 178

114.   ibid., p. 219

115.   ibid.

116.   ibid., p. 217

117.   ibid., p. 222

118.   Penn Jones, Jr., *Forgive My Grief,*vol. II, The Midlothiean Mirror, 1967, p. 27

119.   ibid.

120.   ibid., p. 12

121.   ibid., p. 37

122.   ibid., p. 96

123.   U.S. Senate Select Committee to Study Governmental Operations With Respect to Intelligence Activities., vol. IV, *FBI,* p. 182.

124.   United States Senate Joint Hearings before the Select Committee on Intelligence and the Subcommittee on Health and Scientific Research of the Committee on Human Resources: Project MKULTRA, the CIA's Program of Research in Behavioral Modification, p. 3

125.   ibid., p. 2

126.   ibid., p. 5

127.   ibid., p. 7

128.   ibid., p. 10

129.   ibid., p. 79

130.   ibid.

131.   ibid., p. 81

132. ibid., p. 117

133. ibid., p. 123

134. *Covert Action in Chile*. U.S. Senate, Staff Report of the Committee to Study Governmental Operations with Respect to Intelligence Activities. Government Printing Office: 1975, p. 12

135. ibid., p. 26

136. ibid., p. 33

137. ibid., p. 25

138. *Alleged Assassination Plots*, p. 226

139. ibid., p. 246

140. ibid., p. 39

141. ibid.

PART VI—PRELUDE TO THE ASSASSINATION

1. House of Representatives: Select Committee on Assassinations, *Subcommittee— JFK Assassination*, 95th Congress, 2nd session, vol. III, p. 305, Government Printing Office, 1979

2. ibid., p. 321

3. United States Select Committee to Study Governmental Operations with respect to Intelligence Activities, vol. III, *Alleged Assassination Plots Involving Foreign Leaders*, Government Printing Office: 1975, p. 80

4. ibid., p. 84

5. *Hearings Before the President's Commission Investigating the Assassination of President John F. Kennedy*, vol. II, Government Printing Office: 1964, p. 440

6. *Report of the Warren Commission on the Assassination of President Kennedy*, Bantam Books, 1964, p. 114

7. *Report*, p. 62.

8. *Hearings*, vol. VII, p. 298

9. *Subcommittee—JFK Assassination*, p. 230

10. *Report,*p. 48

11. *Hearings*, p. 103

12. ibid., p. 107

13. *Report*, p. 656

14. ibid., p.657

15. *Alleged Assassination Plots*, p. 46

16. *Hearings,*vol. XI, p. 267

17. ibid., p. 265

18. ibid., p. 267

19. ibid., p. 254

20. ibid., p. 280

21. ibid., p. 282

22. ibid., p. 282-283

23. ibid., p. 291

24. ibid., vol. X, p. 370

25. ibid., p. 376

26. ibid., p. 363

27. ibid., p. 381

28. ibid., p. 383

29. ibid., p. 392

30. ibid., p. 387

31. ibid.

32. ibid., vol. IX, p. 396

33. ibid., p. 344

34. ibid., p. 345

35. ibid., p. 346

36. ibid., p. 354

37. ibid., p. 353

38. ibid., p. 355

39. ibid.

40. ibid., vol. II, p. 503

41. ibid., vol. I, p. 113

42. *Subcommittee—JFK Assassination*, op. cit., p. 231

43. ibid.

44. *Appointment Book of the President*, November 19, 1963

45. *Subcommittee—JFK Assassination*, vol. III, p. 305

46. ibid.

47. ibid.

48. ibid.

49. ibid., p. 233

50. ibid., p. 192

51. ibid.

52. ibid.

53. ibid., p. 193

54. ibid.

55. ibid., p. 194

56. *Hearings*, vol. V, p. 253.

57. ibid., p. 242

58. ibid., p. 243

59. *Dallas Morning News,* November 22, 1963

60. *Hearings,* vol. XIX, p. 483

61. ibid., vol. XVII, p. 392

62. ibid.

63. ibid., vol. VI, p. 289

64. ibid., p. 288

65. *San Francisco Chronicle,* November 23, 1963

66. *Hearings,* vol. XVII, p. 395

67. *Subcommittee—JFK Assassination,* p. 230

68. ibid., p. 234

69. ibid., p. 233

70. *Hearings,* vol. XVIII, p. 619

71. ibid., vol. XXI, p. 563

72. ibid., vol. VII, p. 538

73. ibid., vol. IV, p. 169

74. ibid., vol. XXI, p. 569

75. ibid., vol. IV, p. 332

PART VII—THE ASSASSINATION OF A PRESIDENT

1. *Hearings Before the President's Commission Investigating the Assassination of President John F. Kennedy,* vol. II, p. 194

2. ibid., p. 201

3. ibid., vol. III, p. 279

4. ibid., vol. VI, p. 266

5. ibid., vol. VII, p. 535

6.   ibid., p. 536

7.   ibid., p. 535

8.   *New York Times*, August 28, 1978

9.   *Hearings*, vol. VI, p. 312

10. ibid., vol. VII, p. 347

11. ibid., vol. VI, p. 281

12. ibid., p. 282

13. ibid., p. 213

14. ibid., vol. VII, p. 106

15. ibid., p. 107

16. ibid., vol. VI, p. 246

17. ibid.

18. ibid., vol. III, p. 144

19. ibid.

20. ibid., p. 145

21. ibid., p. 158

22. House of Representatives, Select Committee on Assassinations: JFK Assassination Final Report, p. 184

23. ibid.

24. ibid., p. 223

25. ibid.

26. ibid., p. 222

27. *Hearings*, vol. XIX, p. 167

28. ibid., vol. XXI, pp. 203-204

29. ibid., vol. VI, p. 137

30. ibid., vol. XX, p. 641

31. ibid., vol. VI, p. 146

32. ibid., vol. XXI, p. 216

33. ibid., vol. VI, p. 134

34. ibid.

35. ibid., vol. II, p. 259

* * *